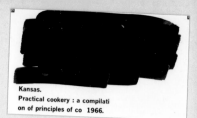

DATE DUE

JUL 1 1 1975			
OCT 1 7 1975			
NOV 1 4 1975			
OCT 2 2 1976			
FEB 1 1 1977			
JUL 1 5 1977			
30 508 JOSTEN'S			

Practical Cookery

Practical

A Compilation of Principles

John Wiley & Sons, Inc.

Cookery

of Cookery and Recipes

Department of Foods and Nutrition

College of Home Economics

Kansas State University

New York · London · Sydney

10   9

Library of Congress Catalog Card Number: 20–21946
Printed in the United States of America

ISBN 0 471 45640 3

Preface

PRACTICAL Cookery was first published in 1912 and has had 23 revisions. It has been widely used by classes in food preparation and by the homemaker. The material of the present edition has been revised extensively.

The primary aim of the authors is to prepare a book for the person inexperienced in food preparation. Each section begins with a general discussion of the characteristics of the food to be prepared followed by basic recipes and suggested variations. Basically the same arrangement has been followed as in preceding editions.

Acknowledgments are made throughout the book.

Members of the Department of Foods and Nutrition
KANSAS STATE UNIVERSITY

Manhattan, Kansas
December 1965

Contents

Practical
Cookery

General
Information

NUTRITIOUS, attractive, and flavorful meals are the goals of every woman interested in the well-being of those who depend upon her for food. Meals are no more appetizing than are the individual foods used in their preparation.

The preparation of palatable foods depends upon many factors, one of which is the quality of the food brought into the kitchen. In general, one selects the highest quality foods that the family can afford, but for many purposes second and third grade foods give equally satisfactory results and may be much more economical. Canned fruits of second or third grade may be better in certain desserts than the very sweet first grade product. Less tender cuts of meat and meats of medium grade are cheaper than tender cuts of high grade, and for certain purposes may be as good or better. On the other hand, flour milled for a specific purpose may be expected to give superior results and whenever possible it is wise to purchase the type prepared for a particular product such as bread or cake. Likewise, certain fats may be desirable for one-bowl cakes; others with a high smoking point may be better for frying.

This book is concerned with the utilization of foods either alone or in combination. Limitations of space make extensive discussion of the selection and purchase of food impracticable. Emphasis is placed upon the preparation and service of food in the home.

The major problem of the cook, whether an amateur or an experienced homemaker is to have all foods ready for a meal at one time. The acceptability of a food is closely related to the temperature at which it is served. Hot foods should be hot, cold foods cold, and neither type should stand

1

long enough to lose quality. Yeast breads, cakes, cookies, and many other foods served at room temperature may be prepared several hours or, in some instances, a day or two before the meal. On the other hand, baked potatoes, broiled steak, and baking powder biscuits are less desirable if not served immediately. Many casserole dishes may stand for some time without loss of quality. Certain chilled desserts, salads, and relishes may be prepared well in advance and kept in the refrigerator until mealtime, whereas others must be combined shortly before serving.

In planning individual meals, the skill and ease with which various foods can be prepared should be considered carefully, but in planning the menus for the day, nutritive value should receive primary consideration. Perhaps the easiest way to be sure that all the necessary nutrients are included is to keep the Basic Four food groups in mind. Basic Four food groups are presented in detail in the United States Department of Agriculture Leaflet No. 42 "Food for Fitness . . . A Daily Food Guide," which can be obtained from the Government Printing Office, Washington, D.C.

The next problem is to introduce foods representing each of these groups into three meals: breakfast, lunch, and dinner or supper. In planning the three menus for the day consider the following:

1. The nutritional needs of the group for the day.
2. The likes and dislikes of the group.
3. The staying quality of the food. Use a protein food and some fat in each meal.
4. The suitability of combinations. It is desirable that foods harmonize and also provide contrasts in texture, flavor, color, form, and temperature.
5. The seasonability, whether or not a food is appropriate to the season and the weather.
6. The cost not only per pound or unit but also in terms of the nutritive value as compared with other foods belonging to the same group.
7. The time required and the equipment available for preparation.
8. The speed with which a food loses quality after preparation.
9. The ease of serving.

Having decided upon the foods to be served, proper preparation is important in determining both acceptability and nutritive value.

The recipes in this book when followed carefully, will result in palatable foods of high nutritive value. Ease of preparation has also been considered. Long tedious processes, so common in early cookbooks, have been eliminated whenever feasible. Recipes for one-bowl cakes, directions for mixes, and other short cuts have been introduced, and suggestions for garnishes have been included.

Having selected a recipe, read it over carefully. Refer to the appropriate section of the book if there are unfamiliar terms or processes. Then assemble necessary supplies and equipment. Choose the correct size of bowl or saucepan for the quantity of food to be prepared, and use the type and size of pan indicated for such products as pies, cakes, and bread. Arrange supplies and equipment in the order required for efficient work and proceed as directed in the recipe.

These preliminary steps increase the ease of preparation, help insure good products, and make for satisfactory meals from the standpoint of the one who prepares them and also of those who consume them.

PROCESSES IN FOOD PREPARATION

Bake. To cook by dry heat. Usually done in an oven but occasionally under coals, in ashes, or on heated stones or metals.

Baste. To pour liquid composed of drippings, fat, and water, or sugar and water over a food while cooking.

Beat. To mix with an over-and-over motion to smooth a mixture and to introduce air. This type of beating may also be accomplished by a rotary beater or electric mixer.

Blanch or Scald. To pretreat with steam or boiling water, (1) to partially inactivate enzymes and shrink food before canning, freezing, or drying, by heating with steam or boiling water; (2) to aid in removal of skins from nuts and fruits by dipping into boiling water from 1 to 5 minutes; (3) to reduce strong flavor or set color of food by plunging into boiling water.

Blend. To mix two or more ingredients until they are well combined.

Boil. To cook in boiling liquid. A liquid is boiling when bubbles are breaking on the surface and steam is being released. In a slowly boiling liquid, bubbles are small; in a rapidly boiling liquid, large. As boiling changes from slow to rapid, more steam is formed but there is no increase in temperature. Boiling temperature of water at sea level is 212°F or 100°C. It is reduced by rise above sea level, approximately 1°C for every 1,000 feet of elevation. It is increased by solution of solids in the water and by pressure of enclosed steam as in a pressure saucepan. Sometimes the term is applied incorrectly to foods cooked in moist heat below the boiling point, such as "boiled beef."

Braise. To brown meat in a small amount of fat, then cook slowly in a covered container with a small amount of liquid or in steam.

Broil or Grill. To cook by direct heat.

Cream. To work one or more foods until soft and creamy. The hands, a spoon, electric mixer, or other implements may be used.

Cut. (1) To divide food material with knife or scissors; (2) to incorporate fat into dry ingredients with a pastry blender or two knives, with the least possible amount of blending.

Cut and Fold. A combination of two motions—to cut vertically through mixture and to turn over and over by sliding tool across bottom of mixing bowl at each turn. Proper folding prevents loss of air.

Dice. To cut into cubes.

Dredge. To sprinkle or coat with flour or other fine substance.

Egg and Crumb. To coat a food with flour or bread crumbs, then with diluted slightly beaten egg, and finally with crumbs. This method forms a coating that browns easily and tends to prevent soaking of food with fat.

Fricassee. To braise. The term is usually applied to fowl, rabbit, or veal, cut into pieces. Browning may be omitted.

Frizzle. To cook in a small amount of fat until the edges curl. Often applied to dried beef.

Fry. (1) To cook in fat deep enough to float the food. Also called "deep-fat fry" or "French-fry"; (2) to cook in small amount of hot fat or drippings. Also called "pan-fry" or "sauté."

Glaze or Glacé. To coat with a thin sugar syrup.

Grate. To rub foods against grater to divide into small particles.

Grill. See Broil.

Grind. To put through a food chopper.

Knead. A process of mixing that consists of a pressing motion accompanied by folding and stretching. In this way flour may be added to doughs that are too stiff to beat or stir.

Lard. To insert lardoons—small strips of fat—into uncooked meat or fish either by placing in gashes cut into the food or by running them in with a larding needle. Also applied to placing strips of fat, such as bacon, on top of meat before cooking.

Marinate. To allow food to stand in an oil and acid mixture such as French dressing.

Melt. To liquefy by heat.

Mill. To beat. It is best done with a rotary beater. Milk dishes, such as cocoa, are milled to remove scum formed during heating.

Mince. To cut or chop into very small pieces.

Pan. To cook certain vegetables cut into small pieces in a small amount of fat and other seasonings with little or no added water. A tightly covered pan and carefully regulated heat are desirable.

Pan-Broil. To cook uncovered on hot metal such as a grill or frying pan. The utensil may be oiled just enough to prevent sticking. Excess fat accumulated while cooking should be poured off.

Pan-Fry. To cook in a small amount of fat. *See* Fry.

Parboil. To boil until partially cooked. Foods with strong or salt flavor are often parboiled, as are tough foods that are to be roasted or cooked in hot fat.

Pare or Peel. To remove outer cover.

Pasteurize. To preserve food by heating sufficiently to destroy pathogenic microorganisms and arrest fermentation. Applied to liquids, such as milk and fruit juices. The temperature varies with the food but commonly ranges from 140 to 180°F.

Plank. To cook or serve on a plank made especially for the purpose.

Poach. To cook food by slipping it into hot liquid. Temperature varies with material to be poached.

Render. To free fat from connective tissue by means of heat.

Roast. To bake. Applied to certain foods such as meats and chestnuts. In its original sense it was similar to broil, for it meant to cook before an open fire.

Sauté. To cook in a small amount of fat. *See* Fry.

Scald. (1) To heat a liquid, usually milk, until bubbles appear around edge. Do not boil. (2) To blanch, as when preparing vegetables for freezing.

Scallop. To bake one or more foods with a sauce in a baking dish, usually topped with crumbs.

Score. To make light cuts in a surface. To cut ⅛-inch gashes at ½- to 1-inch intervals in the fatty edge of steaks and chops to prevent edges from curling during cooking.

Sear. To brown the surface quickly by intense heat in order to develop color and flavor and to improve appearance. Usually applied to meat.

Simmer. To cook in liquid below the boiling point. A liquid is simmering when bubbles form slowly and break just below the surface, about 185°F.

Steam. To cook in steam, with or without pressure. Steam may be applied directly to the food as in a steamer or pressure cooker, or to the vessel as in a double boiler. Temperature of steam at atmospheric pressure is the same as that of boiling water, but because of rapid condensation the temperature at which food is cooked is lower. Thus a longer time is required for steaming than for boiling.

Steep. To extract flavor, color, or other qualities from a substance by allowing it to stand in liquid below the boiling point.

Sterilize. To destroy microorganisms. For culinary purposes this is done most often at a high temperature with steam, dry heat, or by boiling in a liquid.

Stew. To simmer in a small amount of liquid.

Stir. To mix with a circular motion, to blend food materials, or to obtain a uniform consistency as in sauces.

Whip. To beat rapidly to produce expansion due to incorporation of air. Applied to cream, eggs, and gelatin dishes.

SOME TECHNIQUES OF FOOD PREPARATION

To Make Butter Balls. Scald special butter paddles. Chill in ice water. Allow ½- to 1-tablespoonful of butter for each ball. Unless very firm, chill butter in cold water. Roll each piece between smooth sides of paddles until round. This may be done more successfully if only one paddle is rotated. When shaped, roll between grooved sides to give markings. Drop into ice water until ready to serve.

To Make Butter Curls. Butter curls are made with a special device known as a butter curler, a knife with a curved blade and notched edge. To make butter curls, start with an unbroken 1-pound or ¼-pound print of butter at room temperature (68 to 71°F). Dip curler into hot water, then cool slightly. If the curler is too hot, the butter will melt when it comes in contact with the metal. With a light stroke, draw curler, holding it almost horizontally, lengthwise across surface of butter. A strip of butter so separated rolls into a curl with corrugated markings. Place finished curls in ice water to harden.

To Cut Foods Such as Celery or Rhubarb. Arrange stalks in bunch, hold firmly on board with one hand, and cut in desired lengths with long sharp knife.

To Melt Chocolate. Since chocolate burns easily, melt it over hot water or in a slow oven. A rubber scraper aids in removal from pan.

To Roll Dough. Lightly flour bread board and rolling pin. Board may be covered with a pastry cloth and rolling pin with a stockinette (or child's white stocking with foot removed). Both pastry cloth and stockinette should be lightly floured. Shape dough into a ball, and place on board. To roll the dough start from the center with each stroke of the rolling pin and roll in the direction to give the desired shape. In order to keep the dough consistently thick, the pin should never be rolled off the dough onto the board. The rolling pin should be lifted at the end of each stroke and started over again.

To Chop Ice. If regular ice crusher is not available, place in heavy burlap or canvas bag and pound with wooden mallet.

To Chop Nuts. If special nut-chopping device is not available, cut with long sharp knife on cutting board.

To Chop Sticky Foods. Cut dates, raisins, marshmallows, and similar foods with scissors dipped in warm water.

To Separate Head Lettuce. Cut out core; remove coarse outer leaves. Hold head, cut part up, under cold running water to loosen leaves.

To Mince Parsley and Other Herbs. Form into tight bunch. Hold firmly in one hand, and cut with scissors or on board with sharp knife.

To Use a Pastry Bag and Tube. Fit tube into place. Turn upper part of bag to the outside to prevent smearing while filling. Fill bag not more than one-half full, and twist top tightly above mixture. Hold in one hand in such a manner that sufficient pressure can be exerted at top of bag to force out contents. Guide with one hand while pressing with other. Separate tube from mixture by pressing it down slightly and raising it quickly. A metal syringe may be used instead of cloth bag.

To Peel Tomatoes. Hold on fork over a flame or electric unit, turning constantly until skin breaks, or dip in boiling water. Remove loosened skin with paring knife.

To Reheat Rolls. Place in tightly covered pan or wrap in paper bag or aluminum foil, and set in moderate oven (375°F) until heated through (about 10 minutes). If dry, rolls may be sprinkled sparingly with water before reheating. A few rolls may be heated in the top of a double boiler over boiling water.

To Cut Balls with a French Cutter. Place cutting edge of the ball cutter against the peeled surface of the fruit or vegetable. Exerting even pressure on the knife, roll from right to left and left to right alternately so that the knife cuts into the food first on one side and then on the other. Continue until the food shows through the hole on the back of the cutter. Still exerting pressure on the knife, lift the handle until it is at right angles with the food. Turn the handle completely around in the hand, and lift out the ball.

To Grate Lemon or Orange Rind. Grate before paring or cutting the fruit. Rub the washed fruit against surface of grater, taking care to remove only the outer colored portion of the rind.

OVEN TEMPERATURES

Oven temperatures are designated variously. A convenient classification is slow, moderate, hot or quick, and very hot. The temperatures may be indicated as follows:

Slow	250 to 325°F
Moderate	325 to 375°F
Hot or quick	375 to 425°F
Very hot	425 to 500°F

MEASUREMENTS

All measurements should be level. This procedure makes exact recipes possible and tends to assure success because the quantity measured is more uniform. Choose standard measuring equipment. Standard measuring cups hold ¼ quart, 237 milliliters, or 16 tablespoons. Accurate markings of fractional measures or sets of cups holding graduated amounts are essential. A set of graduated measuring spoons with the tablespoon holding 3 teaspoons or 14.8 milliliters and the teaspoon and fractional teaspoons holding proportionate amounts is also helpful. Dry materials such as flour and white sugar are measured lightly and never shaken or pressed down, but brown sugar is pressed firmly into the cup. Flour is measured after sifting once. Dry ingredients are placed lightly into the cup with a spoon. A straight-edged knife or spatula is used to level the surface. A spoonful of dry material is measured by filling to overflowing and leveling with a straight-edged knife, not by pressing with the blade. Liquids, including oils, are poured into a transparent cup with an extension above the last mark. Fill measuring cup with liquid until bottom of the meniscus is level with the desired mark. Solid fats are measured by packing tightly into cup or spoon, leaving no air spaces, and leveling with a straight-edged knife or by placing cold water in a measuring cup, leaving space equal to required amount of fat. Fat is added until water rises to the 1-cup mark, always keeping the fat below the water level. The water is then drained off.

Table of Abbreviations and Equivalents *

ABBREVIATIONS	EQUIVALENTS
c = cup	3 tsp = 1 Tbsp
Tbsp = tablespoon	16 Tbsp = 1 c
tsp = teaspoon	2 c = 1 pt
spk = speck	2 pt = 1 qt
oz = ounce	4 qt = 1 gal
lb = pound	2 gal = 1 pk
qt = quart	4 pk = 1 bu
pt = pint	16 oz = 1 lb
gal = gallon	28.35 g = 1 oz
pk = peck	453.6 g = 1 lb
bu = bushel	2.2 lb = 1 kg
g = gram	5 ml = 1 tsp
kg = kilogram	20 drops = 1 ml

* The equivalents are the same for both solids and liquids.

Approximate Measure of a Given Unit of Some Food Materials

FOOD	UNIT	MEASURE
Bread, loaf, white	16 oz	16 slices *
Bread, loaf, sandwich	22 oz	30 slices *
Bread, loaf, whole wheat	16 oz	16 slices *
Cheese, cream, soft	pkg, 3 oz	⅓ c
Egg, whole, unbeaten		3 Tbsp
Egg, white, unbeaten		2 Tbsp
Egg, yolk, unbeaten		1 Tbsp
Milk, condensed	can, 15 oz	1⅓ c
Milk, evaporated	tall can, 14¼ oz	1⅔ c
	small can, 6 oz	⅔ c
Olives, small	qt	116 to 140
Olives, mammoth	qt	65 to 75
Oysters	pt	20 large
		30 small
Yeast, active dry	pkg, ¼ oz	1 Tbsp

* Without end slices.

Approximate Equivalents of Some Food Materials

FOOD	MEASURE	EQUIVALENT
Baking powder	1 tsp	¼ tsp soda + ½ tsp cream of tartar
Butter	1 c	⅞ to 1 c hydrogenated fat + ½ tsp salt ⅞ c oil + ½ tsp salt ⅞ c lard + ½ tsp salt ⅞ c clarified chicken fat + ½ tsp salt 1 c margarine
Chocolate	1 oz or square	3 Tbsp cocoa + ½ Tbsp fat
Cream, thin (18 to 20% fat)	1 c	⅞ c milk + 3 Tbsp fat
Cream, heavy (36 to 40% fat)	1 c	¾ c milk + ⅓ c fat
Egg	1 whole	3 Tbsp slightly beaten 2 yolks + 1 Tbsp water (in cookies) 2 yolks (in custards, cream fillings, and similar mixtures)
Dried whole egg *	2 Tbsp (13.5 g) packed + 2½ Tbsp (36.7 g) water	1 whole egg
Dried egg yolk *	1½ Tbsp (9 g) + 1 Tbsp (14.7 g) water	1 yolk or 1 Tbsp yolk
Dried egg white †	1 Tbsp (3.7 g) + 2 Tbsp (29.4 g)	1 white or 2 Tbsp white
Flour, all-purpose	1 c	1 c + 2 Tbsp cake flour ⅞ c cornmeal 1 c graham flour 1 c rye flour 1½ c bran 1½ c bread crumbs 1 c rolled oats

* To reconstitute, add a little of the lukewarm water to the dried egg. Stir and blend until a medium thick paste is formed and there are no lumps of egg powder. Gradually add remainder of water, and stir or beat until mixture is smooth. For baking, egg may be sifted with dry ingredients, or follow directions on package.
† Sprinkle dried egg whites on lukewarm water and let stand for 15 minutes, then stir, or follow directions on package.

Approximate Equivalents of Some Food Materials (Continued)

FOOD	MEASURE	EQUIVALENT
Flour, cake	1 c	⅞ c all-purpose flour
Flour (for thickening)	1 Tbsp	½ to ¾ Tbsp cornstarch
		1 Tbsp granular tapioca
		1 whole egg, 2 egg whites, or 2 egg yolks
		2 Tbsp granular cereal
Milk, sour	1 c	1 c sweet milk + 1 Tbsp lemon juice or vinegar
Milk, evaporated	½ c + ½ c water	1 c liquid whole milk
Milk, nonfat instant dry milk crystals *	1 c	⅓ c and ice water to make 8 oz or follow manufacturer's directions
Milk, liquid, skim	1 qt + 1½ oz (3 Tbsp) butter	1 qt liquid whole milk
Sugar	1 c	1⅓ c brown sugar, lightly packed
		1½ c powdered sugar
		1 c honey less ¼ to ⅓ c liquid
		1⅓ c molasses minus ⅓ c liquid
		1¼ to 1½ c corn syrup minus ¼ to ½ c liquid
Tapioca, granular	1 Tbsp	2 Tbsp pearl tapioca
Yeast, active dry	1 pkg (¼ oz)	1 cake compressed

* When nonfat dry milk is used in baked products, the milk may be sifted with the dry ingredients. If it is used regularly for various purposes, it is simpler to reconstitute the milk, 1 or 2 quarts at a time, and use it as liquid milk. To reconstitute milk add milk to surface of water and stir to dissolve. Nonfat dry milk may be used up to double strength in beverages, cream soups, and some desserts to increase nutritive value and palatability.

Approximate Measure and Number of Servings per Pound of Some Food Materials as Purchased

FOOD	MEASURE	NUMBER OF SERVINGS
Almonds, in shell	1⅓ c or 5 oz, shelled	
Almonds, shelled	3½ to 4 c	
Apples	2½ to 3, medium	

**Approximate Measure and Number of Servings per Pound
of Some Food Materials as Purchased (Continued)**

FOOD	MEASURE	NUMBER OF SERVINGS
Apricots, dried	3 to 3½ c, 50 halves	9 to 10
Apricots, fresh	8, medium	
Artichokes, globe or French	2, medium	2
Artichokes, Jerusalem	4	4
Asparagus, fresh	20 stalks, medium, or 2 c, 1-inch pieces, cooked	
Avocado	2, medium	
Bacon, uncooked	15 to 25, full slices	
Bananas	3, medium	3
Beans, kidney	2⅓ c, uncooked 7 c, cooked	11
Beans, lima, small	2⅓ c, uncooked 6 c, cooked	10
Beans, navy	2⅓ c, uncooked 6 c, cooked	10
Beans, soy	2⅓ c, uncooked 6½ to 7 c, cooked	11 to 12
Beans, string	¾ to 1 qt	5 to 6
Beef, cooked, diced	3 c	4 to 5
Beef, ground, raw	2 c	4
Beets, young	6, small (1 bunch)	3 to 4
Beets, mature	3 to 4, medium	3 to 4
Blackberries, fresh	3 c	3
Bran flakes	12 c	20 to 24
Bread, crumbs, soft	9 c	
Bread, crumbs, dry	5⅓ c	
Broccoli	2 to 4 heads	3 to 4
Brussels sprouts	30 heads, medium, 1 qt	5 to 6
Butter	2 c	48 to 60 squares
Cabbage	½ head, small	3 to 4
Cabbage, Chinese	½ stalk, medium, or 2 c, cooked	
Cabbage, shredded, cooked	2½ c	5
Cabbage, shredded, raw	4 to 5 c	10 to 12
Cantaloupe	1, small	2
Carrots, mature	4, medium	4
Carrots, young	6 to 8, small	3 to 4
Cauliflower	1 head, small	3 to 4

Approximate Measure and Number of Servings per Pound of Some Food Materials as Purchased (Continued)

FOOD	MEASURE	NUMBER OF SERVINGS
Celery	1 bunch, medium	4
	2 c ½-inch pieces	
Cheese, American, grated	4 c	
Cheese, cottage	2¼ c	5
Cherries, candied	160 cherries; 7 oz = 1 c	
Chicken, cooked, diced	3 c	4 to 6
Chocolate	16 squares	
Cocoa	4½ c	
Coconut		
dry, shredded	6 to 7 c	
moist, canned	5⅓ c	
Coffee, ground	5 to 5½ c	50
Corn	2 ears, medium	2
Cornflakes	16 c	12 to 16
Cornmeal	2 c, uncooked	16 to 24
	12 c, cooked	
Corn syrup	1⅓ c	
Cornstarch	3 to 3¼ c	
Crackers, Graham	50 to 80	
Crackers, white, 2 inches x 2 inches	108	
Cranberries, uncooked	4 c	16
Cream of wheat	2⅔ c, uncooked	16 to 20
	11 c, cooked	
Cucumbers	2, 6 inches long	
Currants, dried	3 c	
Dates, unpitted	2½ c (60 dates)	
Eggplant	1, medium	4 to 5
Egg yolks	2 c (24 to 28 yolks)	
Egg whites	2 c (16 whites)	
Eggs, whole	8 to 10 in shell	8
Endive, curly	1 head	
English walnuts, shelled	3 to 4 c	
English walnuts, in shell	1⅕ c, nut meats	4 to 6
Farina	3 c, uncooked	15 to 20
	15 c, cooked	
Figs, dry, small	2¾c (44 figs)	
Flour, all-purpose, sifted once	4 c	

Approximate Measure and Number of Servings per Pound of Some Food Materials as Purchased (Continued)

FOOD	MEASURE	NUMBER OF SERVINGS
Flour, cake, sifted once	4¾ c	
Flour, whole wheat	3¾ c	
Flour, white bread, sifted once	4 c	
Gelatin, flavored	2⅓ c; 1 pkg = ½ c	
Gelatin, granulated	3¼ c; 1 envelope = 1 Tbsp	
Grapefruit, size 64	1 grapefruit	
Grapenuts	4 c	12 to 16
Green peppers	4 to 5, medium	
Greens	2 to 5 qt	3 to 4
Ham	1 c, cooked	
Hominy grits	3 c, uncooked	16
	13 c, cooked	
Honey	1⅓ c	
Kohlrabi	4 to 6, medium	4
Lard	2 c	
Lemon juice	2 c, 8 to 10 lemons	
Lemon, size 300	4 lemons, medium	
Lentils, dried	2 c, uncooked	8 to 10
	4 c, cooked	
Lettuce	1, large	6 to 8
Lettuce, leaf	24 to 48 leaves	6 to 8
Macaroni, 1-inch pieces	4½ c, uncooked	12 (⅔ c)
	9 c, cooked	
Marshmallows	80	
Mayonnaise	2 c	
Meat, cooked, diced	3 c	4 to 5
Meat, ground, raw	2 c	4
Milk, powdered, skim	4 c	5 qt liquid
Mincemeat	2 c	
Molasses	1⅓ c	
Mushrooms	30 to 40 caps, medium	
Mushrooms, fresh, sliced, with stems	5 to 6 c	
Mushrooms, canned	2 c	
Noodles	6 to 8 c, uncooked	14 (⅔ c)
	14 c, cooked	
Nuts, chopped	4 c	

**Approximate Measure and Number of Servings per Pound of Some
Food Materials as Purchased (Continued)**

FOOD	MEASURE	NUMBER OF SERVINGS
Oats, rolled	4¾ c, uncooked	12 to 15
	9 c, cooked	
Oil, salad	2⅛ c	
Okra	24 pods, medium	5 to 6
	3 c, sliced	
Onions, small	24	6
Onions, large, mature	4	4
Orange juice	2 c	3 to 4
Oranges, size 150	2	2
Parsnips	4, medium	4
Peaches, dried	3 c	
Peaches, fresh	3 to 4, medium	
Peanut butter	1¾ c	
Peanuts, in shell	2 to 2¼ c nut meats	
Peanuts, shelled	3 c	
Pears, fresh	3 to 4, medium	3 to 4
Peas	1 qt or 1 c, shelled	2 to 3
Pecans, in shell	2¼ c nut meats	
Pecans, shelled	4 c	
Pettijohns	4½ c, uncooked	18 to 24
	12 c, cooked	
Pickles, 3 inches long	3 c, 36 halves	36
Pimientos, chopped	2½ c	
Pineapple, fresh	½, medium	3 to 4
Potato chips	5 qt	15 to 20
Potatoes, white	3 to 4, medium	3 to 4
Potatoes, sweet	3, medium	3 to 4
Prunes, dried	2 c, size 30 to 40	7 to 8
Pumpkin	2½ c, uncooked	
	1 c, cooked	
Radishes	20 to 30, small	10
Raisins, seeded	2½ c	
Raisins, seedless	3 c	
Ralston, instant	3 c, uncooked	16 to 18
	9 to 10 c, cooked	
Raspberries	3⅜ c	4 to 5
Rhubarb	4 to 8 stalks	3 to 4
	4 c, 1-inch pieces	

Approximate Measure and Number of Servings per Pound of Some Food Materials as Purchased (Continued)

FOOD	MEASURE	NUMBER OF SERVINGS
Rice	2 c, uncooked	12 to 16
	8 c, cooked	
Rice, flakes	13 c	20 to 25
Rice, puffed	27 c	25 to 35
Rutabaga	1 to 2 rutabagas	3 to 4
Salsify	8, or 1 to 2 bunches	4
Sauerkraut	3 c, packed	
Sausage, small link	14 to 16 links	4
Shredded wheat	16 biscuits	16
Soybeans, green	1 qt	2 to 3
Spaghetti	4¼ c, uncooked	15
	9 c, cooked	
Squash, acorn	1, medium	2
Squash, summer	1, medium	3 to 4
Squash, winter	2½ c, uncooked	2 to 3
	1 c, cooked	
Strawberries	2¼ c	3 to 4
Sugar, brown	3 c, lightly packed	
	2⅓ c, packed	
Sugar, granulated	2 c	
Sugar, loaf, ½-inch cubes	96 to 116	
Sugar, loaf, domino	90 dominoes	
Sugar, powdered, sifted	3½ c	
Tapioca, granular	3 c	
Tapioca, pearl	2¾ c	
Tea	6 c	300
Tomatoes, fresh	3 to 4, medium	3 to 4
Turnips	2 to 4	3 to 4
Water cress	5 bunches, small	
Yeast, compressed	32 cakes	
Yeast, active dry	64 packages	

Approximate Amounts of Meat, Fish, and
Poultry to Allow Per Person When Buying

FOOD	AMOUNT
Meats	
Chops	1 to 2, according to size
Roasts	¼ to ½ lb
Loin steaks	¼ to ½ lb
Round steak	¼ to ⅓ lb
Boned or ground meat, liver, sausage	¼ lb
Chickens, dressed, undrawn	
Stewing (2½ to 5 lb)	½ lb
Roasting (2½ to 5 lb)	¾ lb
Frying (2½ to 3½ lb)	¾ lb
Broiling (1 to 2½ lb)	¾ to 1 chicken, according to size
Fish	
Steaks and fillets	¼ to ⅓ lb

WEIGHT AND MEASURE OF STANDARD SIZES OF CANNED GOODS

It is difficult to state weight and measure of standard size cans exactly, for they vary with different types of foods and with packs in different canneries. It is well to remember that jams, marmalades, and preserves have somewhat greater weight for a given size of jar, and fish and some other foods are lighter than average. Fruits and vegetables tend to be more or less uniform in weight.

Some common can and jar sizes are:

SIZE	NET WEIGHT	MEASURE
No. 300	14 to 16 oz	1¾ c
No. 303	16 to 17 oz	2 c
No. 2½	1 lb 13 oz	3½ c

Beverages

WATER is the natural beverage and forms the greater portion of all others. A few beverages are valued only for their flavors or stimulating qualities, others are quite nutritious, and some combine these properties. Temperature is important in the acceptance of beverages. Hot beverages should be served hot and "iced" beverages very cold.

Beverages may require merely a mixing together of the ingredients; in some cases their preparation may involve a special process. Some terms used in preparation of beverages are:

Infusion. Boiling water is poured over material; mixture is then covered and allowed to stand until flavor is extracted. Example: steeped tea or coffee.

Filtration. Hot or boiling water is poured slowly over material enclosed in some kind of sieve. Example: drip or filtered coffee.

Percolation. Hot water is allowed to circulate through material held in a strainer until desired strength is obtained. Example: percolated coffee.

COFFEE

General Suggestions. Ground coffee sealed in a metal or glass container or coffee beans to be ground after purchase may be selected. Ground coffee, when not sealed in the original container, keeps its flavor better if stored in a tightly closed container.

Coffee should be ground as fine as it can be used with equipment at hand. Regular (medium), drip (medium-fine), and pulverized (fine) are common commercal grinds. Finely ground coffee makes a stronger and richer beverage than coarsely ground coffee. It should be used when the method of preparation does not allow long contact of water with coffee.

Glass, enamel, aluminum, and stainless-steel pots commonly are used in making coffee. A coffee pot of suitable size should be selected. Manufacturers suggest that for best results the pot should be at least ½ full. The pots should be clean. Water should be freshly boiled. Long boiling makes it flat and insipid and affects flavor of beverage. Many automatic coffee makers require starting with cold water. Measurements should be accurate. Each step should be carefully timed. Coffee should not boil. Boiling extracts bitter flavoring components, such as tannins, and increases the loss of aromatic components commonly referred to as caffeol. The beverage should not stand on the grounds, as this also extracts tannins.

Proportions. Proportions of coffee suggested for 1 measuring cup of water vary with strength desired and with grind of coffee. They are approximately as follows:

Weak	1 tablespoon
Medium	1¼ to 1½ tablespoons
Strong	1½ to 2 tablespoons
After-dinner	2 to 3 tablespoons

Service. Two measuring cups of water make three servings in regular coffee cups or six to eight in after-dinner coffee cups. Coffee may be served black, with cream and sugar, or with hot milk (café au lait). Plain cream or a garnish of whipped cream or ice cream may be used in iced coffee.

STEEPED COFFEE ("BOILED" COFFEE)

METHOD I. Pour freshly boiled water over regular grind coffee. Stir. Cover. Set over low heat and steep 5 to 8 minutes. *Do not boil.* Add dash of cold water. Let it settle 3 to 5 minutes. Strain. Serve at once.

METHOD II. Add a slightly beaten egg with the crushed shell, or slightly beaten egg white, or several crushed shells, to dry coffee. The particles of coffee adhere to egg as it coagulates, and settling is more easily accomplished. Proceed as for Method I.

METHOD III. Use cold instead of boiling water. Heat mixture to just below boiling point, and simmer 5 to 8 minutes. *Do not boil.* Allow to settle, adding cold water if egg has not been used.

DRIP COFFEE (FILTERED COFFEE)

Measure drip grind coffee into strainer of drip pot. If a filter paper is required, place coffee on top of filter. Insert water spreader. Measure boiling water into upper compartment. Cover and keep hot until dripping is completed. If a stronger beverage is desired, coffee may be poured through a second time, but volatile oil will be lost and flavor affected. Remove grounds. Cover pot. Serve at once.

VACUUM DRIP COFFEE

If directions are available for equipment used, follow those. Measure water into the bottom section of the vacuum coffee maker and put the top section in place with rod or filter. Measure fine grind coffee into the upper bowl, place pot on burner. Heat slowly. When all but a thin layer of water has been forced into the upper section, turn heat very low and allow water to remain in upper bowl 2 or 3 minutes. Stir just once. Remove from heat. As soon as coffee has filtered back into the bottom section, remove the top section. Keep covered. Serve at once.

PERCOLATED COFFEE

Place cold water in pot and regular grind coffee in strainer. Heat. Let water circulate slowly through coffee until it is of desired strength as determined by color and flavor. This will require about 5 minutes. Avoid boiling of beverage in pot.

AFTER-DINNER COFFEE

Make strong coffee. Serve black in demitasse cups.

CAFÉ AU LAIT

Make coffee of medium strength. Serve with an equal quantity of *hot* milk.

ICED COFFEE

Partially fill tall glasses with cracked ice or ice cubes. Fill with strong freshly made hot coffee. Garnish with whipped cream or ice cream if desired.

TEA

General Suggestions. China, glass, earthenware, or enamel pots are recommended for making tea. Metal is apt to affect flavor. The pot should be scalded to heat it. Water should be freshly boiled. If loose tea is used the tea should be poured off leaves as soon as sufficiently steeped. Strainers, tea balls, or tea bags should not be filled more than ½ full so the leaves can swell. They should be removed after steeping.

Proportions. Proportion of tea to water cannot be stated definitely, as it depends largely upon kind of tea and personal taste. A common rule allows ½ to 1 teaspoon tea to 1 measuring cup water.

Service. Two measuring cups of water yield 3 average servings. Tea may be served with milk or cream, sugar, thinly sliced orange or lemon, candied cherries, ginger, orange peel, mint leaves, or similar accompaniments.

HOT TEA

Scald pot, put in tea, pour boiling water over it. Cover, steep in warm place 1 to 3 minutes. *Do not boil.* Strain, serve at once. Strength may be regulated to suit each individual by combining with freshly boiled water at the table.

SPICED TEA. Simmer ⅛ to ¼ teaspoon whole allspice, ⅛ to ¼ teaspoon whole cloves, ¼ stick cinnamon, ⅛ lemon rind, and ¼ orange rind per measuring cup of water for 20 minutes. Add 1 teaspoon tea per measuring cup water, cover and steep 1 to 3 minutes. Strain out leaves and spices. Add 1 tablespoon orange juice and 2 teaspoons lemon juice per cup. Add sugar to taste. Serve hot or cold.

ICED TEA. Partially fill iced tea glasses with crushed ice or ice cubes. Fill with hot, strong freshly made tea. If tea is cooled first, some flavor is lost.

Some infusions become cloudy when cold. If tea is brewed with softened water, this problem can be avoided. Clear tea is also assured if tea is added to cold water. In the cold water method, allow 4 teaspoons of tea per measuring cup of water. Let stand in the refrigerator 12 to 24 hours. Strain and serve. This method requires more tea and produces a slightly different flavor.

Served with sliced lemon or orange. A sprig of mint is an attractive garnish. Lemon cubes made by freezing lemonade may be used. Plain or colored ice cubes containing slices of lemon, orange, whole cherries, or sprigs of mint add variety.

INSTANT BEVERAGES

Instant coffee, tea, and cocoa are available on the market. Follow the directions on the package for preparation. These beverages may be served either hot or cold and with various garnishes and flavorings added.

MILK BEVERAGES

CHOCOLATE

1 square unsweetened chocolate
3 tablespoons sugar
A few grains salt

½ cup hot water
3½ cups milk, scalded

■ Place chocolate, sugar, salt, and water in saucepan. Cook over low heat until smooth and glossy, stirring constantly. Add milk, reheat, beat with rotary beater just before serving. Flavor improves if mixture is allowed to stand ½ hour or more over hot water. A few drops of vanilla may be added just before serving. Garnish with whipped cream or marshmallow if desired. Four cups.

CHOCOLATE SYRUP (FOR HOT OR COLD CHOCOLATE)

1 square unsweetened chocolate	¹⁄₁₆ teaspoon salt
	¾ cup hot water
¼ cup sugar	¼ teaspoon vanilla

■ Place chocolate, sugar, salt, and water in saucepan. Cook over low heat until smooth and glossy, stirring constantly. Cool and flavor. Store in refrigerator. Allow 1½ tablespoons syrup to 1 cup milk. One cup syrup, scant.

CHOCOLATE MILK

Flavor milk to taste with Chocolate Syrup (p. 21).

CHOCOLATE MILK SHAKE

Make Chocolate Milk (p. 21). Shake in beverage mixer or beat with rotary beater until foamy. One-fourth cup ice cream for each cup milk may be added before beating. Serve ice cold.

CHOCOLATE MALTED MILK

3 tablespoons malted milk	2 tablespoons Chocolate
⅔ c, water or milk	Syrup (p. 21)

■ Mix malted milk with a little of the liquid. When smooth, add syrup and remainder of liquid while stirring. Serve hot or cold.

FRENCH CHOCOLATE

Place a generous tablespoon of Chocolate Sauce (p. 103) in each serving cup. Add hot milk to fill cup. Stir until mixed.

COCOA

3 tablespoons cocoa	½ cup water
3 tablespoons sugar	3½ cups milk, scalded
A few grains salt	

■ Mix cocoa, sugar, and salt. Add water. Continue as directed for Chocolate (p. 20). Four cups.

CREAMY COCOA. Prepare as for Cocoa, mixing 1 tablespoon flour or ½ tablespoon cornstarch with sugar, salt, and cocoa. This makes a thicker beverage that does not separate readily.

COCOA WITH EGG. Prepare as for Cocoa, allowing ½ egg for each cup of liquid. Beat egg until light and frothy. Add hot cocoa mixture gradually, beating constantly. Serve at once.

COCOA WITH NONFAT DRY MILK. Use 2⅔ cups instant nonfat dry milk and 3½ cups water in place of milk in recipe for Cocoa. Continue as for Cocoa. This gives a highly desirable beverage containing approximately twice the milk solids of standard cocoa.

MEXICAN CHOCOLATE

2 squares unsweetened chocolate	2 teaspoons cinnamon
2 tablespoons hot water	2 cups strong coffee
⅔ cup sugar	3 cups hot milk
½ teaspoon salt	1 teaspoon vanilla

■ Place chocolate and hot water in saucepan, cook over low heat until chocolate melts. Combine the sugar, salt, and cinnamon and add to the chocolate. Add coffee and stir until smooth. Cook 5 minutes longer. Combine hot milk to which vanilla has been added and the chocolate mixture. Cook over low heat for 10 minutes to blend flavors. Whip to a froth and serve. Five and one-third cups.

EGG-NOG

¾ tablespoon sugar	1 egg, well beaten
A few grains salt	⅔ cup milk
¼ teaspoon vanilla	A few grains nutmeg

■ Add sugar, salt, and vanilla to egg. Mix well. Add milk gradually. Strain, chill, and serve sprinkled lightly with nutmeg. Egg white may be beaten separately if desired and folded in last.

Egg-Nog may be prepared in a shaker containing a small amount of cracked ice. A glass jar may be used when a shaker is not available.

CHOCOLATE EGG-NOG. Add 2 tablespoons Chocolate Syrup (p. 21) to Egg-Nog. Omit sugar.

COFFEE EGG-NOG. Use Egg-Nog recipe, substituting strong coffee for ½ the milk. Cream may be used instead of milk.

MALTED MILK EGG-NOG. Add 1 tablespoon malted milk to Egg-Nog, mixing it with sugar and egg yolk. Substitute 1 tablespoon cream for equal amount of milk.

ORANGE, GRAPE, OR PINEAPPLE EGG-NOG. Make as for Egg-Nog, substituting respective fruit juices for ½ the milk. One tablespoon or more of cream may be added if a richer beverage is desired. A few grains of nutmeg or cinnamon may be sprinkled over Orange Egg-Nog before serving. Increase sugar in Grape Juice Egg-Nog to 1 tablespoon.

FRUIT BEVERAGES

General Suggestions. Carbonated water or gingerale may be substituted for part of the water in fruit beverages. Sugar syrup may be used to advantage for sweetening, as it insures dissolving the sugar. Syrup may be kept on hand for use as needed. Lemon juice improves the flavor of almost all other fruit juices and is therefore desirable to use with them.

Service. Slices of lemon or orange, maraschino cherries, fresh strawberries, or sprigs of mint are frequently used as garnishes for iced drinks. See suggestions for garnishing Iced Tea (p. 20).

SUGAR SYRUP

1 cup sugar   1 cup water

■ Boil sugar and water together to make a thin syrup. Pour into clean hot bottles or jars. Seal. This may be kept on hand for use in beverages and frozen desserts.

If thicker syrup is desired, increase sugar to 1½ cups and add 1 tablespoon corn syrup to prevent crystallizing. Approximately 1¼ cups.

LEMONADE I

½ to ¾ cup sugar   1 quart water
¾ cup lemon juice

■ Mix sugar and lemon juice. Add water and stir until sugar is thoroughly dissolved. Chill. Five cups.

LEMONADE II

¾ cup lemon juice   3 cups water
1 cup sugar syrup (p. 23)

■ Mix ingredients thoroughly. Chill. Five cups, scant.

FOUNDATION PUNCH I

3 cups orange juice, strained   2 cups sugar
1½ to 2 cups lemon juice,   Water to make 1 gallon
   strained

■ Make sugar into a syrup with 2 cups of water. Cool. Combine with fruit juice and remaining water. Pour a small quantity into punch bowl, add a block of ice, pour remainder of punch over ice. Tea may be substituted for part of water. Other fruit juices, sweetened to taste, may be added for variety. Approximately 1 gallon.

FOUNDATION PUNCH II

2 6-ounce cans frozen, concen-   2 cups sugar
   trated orange juice   Water to make 1 gallon
2 6-ounce cans frozen, concen-
   trated lemon juice

■ Follow directions for Foundation Punch I.
CHERRY PUNCH. Allow 3 parts Foundation Punch to 1 to 2 parts cherry juice.
CRANBERRY PUNCH. Allow 3 parts Foundation Punch to 1 part cranberry juice.

GINGER ALE PUNCH. Use Foundation Punch, substituting 1 large bottle ginger ale for an equal amount of water.

GRAPE PUNCH. Allow 1 part Foundation Punch to 1 to 2 parts grape juice.

MINT PUNCH. Allow 1 gallon Foundation Punch to 1 dozen small sprigs fresh mint. Pour hot syrup used in making Foundation Punch over mint. Let stand 5 minutes. Strain and cool before adding to fruit juice. A garnish of fresh mint is good.

PINEAPPLE PUNCH. Allow 3 parts Foundation Punch to 1 to 2 parts pineapple juice.

RASPBERRY PUNCH. Allow 1 part Foundation Punch to 1 to 3 parts raspberry juice.

STRAWBERRY PUNCH. Allow 1 part Foundation Punch to 1 part fresh strawberry juice.

TEA PUNCH. Allow 3 parts Foundation Punch or Lemonade to 2 parts tea.

SPICED GRAPE JUICE

3 cups sweetened grape juice, or 1 6-ounce can concentrated, frozen grape juice, and 3 cans of water	1 teaspoon whole cloves 3 1-inch sticks cinnamon 4 pieces orange rind, 1-inch square

Mix all ingredients. Simmer 10 minutes. Strain. Serve hot. Whole spices are used to insure a clear beverage. Three cups.

SPICED APPLE JUICE. Substitute apple juice for grape juice.

SPICED CIDER. Substitute cider for grape juice.

ORIENTAL PUNCH (HOT SPICED FRUIT PUNCH)

1 cup sugar	1 sprig mint
1 cup water	½ cup lemon juice
6 cloves	1½ cups orange juice
1-inch stick cinnamon	Green coloring, if desired
½ tablespoon chopped ginger root	

■ Simmer sugar, water, cloves, cinnamon, ginger, and mint together slowly for 10 minutes. Add fruit juices, heat to simmering. Strain, color if desired. Serve hot. Three cups.

HOT CRANBERRY PUNCH

2 quarts fresh cranberries	6 3-inch sticks cinnamon
4 whole oranges, sliced	20 whole cloves
4 whole lemons, sliced	5 to 6 cups sugar
7 quarts water	

■ Wash cranberries. Combine all ingredients except sugar. Cover and simmer 20 to 30 minutes. Strain. Add sugar. Reheat and serve hot. Approximately 2 gallons.

Cereals

BREAKFAST cereals that require cooking are usually either whole, cracked, flaked or rolled, or granular. Familiar examples of each are:

Whole	Cracked	Flaked or Rolled	Granular
Wheat	Wheat	Rolled oats	Cornmeal
Barley	Oats	Rolled wheat	Cream of wheat
Rice	Hominy grits	Flaked hominy	Granular whole wheat
Hominy			Cream of rye

Breakfast cereals also may be classified as *long cooking* or *quick cooking* according to method of manufacture used. The present tendency is to use quick-cooking cereals that require only a few minutes to complete cooking. In some cases, as with oats, the texture is different and some prefer the flavor of the long-cooking cereals.

General Directions for Cooking

Cereal cookery is usually accomplished by boiling or steaming in a double boiler, in a saucepan directly over low heat, or in a pressure saucepan. Long cookery by boiling is most suitable to granular cereals where shape retention is not a problem, but coarsely ground and whole cereals require longer cooking than granular cereals. The flavor of cereals is thought to be improved with long cooking. Experiments show it has little effect upon completeness of digestion.

The amount of water determines largely the volume of finished product.

Cereal swells to the extent of water used until the limit of the grain is reached. Individual tastes differ as to consistency desired. Granular cereals, as a rule, absorb more water than whole or flaked. Granular cereals and water must be combined carefully to prevent lumping.

Specific Directions for Cooking and Serving

If cereals are to be cooked over boiling water, use top of double boiler for combining water, salt, and cereal. Most cereals are purchased in packages that give proportions and directions for cooking that particular cereal. It is wise to follow these directions.

METHOD I. Have salted water boiling rapidly. Add cereal slowly, stirring to prevent lumping. Stir whole and flaked cereals as little as possible with a fork to prevent breaking the grains. Cook slowly over direct heat for desired time, stirring as necessary. If preferred, place thickened cereal over boiling water, cover, and cook for longer time.

METHOD II. Put cereal and salt in utensil in which it is to be cooked. Stir cold water into cereal. Cover. Heat very slowly to boiling point. Do not stir. Continue cooking required time.

METHOD III. Stir cereal into water somewhat below boiling point. Continue stirring until boiling point is reached. Reduce heat and cook required time.

Any cooked cereal may be made more nutritious by cooking in part or all milk. It is then better to cook in a double boiler as milk scorches easily. Fruit may be combined with cereals to give variety. Raisins and coarsely chopped figs, prunes, or dates are desirable. Allow 1 tablespoon raisins or 2 each of figs, prunes, or seeded dates for each serving of cereal. Add raisins and figs at beginning of cooking, dates at end. Prunes may be cooked separately and served over cereal. Other fruit sauces as well as sliced bananas and fresh berries may be used in this way.

Leftover cereals may be molded and served cold, or sliced and browned in a small amount of fat, or used in muffins and griddle cakes or in soups.

FRIED CORNMEAL MUSH (SAUTÉED)

Pack very thick hot mush into molds rinsed with cold water. Cool. Cover or brush surface with a small amount of fat to prevent formation of crust. Remove from mold, cut into ⅓-inch slices. Brown in a small amount of hot fat. If slices are dipped in flour or cornmeal, or egged and crumbed (p. 98), before cooking, mush will be drier and fat is less apt to spatter. (Very thick mush is cooked successfully this way.)

SCRAPPLE

2 pounds pork neck bones	2 cups cold water
1 quart water	Pepper, if desired
1 teaspoon salt	Sage, if desired
2 cups cornmeal	

■ Simmer pork neck bones in 1 quart water and salt until meat falls from bones. Remove meat from bones. Add water to bring volume of stock to

1 quart. Heat to boiling point. Mix cornmeal with cold water. Stir meat and cornmeal mixture into boiling stock. Cook, stirring until thick. Add more salt if needed. Continue cooking for 5 minutes. Pour into 9 x 5 x 3-inch loaf pan. Chill until firm. Slice, fry in small amount of hot fat as for Mush (p. 26). Serve hot.

WILD RICE

⅓ cup wild rice soaked   1⅓ tablespoons butter or
    1 hour in warm water   margarine
⅔ cup boiling water   ⅓ teaspoon salt

■ Place soaked rice in top of double boiler with boiling water, butter, and salt. Cover. Cook approximately 2 hours.

STEAMED RICE (CHINESE METHOD)

1 cup rice   ½ teaspoon salt
1¾ to 1½ cups cold water

■ Place rice with water and salt in a pan with tight-fitting cover. Heat to boiling, then open cover slightly and reduce heat to prevent boiling over. Cook slowly until water is nearly all evaporated, then cover tightly, and reduce heat sufficiently to prevent burning. Cook 20 minutes longer. Turn off heat entirely, but do not open cover for 5 minutes. Remove cover, stir gently with fork. Each grain of rice should be dry and unbroken. The amount of water to be used is determined by rice, as some varieties are drier than others; also some persons prefer a drier product. *Do not stir rice during cooking process.* Three cups.

SPANISH RICE I

⅓ cup rice   1 cup or more small
2 cups canned tomatoes   pieces cheese
1 cup hot water   2 tablespoons fat
3 tablespoons chopped onion   2 teaspoons salt
1 tablespoon chopped green   1 speck cayenne
   pepper

■ Mix all ingredients in oiled baking dish. Bake uncovered at 325°F about 1 hour or until rice is soft. Stir occasionally as needed. Chopped celery may be added. Three cups.

SPANISH RICE II

6 strips bacon, cut fine   2 cups canned tomatoes
1 medium onion   Salt to taste
3 cups cooked rice (p. 27)

■ Cook bacon in frying pan until it begins to brown, stirring as necessary. Drain. Slice onion, add to bacon. Cook over low flame until onion is tender, stirring as necessary. Add rice and tomatoes. Mix. Season to taste. Put into oiled casserole and bake at 325°F, 30 minutes. Four cups.

BOILED MACARONI, SPAGHETTI, OR NOODLES

8- or 9-ounce package maca- roni, sphagetti, or other paste, or 5- or 6-ounce package noodles	2 quarts water 2 teaspoons salt

■ Bring water to boil in deep kettle. Break macaroni, spaghetti, or noodles into pieces as desired. Drop gradually into boiling water. Cook uncovered at fast boil, stirring occasionally with fork to prevent sticking. Cook just until tender (9 to 12 minutes for pastes, 5 to 7 minutes for noodles). Drain immediately in colander or sieve. Rinsing is not necessary if it is to be served with sauce. Approximately 4 cups cooked macaroni or spaghetti or 2½ cups cooked noodles.

MACARONI AND CHEESE

2 cups cooked macaroni (4 ounces, uncooked) 1 cup grated cheese	1½ to 2 cups Medium White Sauce (p. 94) Buttered Crumbs (p. 60)

■ Place alternate layers of macaroni, cheese, and white sauce in oiled baking dish. If preferred, cheese may be added to hot white sauce and stirred until melted to give a smoother mixture. Cover top with buttered crumbs. Bake at 375°F until sauce bubbles and crumbs brown. Three cups.

MACARONI WITH TOMATO SAUCE

2 cups cooked macaroni (4 ounces, uncooked)	2 cups Tomato Sauce (p. 99) Buttered Crumbs (p. 60)

■ Add macaroni to sauce. Put into oiled baking dish. Cover with buttered crumbs. Bake at 375°F until sauce bubbles and crumbs brown. Three cups.

BARLEY VEGETABLE SOUP

2 tablespoons quick cooking pearl barley 1 bouillon cube 1 cup boiling water ½ cup canned tomatoes	1 cup mixed cooked veg- etables (carrots, celery, and onion) Salt to taste

■ Cook barley until tender. Dissolve bouillon cube in boiling water (water left from cooking vegetables may be used). Add tomatoes, cooked vegetables, and barley. Salt to taste. Reheat and serve. Sprinkle a little chopped parsley on top.

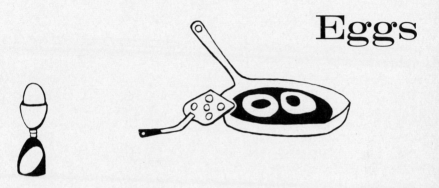

Eggs

Selection. A fresh egg is heavy in proportion to size. For cooking in the shell and poaching only fresh eggs are suitable.

Eggs may be selected on the basis of quality and size. Quality is indicated by grade. Grades AA and A are the best grades and are preferred for poaching, frying, or cooking in the shell. For other cooking purposes, Grade B may be satisfactory and less expensive. The common sizes of eggs include extra large, large, medium, and small.

Care. Eggs should be stored in a refrigerator away from strong-flavored foods. Egg yolks, if unbroken, may be refrigerated for a short time if covered with cold water. If broken, they may be beaten and covered tightly without addition of water. Egg whites, if covered and chilled, will keep some time. They may be frozen for longer storage.

Uses. Eggs are a valuable protein food. Eggs may be served as a main dish or they may function in food preparation as thickening, binding, or emulsifying agents, or to incorporate air. One egg, 2 egg whites, or 2 egg yolks are equivalent approximately to 1 tablespoon of flour in thickening power. For thickening, the texture is better if the egg is beaten only enough to mix. Eggs bind food materials together as in noodles, stuffing, meat loaf, or crumbs on a croquette or chop. The yolk serves as an emulsifier and is used as such in mayonnaise and Hollandaise sauce. Eggs may serve as a leavening agent when considerable air is incorporated in beating. A maximum amount of leavening results when whites and yolks are beaten separately.

Beating. Egg whites whip quickly and volume is larger if they are at room temperature before beating. Egg whites that are to be beaten should be entirely free from bits of yolk as the fat of the yolk reduces ability to hold air. Egg whites should not be beaten until ready to use as there is separation of liquid after standing. Too much beating makes egg whites dry. Egg whites are beaten sufficiently for most purposes when they hold moist, firm rounded peaks. Addition of sugar or acid, such as lemon juice or cream of tartar, in limited amounts increases the ability of egg whites to hold air. When using an electric mixer, sugar may be added to egg whites at the beginning of the beating. When egg whites are beaten by hand, sugar is usually added gradually after soft peaks have formed or during the last half of beating.

Cookery. Eggs should be cooked at low temperatures; high temperatures make them tough and leathery. Egg white begins to coagulate at about 140°F and will change to a tender jelly-like substance at this temperature; at higher temperatures, it is firmer. Egg yolks coagulate at a slightly higher temperature, beginning at about 149°F. The whole egg coagulates at approximately the same temperature as egg yolk. Eggs and foods containing eggs therefore are cooked at low temperatures. Egg dishes cooked in the oven may be set in a pan of hot water that *is not allowed to boil.* In starch-thickened mixtures, eggs are added near the end of the cooking process to avoid overcooking.

Service. Eggs are garnished suitably with toast, slices of crisp bacon, and parsley. Sauces or purées are often served with poached eggs or omelets.

Frozen Eggs. Egg whites and beaten whole eggs may be frozen. Yolks also may be frozen if salt or sugar is added to prevent a pasty consistency. Frozen eggs are defrosted and used in the same way as fresh ones. Frozen whites beat up quickly and to a good volume.

Dried Eggs. Although differing considerably from fresh eggs, dried eggs of good quality may be substituted for fresh ones in many recipes. Directions on package should be followed when using dried eggs.

SOFT-COOKED EGGS (CODDLED)

Allow 1 pint water for first egg, and 1 cup for each additional egg. Heat water to boiling in deep saucepan. Remove from heat. Put eggs gently into water, 1 at a time, from a tablespoon. Cover, let stand in warm place 4 to 10 minutes according to consistency desired.

HARD-COOKED EGGS

METHOD I. Prepare as for Soft-Cooked Eggs (p. 30). Let stand 30 to 45 minutes.

METHOD II. Cook in double boiler. Place boiling water in both top and bottom. Let stand 20 to 30 minutes.

METHOD III. Cover eggs with water (water level should be at least 1 inch above eggs), heat until water just begins to boil. Turn off heat. Cover and let stand 20 to 25 minutes.

POACHED EGGS

Fill oiled shallow pan with water to depth sufficient to cover eggs completely, about 1½ inches. Salt or white vinegar may be added if desired (1½ teaspoons salt or 1 teaspoon vinegar to 1 quart water). Heat water to boiling. Break an egg carefully into a shallow cup; slide gently into water. Repeat for each egg used. Water may be stirred before first egg is added. The swirl of water, if the egg is added at the right moment, will tend to keep it in compact form. Reduce heat to below boiling point, and cook until white is jelly-like and a film forms over yolk. Remove eggs individually with a perforated skimmer. It is easier to obtain an even shape if eggs are cooked in oiled muffin rings or in a special egg poacher suspended over hot water. Slip onto slices of hot, buttered toast. Season with butter, salt, and pepper. Poached eggs may be served on broiled ham, corned beef hash, or on spinach.

BAKED EGGS (SHIRRED)

2 tablespoons soft bread crumbs	1 tablespoon thin cream
1 egg	Salt to taste
	Pepper to taste

■ Cover bottom of individual oiled baking dish with ½ of the crumbs. Break egg, slip onto crumbs. Season, cover with remaining crumbs, add cream. Set in pan of hot water. Bake at 350°F until white is firm, approximately 20 minutes.

Crumbs may be omitted, and ½ teaspoon butter substituted for cream. Serve in baking dish.

Crumbs may be covered with bits of crisp bacon or with 1 tablespoon minced cooked ham, liver, chicken, sausage, or mushrooms browned in butter; or omit crumbs, and add 2 tablespoons of tomato sauce. Omit cream when tomato sauce is used.

FRIED EGGS (SAUTÉED)

METHOD I. Heat frying pan. Add 1 tablespoon or more of fat. Bacon or ham drippings are good. Butter or margarine may be used. Break eggs in saucer. Slip in pan, 1 at a time, and cook slowly until white is set. Lift fat with spoon, and pour over egg until a film forms over yolk or, if preferred, turn eggs once while cooking. Add more fat if needed. Season to taste. Fat should not be hot enough to brown egg or it will be tough. Cooking time approximately 8 minutes.

METHOD II. Use skillet with tight-fitting lid. Proceed as for Method I until whites are just set. Then add 1 tablespoon water. Cover tightly and turn off heat. The steam from the water will finish cooking the eggs and will produce a fine film over the yolks. Lift eggs out with pancake turner onto heated plates and serve at once.

SCRAMBLED EGGS

1 tablespoon fat	⅜ teaspoon salt
3 eggs	Pepper to taste
3 tablespoons milk or cream	

METHOD I. Place fat in frying pan; heat gently. Beat eggs until whites and yolks are mixed. Beat in milk and seasonings. Pour into heated pan. Cook slowly lifting from bottom of pan with a spatula, until eggs are cooked and of creamy consistency. Two servings.

Some people prefer distinct white and yellow particles in scrambled eggs. In that case, eggs are not beaten before putting into heated pan but are stirred occasionally while cooking.

Small pieces of bacon may be cooked until crisp and brown, allowing ½ slice bacon for each egg; or shredded dried beef may be frizzled in pan before adding egg mixture; or cooked asparagus cut into ½-inch lengths may be added to warm fat in pan.

METHOD II. Heat fat in top of double boiler. Add seasonings to eggs and beat until light. Add milk to eggs and combine thoroughly. Cover and cook over simmering water for approximately 25 minutes. Stir only once or twice. Serve promptly on warm plates.

EGGS À LA GOLDENROD

3 to 4 hard-cooked eggs	5 slices toast
1½ cups Medium White Sauce	Salt to taste
(p. 94)	1 pinch paprika

■ Chop egg whites, add to sauce, season to taste. Arrange 4 slices of toast on serving dish, pour egg mixture over them. Sprinkle with sieved cooked egg yolks. Garnish with parsley and Toast Points (p. 62) made from remaining slice of toast.

DEVILED EGGS

4 hard-cooked eggs, cold	Pepper to taste
Salt to taste	Salad dressing, vinegar, or
⅓ teaspoon dry mustard	cream to moisten

■ Remove shells, cut lengthwise or crosswise through eggs, and remove yolks. Mash yolks, mix with seasonings, and add salad dressing, vinegar, or cream as needed to form a smooth paste. Fill egg whites lightly with mixture. Four servings.

Add 1 tablespoon of minced cooked ham or livers, bits of crisp bacon, frizzled dried beef, anchovies, shrimp, sardines, chopped olives, chives, parsley, pimientos, or similar foods to egg yolk mixture if desired.

OMELETS

General Suggestions. It is not wise to make too large an omelet. Two small ones are more apt to be successful than one very large one. From 4 to 6 eggs are as many as should be used in one omelet.

Proportions. Allow 1 tablespoon liquid, ⅛ teaspoon salt, and a speck of pepper to each egg used. Liquid may be water, milk, tomato, or other fruit juice, or cream. Amount of fat required will vary with size of pan. There should be enough to oil it well on sides and bottom.

To Fold and Turn an Omelet. Hold omelet pan by handle. Loosen omelet in pan, then place spatula under that part nearest handle, tip pan to a nearly vertical position, fold one-half of omelet over the other, and roll onto a hot serving dish. If omelet is very puffy, it may be necessary to make 2 1-inch incisions opposite each other and at right angles to handle in order to make omelet fold well.

FRENCH OMELET

1 egg	1 speck pepper
1 tablespoon liquid	1 teaspoon fat,
⅛ teaspoon salt	approximately

■ Beat egg just enough to mix, add liquid and seasonings. Melt fat in omelet pan, and pour in egg mixture. Cook slowly, keeping heat low. As undersurface becomes set, start lifting it slightly with spatula to let uncooked portion flow underneath and cook. Avoid a scrambled appearance. When whole mixture is of creamy consistency, brown lightly on bottom, then fold and turn onto hot platter.

PUFFY OMELET

1 egg	1 speck pepper
1 tablespoon liquid	Fat
⅛ teaspoon salt	

METHOD I. Separate egg. Add seasoning to yolk and beat. Add liquid (other than milk or cream) to egg white and beat until stiff and slightly dry. Fold egg yolk into egg white. Heat a frying pan containing enough fat to cover the bottom. Turn in omelet mixture. Spread evenly over pan and cook slowly 2 to 5 minutes or until delicately browned underneath. Bake at 350°F (moderate oven) until top is firm and dry, but not brown (10 to 15 minutes). Loosen omelet with spatula, fold, and turn onto hot platter. A larger omelet may need a longer cooking time in the oven.

METHOD II. Separate egg. Add seasonings and milk or cream to egg yolk. Beat egg white until stiff and slightly dry. Continue as for Method I.

Omelets may be varied by: (a) sprinkling grated cheese over omelet before putting in oven and serving with cheese sauce; (b) spreading chopped fish or meat over omelet before folding or by adding chopped fish or meat to the omelet before cooking; or (c) garnishing with sections of orange and sprinkling with powdered sugar. Other fruits such as canned apricots may be served hot with the omelet.

BREAD OMELET

2 tablespoons soft bread	1 egg
crumbs	¼ teaspoon salt
2 tablespoons liquid	Fat

■   Soak bread in the liquid. Separate egg. Add salt and beaten egg yolk to soaked bread. Beat egg white until stiff and slightly dry. Fold egg yolk and bread mixture into egg white. Complete as for Puffy Omelet (p. 33). Spread with jelly before folding and sprinkle top with sugar.

EGG YOLK OMELET

10 egg yolks	1 speck pepper
10 tablespoons liquid	1 teaspoon baking powder
½ teaspoon salt	

■   Beat egg yolks slightly, add liquid gradually, and beat until thick and lemon colored. Add other ingredients. Beat until smooth. Finely diced celery may be added if desired. Cook as for Puffy or French Omelet (p. 33). Four servings.

EGGS AS GARNISHES

Hard-cooked eggs make excellent garnishes for many foods. They may be sliced for use on vegetables and salads. Slices should be uniform to be attractive. More elaborate garnishes are made by cutting egg whites into fancy shapes and arranging them in designs. Hard-cooked eggs are good with cooked greens or on lettuce salad. Cooked egg yolks run through a sieve may be sprinkled over cream soups, creamed vegetables, and certain salads. A single poached egg yolk may be used as a garnish for soup; e.g., Consommé Colbert. Fancy shapes cut from a very thick un-sweetened custard (6 to 8 eggs to 1 cup milk) are used occasionally in bouillon and other clear soups.

Fruit

MOST ripe fruits may be eaten raw. They may be cooked to change flavor or soften the fiber.

Preparation of Fresh Fruit

All fruit should be washed thoroughly to remove dirt, microorganisms, and spray residues. Soft fruits, such as berries, may be washed by placing them in a sieve and running cold water over them. Soft fruits should be washed just before serving as they spoil readily when wet. They may be drained on paper towels. All uncooked fruit should be thoroughly chilled before serving. Fruit knives, scissors, plates, paper napkins, or finger bowls should be provided as necessary for eating raw fruit.

Certain fruits, such as apples, darken if exposed to air after being cut because oxidizing enzymes act on tannins and other substances in the fruit. Silver or stainless-steel knives are desirable for paring such fruits. Darkening can be prevented to a great extent by preparing fruit immediately before serving, protecting it from air, sprinkling it with acid fruit juice such as lemon or pineapple, or treating it with ascorbic acid or with commercial preparations that contain ascorbic acid. Sugar added to fruits such as sliced peaches will prevent oxidation for a time.

AMBROSIA

1 cup orange sections (free
  from membrane)
½ cup Thompson seedless
  grapes

1 banana, sliced
½ cup pineapple tidbits
¼ cup shredded coconut

■   Prepare orange sections. Add grapes, sliced banana, pineapple tidbits, and coconut. Toss lightly. Add sugar if desired. Chill. Arrange fruit mixture in sherbet glasses. Garnish with coconut. Four servings.

COCONUT

To facilitate removal of meat from fresh coconut, punch in eyes and drain out milk. Place coconut in a 350°F oven for 15 minutes. Remove from oven and cool. Crack and remove coconut meat from shell keeping pieces as large as possible. Use a vegetable peeler to cut off outer brown covering on coconut meat.

TOASTED COCONUT STRIPS

Cut thin, long slices from the fresh coconut using a vegetable peeler. Lay loosely on an aluminum tray or heavy baking sheet. Sprinkle with salt. Toast in a 300°F oven until light golden brown in color. Turn several times while browning to obtain an evenly browned product.

CRANBERRY RELISH, UNCOOKED

2 cups cranberries
1 large orange

¾ cup sugar

■   Wash cranberries and orange. Grind, add sugar, and mix well. Cover tightly. Keep in cool place 24 hours before using. One pint.

FROSTED GRAPES

Divide bunches of grapes into small clusters. Use some dark and some light colored varieties of grapes. Wash bunches of grapes and pat dry on a clean towel. Use a pastry brush and brush grapes with egg white beaten until slightly frothy. Sprinkle grapes with granulated sugar and place on a wire rack to dry.

FRUIT CUP (FRUIT COCKTAIL)

Suggested combinations: Oranges, pineapple, and grapefruit; pineapple, oranges, strawberries, and bananas; oranges and coconut; melons alone or in combination. Canned fruits may be used.

Remove membrane from citrus fruits, dice peaches, pineapple, and similar fruits; cut melons into small balls, with a French vegetable cutter (p. 7). Mix; chill at least 1 hour before using.

Finely chopped mint, a sprig of mint, pomegranate seeds, berries, and preserved or candied ginger may be used as garnishes.

Ginger ale, cider, grape juice, or other fruit juice may be poured over the cut fruit. Fruit sherbet or ice may be used as a topping. Serve in sherbet glasses or orange or grapefruit shells.

GRAPEFRUIT HALVES

METHOD I. Wash and wipe grapefruit. Cut in halves crosswise and remove any seeds. With a grapefruit knife or other sharp-pointed knife, cut around edge to separate pulp from skin. Then loosen pulp in each section by cutting close to membranes. Avoid puncturing skin with knife. When all sections have been so treated, gather membranes together and snip them loose from shell with scissors. Remove core at the same time. Replace any disarranged sections, wipe off outside, and place grapefruit on serving plate. Chill. Two servings.

METHOD II. Wash and wipe as for Method I. Cut in halves crosswise and remove seeds. Remove center core with scissors. Cut around pulp in each section, leaving membrane attached to shell. Sugar, halves of seeded white grapes, cherries, pineapple, or cranberry sauce may be used to fill center. Grapefruit may be served on bed of shaved ice or otherwise garnished as desired. Two servings.

GRAPEFRUIT SECTIONS

Choose seedless grapefruit. Wash, wipe, pare as for an apple, removing white portion including membrane with skin so that pulp is exposed. A very sharp knife is necessary. While working, hold grapefruit over plate to collect juice. Remove sections by cutting close to membrane on both sides. Arrange attractively on fruit plate. Two servings.

MELON BALL DESSERT

Cut 1-inch, crosswise slices of a cantaloupe. Remove peeling and seeds. Place each slice on a plate of suitable size. Fill center of cantaloupe slices with balls of honeydew melon sprinkled with fresh blueberries or use balls of honeydew melon and watermelon. Chill, garnish with a sprig of mint and serve.

ORANGE SECTIONS

Prepare as for Grapefruit Sections (p. 37) using seedless oranges.

PREPARATION OF COOKED FRUIT

As a rule, cooked fruits should retain as much color, shape, and flavor as possible. The method of cooking will affect these qualities. Rapid cooking causes some fruits to fall apart; therefore if the original shape is to be retained, slow cooking in sugar syrup is desirable. When it is not necessary to retain the shape of the fruit, sugar may be added at the end of the cooking period to produce a more delicate and natural flavor.

APPLESAUCE

Apples	Water
Sugar to taste	A few grains salt

◼ Wash, pare if desired, quarter, core, and remove any decayed or bruised spots. Cook in only enough water to prevent scorching. When soft, run through a sieve. Add sugar, usually ½ to 1 tablespoon for 1 medium-sized apple. Stir until sugar dissolves. Thin slices of lemon, a few drops lemon juice, or spices such as cinnamon and nutmeg may be added. If the apples are a variety that retain their shape in cooking, they may be cut into uniform slices and cooked in a syrup made of water and sugar. One serving. One-half cup.

APPLE COMPOTE

1 apple	2 tablespoons sugar
¼ cup water	

◼ Use apples that retain their shape in cooking. Wash, pare, core, and place in pan in which sugar and water have been dissolved to form a syrup. Apples should just cover bottom of pan. Cook slowly, until apples are clear and tender and syrup is thick and jelly-like. Turn apples occasionally, being careful to retain shape. Remove apples to serving dish. Pour syrup over them. Lemon or orange juice, with or without some grated rind, may be added to syrup. Nuts, raisins, candied orange peel, or dates may be used to fill cavity in apple.

Whipped cream, chopped nuts, cubes of jelly, or candied orange peel make suitable garnishes. One serving.
SPICED APPLES. Add "red-hot" candies to syrup for Apple Compote. Allow 1 to 2 tablespoons red-hots for 1 large apple. Red coloring and a bit of stick cinnamon may be substituted for candy.

BAKED APPLES

Wash, pare if desired, and core medium-sized apples. Put into baking dish, fill cavities with sugar, add about 6 drops lemon juice for each apple. Add water to depth of 1-inch. Bake at 375°F until soft. Apples may be baked covered or uncovered. If uncovered, baste 3 or 4 times with syrup in pan. Serve hot or cold, with or without sugar and cream. A lemon garnish is pleasing. Orange juice, grated lemon peel, or orange peel may be added before baking. Nuts, raisins, candied orange peel, dates, or mincemeat; or jelly may be used to fill the cavity in apples.

FRIED APPLES (SAUTÉED)

6 medium-sized apples

2 tablespoons fat

6 tablespoons water, if desired

Salt to taste

Sugar, if desired

■ Wash apples, core and cut into ½-inch slices. Put in pan with fat, water if used, salt, and a small amount of sugar, if desired. Cover. Cook slowly until water is absorbed and apples are tender turning occasionally. Six servings.

BAKED BANANAS

Wash slightly underripe bananas. Slice in half lengthwise or leave whole. Place in oiled baking dish. Sprinkle with sugar, bits of butter (about 1 teaspoon for each banana), and if desired, a few drops lemon juice. Bake at 350°F until tender and slightly translucent 15 to 20 minutes. Bananas may be baked in their skins, then peeled and seasoned just before serving; or served in the peel and seasoned at the table much like a baked potato. One serving. One-half banana.

BANANAS BAKED IN CRANBERRY SAUCE. Wash 1 cup cranberries. Add ½ cup water, and cook until soft. Rub cooked cranberries through sieve. Add ½ cup sugar to cranberry pulp, and mix well. Peel and quarter bananas. Place in baking dish, and cover with cranberry pulp. Bake at 350°F until tender. Serve hot or cold. If desired, apricot pulp may be substituted for cranberry pulp.

BROILED BANANAS

Peel slightly underripe bananas and place in shallow pan. Brush with melted butter. Salt lightly. Broil about 10 minutes with low heat. Serve immediately with meat or as dessert. One serving. One-half banana.

FRIED BANANAS

Remove skins. Cut in halves crosswise. Egg and crumb (p. 98). Fry slowly in a small amount of fat until golden brown. One serving. One-half banana.

CRANBERRY SAUCE

4 cups cranberries

2 cups sugar

1 cup water

■ Pick over and wash cranberries. Add water and sugar. Cover. Boil gently 10 minutes or until skins burst. Skim. Cool. Mold as desired. Avoid long cooking since it makes cranberries bitter. One cup raisins may be soaked in cold water and substituted for ½ cup sugar. Six to 8 servings.

CRANBERRY JELLY

4 cups cranberries   1 cup water
2 cups sugar

■   Pick over and wash cranberries. Add water and boil gently until skins burst. If desired, 2-inch stick cinnamon and 2 whole cloves may be added while cooking. When cranberries are soft, rub through sieve, add sugar, and boil until dissolved. Pour into molds or sterilized glasses. Fills 3 or 4 jelly glasses.

BROILED GRAPEFRUIT

Prepare halves of sectioned grapefruit. Sprinkle each half lightly with 2 teaspoons brown sugar and a few grains of nutmeg. Add 1 teaspoon butter. If desired, 1 tablespoon shredded pineapple may be added. Place on broiler pan 2 to 3 inches below unit, and broil 15 minutes with low heat. Serve immediately with meat course or as dessert.

BAKED PEACHES

Select firm ripe fruit. Wash, cut in half, and remove stones. Place in baking dish with hollow side up. Fill hollow with ½ teaspoon butter, brown sugar, a sprinkle of lemon juice, and a dash of cinnamon. Bake at 350°F until peaches are tender, approximately 20 minutes.

BROILED PEACHES

Follow directions for Baked Peaches (p. 40). Broil instead of bake.

BAKED PEARS

Select firm ripe fruit and remove cores. Prepare as for Baked Peaches (p. 40).

BROILED PINEAPPLE

Drain large slices of canned pineapple carefully or use slices of fresh pineapple. Brush with melted butter. Sprinkly lightly with brown sugar. Broil under moderate heat until sugar is melted and pineapple lightly browned. Turn and brown other side. Allow 5 to 10 minutes for each side.

RHUBARB SAUCE

4 cups rhubarb   ¾ to 1 cup sugar

■   Wash rhubarb, cut into ½-inch lengths, retaining skin. Add sugar. Cook *very slowly* without water until juice forms, then more rapidly until tender. A small amount of water may be added if thinner sauce is desired. It will require from 3 to 5 minutes to cook young rhubarb after juice is formed. A small amount may be cooked in double boiler. If desired, bake at 300°F, covering to prevent drying. Two and one-half cups.

Preparation of Frozen Fruit

Frozen fruits should be defrosted in the unopened package. They may be defrosted in the refrigerator, at room temperature, under running cold water, or in front of a fan. If leak-proof, the packages may be inverted several times during defrosting. One pint of frozen fruit may be defrosted in the refrigerator in 4 to 6 hours, at room temperature in 2 to 4 hours, under running cold water (if in watertight package) in ½ to 1 hour, or in front of a fan in 1 to 2 hours. Rapid defrosting causes considerable loss of juice.

Fruits are ready to serve when still slightly icy. They deteriorate quickly when removed from the package, therefore they should be used immediately after defrosting. A soft mushy undesirable texture results when the fruits are entirely defrosted. Therefore it is best to simmer any leftovers for use as a sauce.

Frozen fruits may be used successfully in prepared desserts, jams, jellies, and preserves if allowance is made for the sugar added to the fruit before freezing.

Preparation of Dried Fruit

Wash fruit if necessary. Carefully packaged fruits may not need washing. Soaking shortens the cooking period and tends to give richer juice. To soak fruit cover with water and bring to boil. Remove from heat and allow to stand ½ hour. Cover fruit and simmer gently in water in which soaked until tender. Add liquid as needed to keep fruit covered. Add sugar as needed (¼ to ⅓ cup sugar per pound of fruit) at end of cooking time and continue cooking until sugar is dissolved. If syrup is too thin remove fruit and boil juice until it thickens. Add a little lemon juice, sliced or grated lemon rind, or stick cinnamon and cloves to prunes. A few drops of vanilla may be added to figs. Cooked fruit may be allowed to stand over night to improve plumpness. One pound of dried fruit should yield 8 to 12 servings. Four to 6 cups.

STEWED FRUIT (APRICOTS, FIGS, PRUNES, ETC.)

1 pound dried fruit   ¼ to ⅓ cup sugar, if
Water   desired

■   Wash fruit, if necessary. Carefully packaged fruit may not need washing. Soak if desired. Simmer until tender. Add sugar if desired. Cook until dissolved. If syrup is too thin, remove fruit and boil juice until it thickens. A few drops of vanilla may be added to figs. Add a little lemon juice, sliced or grated lemon rind, or stick cinnamon and cloves to prunes. Twelve servings of apricots, figs, and similar fruits. Six cups. Eight servings prunes. Four cups.

Preparation of Fruit Plates

Fruit plates are combinations of fruits. They may be used on various occasions but are served most often as a main course for luncheon or supper. Small fruit plates make pleasing desserts or refreshments. Sometimes a serving of cheese is placed on plate with fruit, or a cheese tray may be passed. The fruits may be arranged on lettuce or other suitable greens. A sprig of water cress or curly endive or a dip of sherbet gives a contrast in color, flavor, and texture. Cinnamon toast, sweet sandwiches, fruit and nut breads are suitable accompaniments. A beverage and dessert will complete the meal.

Suggestions for Combinations. Wedges of fresh pineapple, orange sections, strawberries with stems, sections of banana, pecan halves, cottage cheese, and water cress.

One-half crosswise slice of honeydew melon, watermelon balls, ½ peach, cream cheese, and curly endive.

Wedge of cantaloupe, wedge of honeydew melon, ½ banana cut in halves lengthwise, pineapple fingers, fresh red raspberries, green or ripe olives, and water cress.

One-half pear, ¼ Japanese persimmon, a pickled peach, wedges of apple with red peeling, dates, white grapes, and lettuce hearts.

One-half peach or pear, section of banana, avocado rings, grapefruit sections, a fresh red or blue plum, and leaf lettuce.

Fresh whole apricots, Bing cherries, pineapple fingers, banana slices, and lettuce or water cress.

Flour Mixtures

FLOUR mixtures are combinations containing liquid and flour. They usually are leavened to improve appearance and taste. They are classified as batters and doughs, on the basis of proportion of flour to liquid. Batters may be beaten with a spoon and doughs are stiff enough to knead.

Batters and Doughs

CLASSES	LIQUID	FLOUR	CONSISTENCY	EXAMPLES
Pour batters	1 part	1 part	Pours in a steady stream	Popovers, griddle cakes
Drop batters	1 part	2 parts	Breaks into drops when poured	Muffins, fritters
Soft doughs	1 part	3 parts	Sticky to touch	Biscuits, yeast rolls
Stiff doughs	1 part	4 parts	Firm to touch	Pie crust, noodles

LEAVENING AGENTS

Flour mixtures may be leavened by steam, air, and carbon dioxide. Steam and air contribute to the leavening of most baked products. Steam is formed from water by heat. Thin batters, such as popovers, are leavened in this way.

Air is introduced by beating the mixture, adding eggs to mixture and then beating, or adding beaten eggs. Carbon dioxide is produced by yeast, baking powder, or soda with an acid. Baking powders are classified as tartrate, phosphate, and SAS-phosphate according to their acid ingredients. Tartrate powders (quick-acting) release the largest amount of carbon dioxide when the mixture is cold and SAS-phosphate (double-acting) the least, therefore the quantity of baking powder needed may vary.

General Proportions for Baking Powder and Soda

Baking Powder. Allow 1 to 2 teaspoons baking powder to 1 cup flour. The larger amount of baking powder may be used in recipes calling for heavy ingredients as graham flour. When food must stand for a time before baking, a double-acting powder is recommended.

Soda. Amount of soda required varies with acid used. There should be just enough soda to neutralize the acid. The following rules may serve as a guide. Allow from ¼ to ¾ teaspoon soda to 1 cup molasses. The average for 1 cup buttermilk is ½ teaspoon. Soda should be mixed with the flour instead of the liquid. When only small amounts of soda are used, there may not be enough gas produced to leaven mixture. In that case, add baking powder as described in the following directions.

Adapting Recipes to Sweet and Sour Milk

Sweet Milk to Sour. Substitute sour milk for sweet and add soda as needed to neutralize acid. To determine equivalent in baking powder, multiply amount of soda used by 4. If this does not equal amount in sweet milk recipe, add baking powder to make up difference.

Sour Milk to Sweet. Substitute sweet milk for sour, omit soda, and allow 1 to 2 teaspoons baking powder to 1 cup flour.

FAT

In quick bread recipes calling for liquid fat, either melted fat or oil may be used. Bacon fat, butter, or other fats may be preferred because of their flavor.

Quick Breads

Q UICK breads contain baking powder or soda as the leavening agent. If breads such as griddle cakes and waffles must stand for a time before baking less carbon dioxide is lost when double-acting baking powders are used.

Self-rising flour is available in some sections of the country. This flour has salt and leavening ingredients added in the correct proportions needed for batters and doughs such as griddle cakes and biscuits. Soda and calcium phosphate are the leavening ingredients most commonly used.

Since the water absorption properties of all-purpose flours vary from one section of the country to another the amount of flour in some recipes may need adjusting. Unless otherwise indicated in the following recipes, all-purpose flour and double-acting baking powder should be used.

POUR BATTERS

POPOVERS

1 cup flour	2 eggs
½ teaspoon salt	1 cup milk

■ Sift salt and flour into mixing bowl. Add unbeaten eggs and ½ of the milk. Beat until smooth, using rotary beater, whisk, or spoon. Add remainder of milk and mix well. Fill well-oiled deep muffin pans or glass custard cups ⅓ to ½ full. Avoid excess fat in pans, as it reduces volume and gives misshapen products. Bake at 400°F about 40 minutes, until they are well risen and brown, then quickly slash the top with a paring knife. Turn off heat, and allow popovers to dry in the oven, approximately 10 minutes. Popovers should be firm to the touch when removed from oven, otherwise they will collapse. Serve promptly. Ten large popovers.

YORKSHIRE PUDDING

Bake Popover Batter (p. 45) in baking dish or roaster in about ¼ cup sizzling hot drippings from roast beef. Bake 20 minutes at 425°F, then reduce heat to 350°F, and bake 20 minutes longer. Cut in squares. Serve immediately with roast beef. Six servings.

CREAM PUFFS

½ cup water	½ cup flour
¼ cup fat	2 eggs
¼ teaspoon salt	

■   Heat water, fat, and salt to boiling point. Add flour all at once. Stir vigorously until mixture leaves sides of pan and clings to spoon. Remove from heat. Cool slightly. Then add unbeaten eggs, 1 at a time, beating thoroughly after each addition. Drop mixture by spoonfuls into oiled muffin pans or onto oiled baking sheet 1½-inches apart. If the baking sheet is used, shape dough into rounds about 2-inches in diameter, and pile it slightly in center. Bake in a 400°F oven, 35 minutes. Turn off heat, and leave puffs in oven until they are dry, about 20 minutes.

When ready to use, make cut in top of each with a sharp knife. Fill with cream filling, whipped cream, fruit, chicken salad, or other desired filling. Sprinkle with powdered sugar, or frost if combination is suitable. They may be split, filled with ice cream, and served with sauce as dessert. Very small cream puffs may be served with tea. In this case, cream cheese is a favorite filling. Cream puffs, filled as for patties, may also be used as an entrée. Eight puffs, medium size.

ÉCLAIRS

Shape Cream Puff (p. 46) mixture with pastry bag into 4 x 1-inch strips, placing them on oiled baking sheet 2-inches apart. Bake as for Cream Puffs about 35 minutes. When done, split lengthwise. Fill with Cream Filling (p. 193). Cover tops with any desired frosting. This is best done by dipping. Eight éclairs.

SOUR MILK GRIDDLE CAKES

1 cup flour	1 cup buttermilk or
½ teaspoon salt	thick sour milk
½ teaspoon soda	1 egg, well beaten
1 to 2 teaspoons sugar	1 tablespoon liquid fat

■   Sift dry ingredients together. Add buttermilk, egg, and fat. Mix just to combine ingredients. Leave slightly lumpy. Drop mixture by spoonfuls on a hot griddle that may or may not be oiled according to kind. When cakes are risen, full of bubbles, and cooked on edges, turn them and cook other side. Serve at once. If a less bready mixture is desired, thin batter with milk. Thin batters should be mixed less than thick ones. Omit egg for a more economical product. Eight to 12 griddle cakes, approximately 4-inches in diameter, depending on thickness of batter.

SWEET MILK GRIDDLE CAKES. Substitute sweet milk for sour. Omit soda and use 1½ teaspoons baking powder in Sour Milk Griddle Cakes.

CORNMEAL GRIDDLE CAKES. Substitute cornmeal for ½ to ⅔ of the flour in Sour Milk Griddle Cakes.

BUCKWHEAT CAKES

½ cake yeast
2½ cups lukewarm water
  (82°F)
1 cup all-purpose flour
2 cups buckwheat flour

1½ teaspoons salt
1 teaspoon soda, dissolved
  in ½ cup hot water
¼ cup liquid fat
1 tablespoon molasses

■   The night before cakes are to be served, soften yeast in ½ cup of the lukewarm water. Add remaining water. Sift salt and flour together. Add to liquid mixture, and beat vigorously until smooth. Cover, and let it rise over night in warm place. If desired, reserve 1 cup of mixture to use as starter for next baking. Add remaining ingredients and stir to mix well. Let stand 30 minutes. Bake as for Griddle Cakes (p. 46). Thirty-six cakes, approximately 4-inches in diameter.

Add any leftover batter to that reserved for starter. Add ½ cup cold water, cover, and place in refrigerator until night before more cakes are to be made. Pour off water that has risen to the top. Use remainder in place of yeast, and proceed as above.

WAFFLES

1¼ cups flour
2 teaspoons baking powder
⅔ teaspoon salt
1 tablespoon sugar, if desired
1 cup milk

3 to 5 tablespoons liquid
  or solid fat
2 egg yolks, beaten thick
2 egg whites, beaten stiff

■   Sift dry ingredients together. Mix milk and fat with egg yolks. If melted fat is used, temperature of milk should be such that it will not solidify fat. Combine mixtures. Stir only until blended. Fold in egg whites. Cook on hot waffle iron that may or may not be oiled according to kind. For a crisp waffle, use larger amount of fat and cook longer. Thin batters need longer cooking than thick ones. Whole eggs may be beaten together, but product usually is less light. Serve with melted butter and honey or syrup. Four waffles approximately 8-inches in diameter.

BACON WAFFLES. Sprinkle small bits of bacon, cooked or uncooked, over waffle batter after filling iron. Allow 1 slice bacon for each waffle.

CHEESE WAFFLES. Use 3 tablespoons fat. Add ½ cup grated cheese to waffle batter.

CHOCOLATE WAFFLES. Sift ¼ cup each of sugar and cocoa with dry ingredients for waffles. Add ¼ teaspoon vanilla.

CHOCOLATE CHIP WAFFLES. Mix ½ cup coarsely grated semisweet chocolate with waffle batter.

CORN WAFFLES. Reduce milk in waffles to ¾ cup. Add 2 cups canned cream style corn and 1 to 2 tablespoons sugar. Bake until thoroughly dry.

HAM WAFFLES. Add 1 cup finely chopped cooked ham to waffle batter.

NUT WAFFLES. Sprinkle halves of English walnuts or pecans over waffle batter after filling iron.

BOSTON BROWN BREAD

1 cup cornmeal	1½ teaspoons soda
1 cup white or rye flour	2 cups sour milk
1 cup graham flour	¾ cup molasses
1 teaspoon salt	

■ Sift dry ingredients together. Blend milk and molasses. Add to dry ingredients. Mix. Turn into well-oiled molds, filling not more than ⅔ full. Cover tightly. Steam molds, the size of a 1-pound baking powder or coffee can, 3 hours. Then remove covers, and dry in oven 15 minutes. Remove from molds. If served hot, slice (with a string). Raisins may be added for variety. Bread may be baked as a loaf instead of steamed. In that case, add 1 tablespoon melted fat. Bake 1 hour at 375°F. Two loaves, approximately 3-inches in diameter, 5-inches long.

SOUTHERN BATTER BREAD (SPOON BREAD)

2 cups boiling water	2 to 4 eggs, well beaten
1 cup cornmeal	2 tablespoons fat
1 cup milk	3 teaspoons baking
1 teaspoon salt	powder

■ Pour *boiling* water over cornmeal; add milk, salt, and egg. Beat well, add fat and baking powder. Pour into oiled baking dish. Bake at 350°F about 40 minutes. Serve from baking dish with a spoon. Serve with butter or crisp bacon. Six servings.

DROP BATTERS

MUFFINS

2 cups flour	1 cup milk
3 teaspoons baking powder	1 egg, well beaten
2 to 4 tablespoons sugar	2 to 4 tablespoons liquid or
1 teaspoon salt	solid fat

■ Sift dry ingredients together. Add milk to egg. Either solid or liquid fat may be used. If solid, cut into dry ingredients. If liquid, add to milk-egg mixture. If melted fat is used, temperature of milk should be such that it will not solidify fat. Combine dry and liquid mixture. *Stir only enough to mix ingredients slightly.* Batter will still be lumpy. Long beating causes tunnels and makes muffins compact. Drop batter into oiled muffin pans filling ⅔ full. Bake at 425°F for 15 to 20 minutes. Remove from pans at once. For richer more cake-like muffins use larger amounts of sugar and fat. Nine large or 18 small muffins.

FRUIT MUFFINS. Add ½ cup currants or finely cut raisins, dates, or prunes. Fresh fruits such as grated raw apple and berries also may be used, adding the larger amount of sugar. Blueberries are good in muffins. Canned fruits may be used if they are well drained.

GRAHAM MUFFINS. Substitute graham flour for ½ the white flour. Molasses may be used instead of sugar.

CORNMEAL MUFFINS. Substitute ⅞ cup cornmeal for 1 cup flour. Cornmeal makes a drier mixture than flour, therefore, a smaller proportion is used. Cornmeal may be substituted for a larger proportion of flour if desired.

BRAN MUFFINS

1½ cups flour	1½ cups bran flakes
3 teaspoons baking powder	1 egg, well beaten
½ teaspoon salt	1 cup milk
3 tablespoons sugar	3 tablespoons liquid fat

■   Sift flour, baking powder, salt, and sugar. Stir in bran flakes. Combine egg, milk, and fat. Add liquid ingredients to dry ingredients, and mix only until dry ingredients are dampened. Fill muffin tins ⅔ full. Bake at 425°F, 15 to 20 minutes. Twelve medium muffins.

CORNBREAD

½ cup sifted flour	1 egg, well beaten
¾ teaspoon soda	1¼ cups sour milk or
1 teaspoon salt	buttermilk
2 tablespoons sugar	2 tablespoons fat, melted
1 cup cornmeal	

■   Mix as for Muffins (p. 48). Pour into 8 x 8 x 1-inch oiled pan. Bake at 425°F, 30 minutes or until done.

GRAHAM NUT BREAD

2 cups white flour	1 cup nuts, chopped
2 teaspoons salt	1½ cups sugar
2 tablespoons baking powder	2 eggs, well beaten
2 cups unsifted graham flour	2 cups milk

■   Sift white flour, salt, and baking powder together. Mix with graham flour and nuts. Add sugar to eggs. Beat well. Add milk alternately with flour mixture to egg mixture. Pour into oiled bread pans 8½ x 4½ x 2½ inches. Let stand 25 minutes. Bake 1 hour at 375°F. Two loaves.

FRUIT BREAD

⅔ cup sugar
2 cups flour
½ teaspoon salt
½ teaspoon soda
1 teaspoon baking powder

1 cup fruit
3 tablespoons buttermilk
2 eggs, unbeaten
⅓ cup fat, melted

■ Sift dry ingredients together. Mix fruit, milk, egg, and fat. Add ½ of the fruit mixture to dry ingredients, and beat 2 minutes. Add remainder of fruit mixture, and beat 2 minutes or until batter is smooth. Pour in oiled loaf pan 8½ x 4½ x 2½ inches. Bake 1 hour at 375°F. One loaf.

APPLE NUT BREAD. Substitute 1 cup shredded raw apple packed, ¼ cup nuts, and ½ teaspoon nutmeg for 1 cup fruit.

BANANA BREAD. Substitute 1 cup mashed banana for 1 cup fruit.

ORANGE DATE BREAD. Substitute ½ cup ground dates, ½ cup ground whole orange, blended with ¼ cup orange juice for 1 cup fruit.

PINEAPPLE APRICOT BREAD. Substitute ½ cup drained crushed pineapple, ½ cup ground, softened dried apricots and 2 tablespoons pineapple juice for 1 cup fruit.

PRUNE ORANGE BREAD. Substitute ⅔ cup ground soaked prunes, ⅓ cup ground orange, and 2 tablespoons orange juice for 1 cup fruit.

DATE NUT BREAD

2 cups boiling water
4 cups dates, chopped
4 cups flour
4 teaspoons soda
1 teaspoon baking powder
½ teaspoon salt

½ cup fat
1 cup sugar
2 eggs, beaten
1 teaspoon vanilla
1½ cups pecans, chopped

■ Add boiling water to dates. Cover. Cool. Sift flour, soda, baking powder, and salt together. Cream fat, add sugar gradually, and cream well after each addition. Add eggs, vanilla, and date mixture; then flour mixture gradually, and finally the nuts. Pour into oiled loaf pans 8½ x 4½ x 2½ inches. Bake at 350°F, 1 to 1½ hours. Two loaves.

SOFT DOUGHS

BAKING POWDER BISCUITS

2 cups flour
3 teaspoons baking powder
1 teaspoon salt

5 tablespoons fat
¾ cup milk

■ Sift dry ingredients together twice. Cut in fat until mixture resembles coarse cornmeal. Add milk all at once, mixing until product leaves sides of bowl. Dough should be as soft as can be handled. Turn onto lightly floured board, knead about 20 seconds (20 times) or until dough is just smooth. Shape into a ball. Pat or roll lightly into a sheet ½- to ¾-inch in thickness. Shape with floured cutter. Place fairly close together on baking sheet. If crusty sides are desired, place farther apart. Bake at 425°F, 12 to 15 minutes. Fifteen biscuits, approximately 1¼-inches high, 2-inches in diameter.

DROP BISCUITS. Make as for Baking Powder Biscuits, using enough milk to make thick drop batter. Drop by spoonfuls ½-inch apart on oiled baking sheet or into oiled muffin pans.

DATE BISCUITS. Make Baking Powder Biscuits. Add ½ cup chopped dates to sifted flour mixture before adding milk.

ORANGE ROLLS. Make Baking Powder Biscuits adding 2 tablespoons sugar to flour mixture. Reduce milk to ½ cup, adding 1 beaten egg. Roll dough ¼-inch thick. Brush with melted butter or substitute. Sprinkle with Orange Sugar (grated rind of 1 large orange to 1 cup sugar). Roll as for Jelly Roll (p. 187). Cut into ¾-inch slices. Place cut-side down in oiled muffin pans. Bake 20 minutes at 425°F. Sixteen small rolls.

PECAN ROLLS. Make Orange Rolls, substituting brown for Orange Sugar and sprinkling with pecans. Put melted butter, sugar, and pecans in bottoms of pans before rolls are added.

QUICK COFFEE CAKE. Make as for Baking Powder Biscuits. Add ½ cup sugar to flour mixture. Combine milk and dry ingredients. Do not knead. Spread evenly in 2 8-inch round pans. Brush each with 1 tablespoon melted butter. Sprinkle with mixture of ¼ cup sugar, 1 teaspoon cinnamon, and 1 tablespoon flour. Bake at 400°F, 15 to 20 minutes. Two coffee cakes, approximately 8-inches in diameter.

DUMPLINGS FOR STEWS. Make as for Drop Biscuits, omitting fat. Add 1 egg if desired. Drop by spoonfuls on top of stew, cook 10 minutes without cover, cover tightly and steam an additional 10 minutes without lifting cover. Remove and serve at once, arranging as a border around stew. They may also be cooked in a steamer or dropped on top of a roast and baked. They may be made as for Biscuits and cut into rounds if preferred.

DOUGHNUTS

2⅝ cups flour	½ cup sugar
3 teaspoons baking powder	½ teaspoon salt
1/16 teaspoon nutmeg	1 tablespoon fat, melted
1/16 teaspoon cinnamon	or softened
1 egg	½ cup milk

Sift flour, baking powder, and spices together. Combine thoroughly beaten egg, sugar, salt, and softened or melted fat. Mix until very light and fluffy, add milk and flour mixtures. Mix just enough to blend. Roll ⅓-inch thick on lightly floured board. Cut with floured cutter. Fry in deep hot fat heated to 375°F, until brown, turning once. Drain on absorbent paper. Twelve doughnuts.

BASIC HOME MIX

BASIC QUICK BREAD MIX

10 cups flour
⅓ cup double-acting baking
  powder

2 tablespoons salt
1½ cups fat which does
  not need refrigeration

■ Sift dry ingredients together twice. Place in large bowl. Cut in fat with pastry blender until mixture resembles coarse cornmeal. Store in covered container at room temperature. Twelve cups of mix.

BISCUITS

2 cups Basic Quick Bread Mix   ⅔ cup milk

■ Add milk all at once. Stir with fork until mixture leaves the sides of the bowl. Turn onto lightly floured board, knead 20 times, or until dough is smooth. Roll or pat to desired thickness, about ½-inch. Cut. Bake at 425°F, 12 to 15 minutes until golden brown. Twelve biscuits, approximately 1½ inches high and 2 inches in diameter.

DROP BISCUITS

2 cups Basic Quick Bread Mix   ¾ cup milk

■ Add milk all at once. Stir until well blended. Spoon lightly into well-oiled muffin tins or onto flat baking sheet. Bake as above.

MUFFINS

2 cups Basic Quick Bread Mix
¼ cup sugar

1 cup milk
1 egg, beaten

■ Add sugar to mix. Combine milk and beaten egg. Add liquids to dry ingredients, and stir until just moistened. Bake in greased muffin tins at 425°F, 12 to 15 minutes. Remove from pans at once. Fourteen to 16 small muffins.

COFFEE CAKE

2 cups Basic Quick Bread Mix
⅓ cup sugar
¾ cup milk
1 egg, beaten
1 teaspoon vanilla

Topping:
¼ cup brown sugar
¼ cup granulated sugar
1 teaspoon cinnamon
¼ cup nuts, if desired
2 tablespoons butter, melted

■ Mix as for muffins. Bake in 8-inch square or 9-inch round greased cake pan. Brush top of batter with melted butter and sprinkle with topping mixture. Bake at 375°F. Eight to 9 servings.

Yeast Breads

YEAST breads are leavened by carbon dioxide as are quick breads. However, in yeast breads carbon dioxide is produced by a living microscopic plant, whereas in quick breads, baking powder or soda is the source of carbon dioxide.

INGREDIENTS

Liquid. Milk, water, potato water, or fruit juice is used as liquid in yeast breads. Fresh fluid milk, evaporated milk, nonfat dry milk, sour milk, buttermilk, and whey add nutritive value. Raw or pasteurized milk and buttermilk should be scalded before using. This stops enzyme action that may produce undesirable flavors. Bread containing sweet milk has a creamy white crumb, brown crust, good flavor, good keeping quality, and browns evenly during toasting. It rises more slowly and has a smaller volume than bread made with water. Sour milk, buttermilk, and whey allow rapid growth of yeast but are apt to affect flavor. Dough containing water rises quickly and the bread has large volume, crisp crust, grayish-colored crumb, and stales rapidly. Potato water supplies excellent yeast food, hastens fermentation, and produces a loaf of good volume that has moist texture but may have a dark-colored crumb. Fruit juice is used in special breads.

Yeast. This microscopic plant grows best between 79 and 90°F (optimal temperature is 82°F). It is destroyed at a temperature above 140°F. Below 79°F growth is retarded, but the yeast plant is not destroyed readily at low temperature. For growth, yeast needs food, air, and moisture. Granular yeast

53

keeps well for several weeks at room temperature. A fresh compressed yeast cake is creamy-white, moist, practically odorless, and crumbly and can be kept a week at refrigerator temperature.

Flour. All-purpose, general-purpose, or family flour may be used for yeast rolls and bread. Good flour for bread is granular and will not hold its shape when pressed between the fingers. It contains proteins that will form gluten of high quality. Gluten enables batters and doughs to hold the leavening gas that makes them light. A good quality gluten is necessary for the porous structure of good bread.

Salt. Salt improves flavor of bread and helps control fermentation rate. It appears to affect the gluten so that it expands smoothly. Excess salt inhibits yeast growth and may cause a firm compact loaf.

Shortening. Though not an essential ingredient, fat appears to condition the gluten so that the leavening gas can expand easily and smoothly. Fat may increase the volume, produce a soft velvety crumb, improve the browning, flavor, tenderness, and keeping quality of the bread and add nutritive value.

Sugar. Sugar furnishes food for yeast, hastens fermentation, and aids browning. Honey, molasses, or corn syrup may be used in dark, whole grain breads, sweet rolls, and coffee cakes.

METHODS OF MAKING YEAST BREADS

Straight Dough Method. For this method, all the flour is mixed with the other ingredients, the dough is kneaded, and allowed to rise prior to being shaped for the pan. Active dry or compressed yeast is used in doughs mixed by this method. If breads or rolls are to be made in less than 3 hours, more yeast and sugar is needed than called for in basic recipes.

If doughs are to be refrigerated, egg, additional sugar, and salt are needed to extend action of yeast in the dough.

The yeast batter method is a modification of the straight dough method and is used for soft sweet doughs as coffee cakes and rolls, that are beaten rather than kneaded. For rolls, the dough should be chilled before it is shaped. Products made by the yeast batter method tend to have coarse texture, yeasty flavor, and poor keeping quality.

Sponge Dough Method. Active dry, dry, or compressed yeast may be used. For this method, only enough flour is added to the yeast and liquid to make a thick drop batter. Sugar, salt, and fat may or may not be added at this stage. The batter is allowed to rise until double in bulk, the remaining ingredients added, the dough kneaded, and allowed to rise before being shaped. This method is used for certain special breads that contain ingredients that retard fermentation and also for development of flavor that results from long fermentation times.

PROCESSES USED IN BREAD MAKING

Kneading. Place bread dough onto a lightly floured board. Work lightly, keeping a small amount of flour on board until loaf is smooth, elastic to the touch, and stiff enough so that it will not stick to a clean board when it is handled. To knead bread properly, fold dough from the back toward center with finger tips, then press down and away from the kneader with palms of hands. Do this twice, then give dough a quarter turn on board and repeat process. Always turn dough in same direction. *Do not use more* flour than necessary.

Rising. Place ball of dough in oiled bowl and turn dough once to oil the top. Cover bowl to prevent formation of crust on dough. Set in warm place (82°F) and allow dough to double in bulk. Dough may then be worked or punched down and allowed to double in volume a second time if a better texture is desired. After dough has been shaped and placed in the baking pan it is allowed to double in volume again before it is baked.

Shaping. After kneading, allow dough to rest a short time before making into a loaf. To shape roll dough with a rolling pin, into a rectangular shape no wider than the pan is long and about ½-inch thick. Roll like a Jelly Roll (p. 187) and seal the edges by pressing tightly together. Tuck in the ends and seal in a similar manner. Place in oiled bread pan smooth side up.

Baking. Bake bread at 400°F (hot oven) or start baking at 400°F and after 10 minutes reduce the heat 10 to 15°F. Allow 40 to 45 minutes for baking a loaf 9½ x 4½ x 3½ inches.

Cooling. Remove bread from pan as soon as baked. Cool on wire rack so that air may pass completely around loaf. If a soft crust is desired, oil top. Do not let strong air currents blow directly upon loaf or crust will crack. Do not wrap bread in a cloth to cool as flavor will be less desirable. When bread is cool, place it in ventilated bread box, plastic bag, or other suitable container.

BREADS

WHITE BREAD

¼ to 2 packages active dry yeast softened in ¼ cup water (105 to 110°F) or
¼ to 2 cakes compressed yeast softened in ¼ cup water (80 to 85°F)
1 cup liquid, lukewarm *
1 tablespoon sugar
0 to 1 tablespoon fat, softened

1¼ teaspoons salt
Flour to make a firm dough, 3 to 3½ cups

* Milk, water, or potato water. The liquid is scalded and cooled unless evaporated or nonfat dry milk is used.

Straight Dough Method. Soften yeast and let stand 5 to 10 minutes. Add remaining liquid, sugar, fat, salt, and about ⅓ of the flour. Beat with a wooden spoon until well blended. Gradually stir in the remaining flour and continue beating until the dough can be lifted in a mass on the spoon, leaving the bowl free of dough. Turn dough onto lightly floured board or pastry cloth. Knead lightly for 5 to 8 minutes until the dough is smooth, satiny, elastic to the touch, and stiff enough that it will not stick to a clean board. Shape into ball and place in oiled bowl. Turn dough over to oil the top. Cover and allow to rise in warm place (80 to 85°F) until dough doubles in bulk or when touched with the finger will leave an impression. Punch down, shape into a smooth ball and let rest 8 to 10 minutes. Shape into loaf, place in oiled bread pan and allow to double in bulk. Bake at 400°F (hot oven) until loaf begins to pull away from pan or sounds hollow when thumped. One loaf.

Sponge Method. Make as for White Bread, Straight Dough Method, adding only enough flour to make a thick drop batter. Cover. Let rise in warm place until bubbly and light. Add remaining flour, and proceed as for Straight Dough Method.

WHOLE WHEAT BREAD. Make as for White Bread, following either method of mixing preferred but substituting whole wheat for ½ of the white flour. If desired, use 1½ tablespoons molasses instead of sugar. Rolled oats or other grains may be used in the same way, but, as a rule, should not replace more than ⅓ of the white flour.

ALL WHOLE WHEAT BREAD. Make as for Whole Wheat Bread, using all whole wheat flour. Loaf will be heavy and small but nutritious and of good flavor.

RAISIN BREAD. Add ½ cup floured chopped raisins to any recipe for 1 loaf of bread.

SWEDISH RYE BREAD. Make as for White Bread, following either method of mixing preferred, but add 2 tablespoons molasses, 2 tablespoons dark corn syrup, and ¾ cup rye flour. Mix and knead as usual. Bake at 400°F for 40 to 45 minutes.

HERB BREAD

1 cake yeast, compressed and ¼ cup water (80 to 85°F) or	1 tablespoon shortening
1 package yeast, granular and ¼ cup water (105 to 110°F)	2 teaspoons sage leaves, crumbled
2 cups milk	⅛ teaspoon cardamon seed, crushed
2 tablespoons sugar	1 teaspoon nutmeg
2 teaspoons salt	¼ teaspoon fennel
6 cups flour	1 tablespoon caraway seed
	¼ teaspoon anise seed

■ Make as for White Bread (p. 55), adding herbs with flour. Mold into 2 loaves, and bake in pans 8½ x 4½ x 2½ inches at 400°F about 1 hour.

CORNELL WHITE BREAD

1 package active dry yeast
1½ cups warm water
1 tablespoon sugar
2 teaspoons salt
3¼ cups unbleached or bleached
   flour

¼ cup stirred soy flour
1½ tablespoons wheat germ
½ cup nonfat dry milk
1 tablespoon oil

■ Mix yeast, warm water, and sugar; allow to stand 5 minutes. Sift salt, flour, and soy flour together, and mix with wheat germ and nonfat dry milk. Mix ½ of the flour-milk mixture with softened yeast. Add oil, then remainder of flour-milk mixture to yeast. Knead vigorously for 5 minutes on board floured with an additional ¼ cup flour. Place dough in large greased bowl and brush lightly with melted fat. Cover. Let rise in warm place until doubled in bulk (35 minutes). Punch down and let rise a second time (20 minutes). Shape dough into loaf, place in greased loaf pan, and let rise in warm place until doubled in bulk. Bake at 350°F for 50 minutes. One loaf.

OATMEAL BREAD. Delete from Cornell White Bread recipe 1½ cups warm water, 1 tablespoon sugar, 3¼ cups flour, 1½ tablespoons wheat germ, and 1 tablespoon oil. Soften 1 cake active dry yeast in ⅜ cup warm water to which ⅙ cup brown sugar was added and let stand 5 minutes. In large bowl, mix 1 cup uncooked quick or regular oats, 1¼ cups boiling water, 1½ tablespoons fat, and 2 teaspoons salt. Cool to lukewarm. Sift together 2¾ cups flour and ¼ cup soy flour; mix with 1 tablespoon wheat germ and ½ cup nonfat dry milk. Stir softened yeast into lukewarm oatmeal mixture. Add ½ dry ingredients. Beat until smooth. Stir in remaining dry ingredients. Knead for 5 minutes on board floured with additional ¼ cup flour. Proceed as for Cornell White Bread. One loaf.

ROLLS

As a rule, roll dough is softer and contains more sugar and shortening than bread.

BASIC SWEET DOUGH

2 packages active dry yeast
   softened in ¼ cup water
   (105 to 110°F) or
2 cakes compressed yeast
   crumbled in ¼ cup water
   (80 to 85°F)

1 cup milk, lukewarm *
½ cup sugar
¼ cup fat, softened
2 teaspoons salt
5 cups flour, approximately
2 eggs

* Milk should be scalded unless evaporated or nonfat dry milk is used.

■ Soften yeast and let stand 5 to 10 minutes. Combine milk, sugar, fat, and salt. Add flour to make a thick batter. Mix well. Add softened yeast and eggs. Mix. Continue beating in flour until dough is smooth and can be lifted in a mass on the spoon, leaving the bowl clean. Turn dough onto lightly floured board and knead until smooth and satiny. Keep as soft as can be handled. Place in lightly oiled bowl and cover. Set in warm place until doubled, then punch down. Let rest 10 minutes and shape as desired. Three and one-half dozen small rolls.

BRAIDS. Roll Basic Sweet Dough ¼-inch thick. Cut into ½-inch strips, then braid using 3 to 4 strands. Have braids wider in center than at ends. When light, bake at 425°F, 15 to 20 minutes.

BUTTER HORNS. Roll ball of Basic Sweet Dough into circular piece ¼-inch thick and 8 inches in diameter. Cut into pie-shaped wedges. Brush with melted fat. Roll up beginning at wide end. When light, bake at 425°F, 15 to 20 minutes.

CINNAMON ROLLS. Roll Basic Sweet Dough ½-inch thick. Spread with melted fat. Sprinkle liberally with mixture of 6 to 8 parts sugar to 1 part ground cinnamon. Raisins or currants also may be used. Roll dough and cut into ¾-inch slices. Put into oiled pan, cut side up. Let rise until light, then bake at 400°F, approximately 35 minutes.

CLOVER LEAF OR SHAMROCK ROLLS. Shape small bits of Basic Sweet Dough into small balls. Place 3 or 4 balls for each roll into oiled muffin pan. When doubled in bulk, bake at 425°F, 12 to 15 minutes.

RAISED DOUGHNUTS. Let Basic Sweet Dough rise until doubled in volume. Roll into a sheet ⅓-inch thick. Cut with floured doughnut cutter. Let rise until doubled in volume. Fry in deep fat at 350 to 360°F placing raised side down into fat. Drain on soft paper. Roll in sugar or dip in glaze. Thirty-six doughnuts, medium size.

FAN TANS. Roll Basic Sweet Dough into very thin rectangular sheet. Brush with melted fat. Cut in strips 1-inch wide. Pile 6 to 7 strips together. Cut into 1½-inch pieces. Place cut side down in oiled muffin pans. When light, bake at 425°F, 12 to 15 minutes.

HOLLAND BRIOCHE CAKES. Add grated rind and juice of 1 lemon to Basic Sweet Dough after enough flour has been beaten in to make drop batter. It may be necessary to increase the flour slightly. When dough is light, roll into a rectangle ¼-inch thick. Spread with melted fat and fold from sides to center to make 3 layers. Cut across into ¾-inch strips. Cover. Let rise until light to touch. Twist ends of each strip in opposite directions, coil, and bring ends together at top. Place on oiled pans, let rise until nearly doubled in bulk. Bake at 400°F, about 20 minutes. Cool, then cover with powdered sugar frosting using lemon juice as the liquid. Thirty cakes.

PARKERHOUSE ROLLS. Roll Basic Sweet Dough ¾-inch thick. Lift dough from board to allow it to shrink before cutting rolls. Shape with round or oval floured cutter. Brush center of each circle with melted fat. Stretch slightly, fold over, and pinch edges together. Place 1-inch apart in oiled pan. Brush tops with melted fat. Let rise until more than doubled in volume, then bake at 425°F, 15 to 20 minutes.

REFRIGERATOR ROLLS. Prepare Basic Sweet Dough, knead, and place in oiled bowl. Oil top of dough, cover tightly, and refrigerate. Two and one-half to

3 hours before rolls are to be served, remove dough from refrigerator, shape, and set in warm place to rise. When doubled in volume, bake rolls.

SALAD OR DINNER ROLLS. Roll Basic Sweet Dough ½-inch thick, cut into small biscuits. Place in rows on floured board, cover with cloth and let rise until very light. With floured handle of wooden spoon, make deep crease in middle of each roll. Brush with melted fat. Fold as for Parker House Rolls. Place close together in oiled pan. Cover, let rise, and bake at 425°F, 12 to 15 minutes.

BREAD STICKS. Fold a beaten egg white into Basic Sweet Dough before adding flour. When light, form into small balls, then roll on unfloured board with hands to make uniform sticks of size and shape of lead pencil. Place in oiled bread stick pan or on baking sheet some distance apart. When light, bake at 425°F, 10 to 15 minutes. Reduce heat at last of baking so that sticks may be crisp and dry.

SALAD STICKS. Use Bread Stick mixture adding more salt. Make as for Bread Sticks. Sprinkle with salt before baking.

SWEDISH TEA RING. To Basic Sweet Dough, add a well-beaten egg when mixture is at batter stage. When dough is light, roll on unfloured board, forming rectangle ⅛- to ¼-inch thick. Spread with melted fat, sprinkle with blanched chopped almonds or other nuts or cinnamon and sugar. Currants may be used instead of nuts. Roll dough and cut a small piece from each end to aid joining. Unite cut ends to form ring. Place on oiled baking sheet. Cut gashes with scissors 1- to 2-inches apart beginning at outside and extending almost to center of roll. Turn each piece, cut side up, to give flower-like effect. When light, bake at 375°F, 35 to 40 minutes.

BEATEN BATTERS

Beaten batters differ from roll doughs in that the proportion of flour to liquid is less for the batters. Beaten batters are not kneaded whereas roll doughs are.

BASIC BEATEN BATTER

1 package active dry yeast softened in ¼ cup water (105 to 110°F) or
1 cake compressed yeast crumbled in ¼ cup water (80 to 85°F)
1 cup lukewarm milk *
¼ cup sugar
1 teaspoon salt

3¼ cups sifted, enriched flour (approximately)
1 egg
½ teaspoon vanilla, if desired
½ cup fat, melted

* The milk is scalded and cooled unless evaporated or nonfat dry milk is used.

■   Soften yeast and allow to stand 5 to 10 minutes. Combine milk, sugar, and salt. Add 2 cups flour and beat well. Add egg, softened yeast, and vanilla if used. Beat well. Stir in fat. Add more flour to make a stiff batter. Beat thoroughly until smooth. Cover and let rise until bubbly (about 1 hour). Use with different toppings to make puffs and coffee cakes. Approximately 2½ dozen 2-inch puffs or 2, 8-inch square, or 9-inch round coffee cakes.

APPLE COFFEE CAKE. When Basic Beaten Batter is light, stir down. Spread in oiled 8-inch square or 9-inch round layer pan. Arrange slices of 4 medium-sized apples on top, begin by laying slices lengthwise around the edge of the pan. Continue arranging slices until entire top is covered. Brush with 4 tablespoons melted butter or margarine and sprinkle with a mixture made using ½ cup sugar and 1 teaspoon cinnamon. Let rise until light (about 30 minutes). Bake at 375°F, 30 to 35 minutes. Two coffee cakes.

APRICOT PUFFS. When Basic Beaten Batter is light, stir down. Drop by spoonfuls into oiled muffin pans. Top each with sweetened cooked apricot half. Let rise until light (about 30 minutes). Bake at 375°F for 20 to 25 minutes. Brush with thin Powdered Sugar Icing (p. 191) and sprinkle with 1 cup shredded coconut. Approximately 24, 3-inch puffs.

CINNAMON NUT PUFFS. When Basic Beaten Batter is light, stir in 2 cups raisins. Drop by spoonfuls into oiled muffin pans. Mix ½ cup sugar, 1 teaspoon cinnamon, and ½ cup nuts, finely chopped; sprinkle over muffins. Let rise until light (about 30 minutes). Bake at 375°F for 20 to 25 minutes. Approximately 32, 2-inch puffs.

SUGAR PLUM COFFEE CAKE. When Basic Beaten Batter is light, stir down. Spread in oiled 8-inch square pan. Arrange 24 sweetened, cooked plums on batter. Let rise until light (about 30 minutes). Sprinkle with a mixture made using 1 cup brown sugar and 4 teaspoons cinnamon. Bake at 375°F, 30 to 35 minutes. Two coffee cakes.

KITCHENETTE DOUGHNUTS. When Basic Beaten Batter is light, drop from teaspoon into deep hot fat (350°F) and fry about 1½ minutes on each side, until light brown. Drain on paper. Toss in paper bag with sugar or dip warm doughnuts into a warm glaze. Six dozen.

DRY BREAD

BREAD CRUMBS

Roll, grate, or run crisp dry bread through food chopper until reduced to crumbs. Sift. These crumbs may be prepared in quantity and stored in a covered container in the refrigerator. Bread crumbs are suitable for egging and crumbing food to be fried, for covering scalloped dishes, and for thickening, as in puddings.

BUTTERED BREAD CRUMBS

Melt 1 tablespoon butter or margarine, add ⅓ cup dry bread crumbs, and stir until well coated. One-third cup crumbs.

CROUSTADES OF BREAD (BREAD BOXES)

Cut slices of bread 2-inches thick. Remove crusts. Cut slices in halves either diagonally or crosswise, or cut into rounds. Cut out inside portion carefully with small, pointed knife, leaving sides and bottom ¼-inch thick. Fry or dip lightly into melted fat and brown at 450°F (hot oven). Use as cases for creamed vegetables, fish, or meat. To garnish, dip top lightly into unbeaten egg white, then into finely chopped parsley.

TOAST

CINNAMON TOAST

Use sliced bread or cut ¼- to ½-inch thick. Remove crusts if desired. Toast lightly and quickly. Brush with melted butter, and sprinkle with a mixture of 1 part cinnamon and 8 parts sugar. Return to broiling oven until sugar forms a glaze. Serve hot with tea, chocolate, or fruit plate.

DRY TOAST

Use sliced bread or cut to desired thickness. Remove crusts if desired. Use electric toaster or place on broiling rack of oven. If soft toast is desired, preheat oven. Place rack about 2-inches below heat. Turn bread often enough to prevent warping and to insure even browning. Toast to a golden-brown color.

FRENCH TOAST

⅔ cup milk　　　　　　　　　6 slices bread
½ teaspoon salt　　　　　　　Sugar, if desired
2 eggs, slightly beaten　　　　Cinnamon, if desired

METHOD I. Add milk and salt to egg. Mix well. Dip bread quickly into mixture. Brown in a small amount of hot fat.
METHOD II. Prepare bread as above. Place in well-oiled baking pan and brush with melted fat. Bacon drippings are especially good. Bake at 450°F for 10 minutes or until nicely browned, turn, and brown other side, about 10 minutes.

MELBA TOAST

Cut bread into ⅛-inch slices. Place on baking sheet or directly on rack of cold oven. Set regulator for 250°F (slow oven) and bake for an hour or until bread is dry and an even golden color. White or rye bread is good. Bread may be brushed with garlic or onion butter before or after toasting. Serve for breakfast or tea or as an accompaniment for soup or salads.

ORANGE TOAST

Use sliced bread or cut to desired thickness. Remove crusts and cut into halves or strips. Mix 1 tablespoon orange juice, 1½ teaspoons orange rind, and ½ cup sugar. Toast bread, spread with butter or margarine and then orange mixture. Return to broiler until sugar forms a glaze.

TOAST CUPS

Cut crusts from slices of fresh bread and spread with melted butter or margarine. Place bread slices in muffin cups. Brown in oven at 425°F for approximately 8 to 10 minutes. Use as cases for creamed vegetables, fish, or meat.

TOAST POINTS

Cut bread as for Dry Toast (p. 61), removing crusts. Toast. While hot, cut diagonally across each way to form 4 small triangles. Use as garnish.

Sandwiches and Canapés

SANDWICHES

Sandwiches are appropriate for many uses—tea, lunch box, picnic, luncheon, or supper. Versatility in sandwiches is obtained with breads, fillings, and sizes and shapes.

Equipment. A sharp knife is essential. One especially designed for cutting bread is useful when making sandwiches. A bread board on which cutting may be done protects the table and the knife. Special cutters permit making a variety of shapes.

Bread. Choose bread of any desired kind. Special sandwich loaves may be obtained. These loaves often are cut into thin slices. Unsliced bread may be cut to desired thickness. To cut well, bread should be about 24 hours old. However, rolled sandwiches are easier to handle, when made from fresh bread as this does not break easily. For a dainty party sandwich, cut very thin slices of bread and remove crusts. If sandwiches are to be cut into fancy shapes, it is more economical to slice loaf lengthwise. Use regular sliced bread and retain the crusts for picnic or lunch sandwiches. Bread may be toasted for variety.

Butter and Fillings. Cream butter until soft and pliable. Allow ¾ teaspoon to 1 slice bread. Mustard, chopped parsley, water cress, chives, onion, garlic, or horseradish may be creamed with butter if such flavor is desired. Apply a thin even coat of butter to both slices of bread or to only one as preferred. If filling is moist, both slices should be buttered to prevent soaking. Butter should extend to, but not over, edges of bread.

The filling should be easy to eat. As a rule it is more satisfactory if ingredients are chopped. Spread filling evenly in desired thickness on 1 slice of buttered bread. Sliced meat should be cut thin. Place several pieces in each sandwich. Spread mayonnaise, if desired, on 1 slice of the buttered bread. A crisp lettuce leaf also may be placed on the bread.

Storing. Freshly made sandwiches are preferable, especially if filling is soft. If necessary to make sandwiches some time before serving, wraps of wax paper, aluminum foil, or polyethylene film will prevent drying. Open faced sandwiches may be placed on a cloth wrung as dry as possible from hot water. This cloth is placed in a fairly deep pan, that can be covered with foil or plastic film without touching the sandwiches. Keep at refrigerator temperature. Sandwiches may be frozen if they are placed in a moisture-vapor-proof container or wrap. Frozen sandwiches are especially convenient when packing lunches. However, do not freeze fillings with mayonnaise, lettuce, tomato, or hard-cooked egg white.

Serving. Serve sandwiches that fit the occasion. A sandwich that is a meal in itself should be the hearty type. Use plenty of meat, cheese, or other high protein foods on buns or generous slices of bread.

Tea sandwiches must be dainty, pretty to look at, and good to eat. Contrast in fillings, shapes, and garnishes add interest. Arrange sandwiches attractively on trays or platters and garnish with water cress, parsley, or celery leaves.

Suggestions for Sandwich Fillings

Fillings should be adapted to the type of sandwich desired. Lunch or picnic sandwiches are filled generously. Those for parties are made with small amounts of filling and are dainty in effect. Variety in sandwiches to be served at one time is best obtained by contrasts of color, flavor, and texture.

Either cooked or mayonnaise dressing may be used in the following combinations unless otherwise specified. Salad dressing usually is added in quantities sufficient to moisten. Lettuce improves almost any savory sandwich and should be added just before serving. Cheese is mashed or grated; nuts and dates are chopped; meats are sliced, chopped, minced, or ground; eggs are hard-cooked and chopped. Seasonings are added to taste in all cases.

Sandwich fillings are seldom made from recipes but represent a combination of ingenuity and available ingredients. Start with the following suggestions and use imagination.

Chopped green pepper, onion, celery, and cabbage, with Thousand Island Dressing (p. 148).

Grated raw carrots, nuts, and salad dressing, with whole wheat bread.

Cucumbers, sliced thin, marinated in French Dressing (p. 147), with or without lettuce; good on brown bread.

Lettuce with salad dressing.

Thinly sliced tomatoes with lettuce and mayonnaise.

Water cress, cut into small pieces, marinated in French Dressing (p. 147).

Tender, crisp nasturtium leaves, lettuce leaf, and salad dressing.

Cooked chicken, chopped and moistened with salad dressing or rich chicken stock. Chopped parsley, celery salt, or onion juice may be used for seasoning. Chopped celery is a good addition.

Boiled ham with salad dressing or prepared mustard.

Boiled ham as above with extra seasoning of catsup, Worcestershire sauce, or Tabasco sauce.

Boiled ham with chopped, sweet pickles, and salad dressing. Allow 1 cup ham to 4 medium-sized pickles.

Boiled ham, hard-cooked eggs, minced chives, and salad dressing or prepared mustard to taste.

Tuna, chopped pickles, crisp bacon, celery, mayonnaise, and lettuce.

Hard-cooked eggs, mayonnaise, and lettuce.

Hard-cooked eggs, tomato catsup, and lettuce.

Sliced, hard-cooked eggs, chopped stuffed olives, mayonnaise, and lettuce.

Cottage cheese with chopped Spanish onion. Add mayonnaise if desired.

Cottage cheese with jelly, jam, marmalade, or finely chopped candied ginger.

Cottage cheese with chopped pickles, olives, nuts, or pimientos, and salad dressing.

Cream or American cheese; chopped, stuffed olives or pimientos, and salad dressing.

Cream cheese, shredded pineapple, and salad dressing, with or without lettuce.

Cream cheese, chopped candied ginger, chopped almonds, and cream to moisten.

Cream cheese, chopped olives, and chopped pimientos.

Cream cheese, nuts, raisins, and mayonnaise.

Peanut butter, apple butter, and dates or other fruits.

Nuts with creamed butter.

Nuts or nut butter and chopped, stuffed or ripe olives in equal quantities. Add salad dressing if desired.

Ripe olives, nuts, salad dressing, and lettuce.

Chopped raisins, alone or with nuts and cream cheese.

Chopped raisins, dates, and nuts with lemon juice to season. Mix with cream or mayonnaise.

Nut bread with orange marmalade.

Fruit bread with cream cheese.

Whipped cream, sweetened and flavored, spread between thin slices of cake. Add nuts, candied cherries, or other fruits, according to taste.

OPEN-FACE SANDWICHES

Open-face sandwiches often are served at afternoon teas and receptions. An open-face sandwich consists of a single ⅜-inch slice of bread cut into any desired shape. They are spread with a suitable filling and garnished if desired.

ROLLED SANDWICHES

Remove crusts from 3 sides of fresh or day-old bread. Leave crust on bottom of loaf. With crust at left, cut loaf into lengthwise slices, ⅛ to ¼-inch thick. Place slices on cloth wrung out of hot water, or run rolling pin the length of each slice to make it easier to handle. Spread with butter and other smooth spread as desired. Olives, gherkins, carrots, frankfurters, or other foods may be placed across end. Starting at end with garnish, roll tightly being careful to keep sides straight. Wrap each roll in wax paper or aluminum foil. Chill several hours. Cut into ¼ to ½-inch slices.

RIBBON SANDWICHES

Butter 2 slices white bread and 1 slice whole wheat on both sides. Butter 2 slices whole wheat bread on 1 side only. Stack whole wheat and white bread slices alternately so that unbuttered sides of whole wheat bread slices are on outside. Firmly press together. Cut off crusts. Wrap tightly in wax paper, aluminum foil, or slightly damp cloth. Chill for several hours. Cut ½-inch slices. Any smooth spread may be used with the butter.

CHECKERBOARD SANDWICHES

Make stacks of Ribbon Sandwiches by alternating 2 slices white and 2 slices whole wheat bread and filling with butter or other smooth spread. Trim, and cut each stack into 3 slices. Using butter or spread as a filling, stack the 3 slices together so that white and whole wheat squares alternate to give a checkerboard effect.

CHEESE LOAF (A ONE-DISH MEAL)

⅔ Pullman loaf unsliced bread
½ cup butter or margarine, creamed

Fillings as suggested
¾ pound cream cheese
Thin cream

FILLING I. One cup ground cooked ham, 2 tablespoons pimientos, and salad dressing to moisten.

FILLING II. Two cups coarsely chopped carrots or other mild, colorful vegetable.

FILLING III. Two hard-cooked eggs, 1 cup chopped sweet pickles, and salad dressing to moisten.

Remove crusts from bread. Cut loaf lengthwise into 3 slices, parallel with bottom of loaf. Spread bread with butter on both sides except bottom and top slices, which are spread only on 1 side. Spread bottom layer with ham mixture. Cover second layer thickly with ground carrots. Spread top layer with egg mixture. Cover entire loaf with the cheese which has been mixed with cream as necessary to make a smooth paste. Decorate top with bits of pimiento. Garnish serving plate with lettuce or parsley. Six slices, 2 inches wide.

Fillings may be varied according to materials available. Chopped pickles may be added as desired. Other combinations for fillings are:

Chopped dates, English walnuts or pecans, with mayonnaise.

Chopped meat or chicken, with celery and mayonnaise.

Lettuce or tomatoes, with mayonnaise.

Peanut butter, bananas, and mayonnaise.

Ground whole orange and raisins.

Sliced tomatoes with chicken salad fillings.

Sliced cucumbers, alone, or with pineapple and mayonnaise.

Sharp cheese spread.

CLUB SANDWICHES

Arrange lettuce, crisp bacon, sliced tomato, and salad dressing on a slice of buttered toast. Cover with another slice of toast. Make second layer of lettuce, sliced chicken, cucumber, and salad dressing. Cover with third piece of toast. Garnish with parsley and olives or pickles. Serve while toast and bacon are hot. Bread may be toasted on one side only if desired. Toasted side is then placed uppermost. Fasten sandwich together with toothpicks, and cut into triangles.

Such a sandwich is suitable as a main dish for luncheon or supper. It requires a fork and usually a knife for satisfactory service.

CHEESE, TOMATO, AND BACON SANDWICHES

6 slices of bread	6 large slices tomato
2 tablespoons butter or	6 thin slices cheese
margarine	6 slices bacon

■ Toast bread lightly. Butter. Place a slice of tomato on each slice of bread, place cheese on tomato, and add a slice of bacon cut in half. Toast in broiling oven until cheese is melted and bacon crisp.

DEVILED TOMATO SANDWICHES

6 medium-sized tomatoes	1 tablespoon prepared
6 tablespoons bread crumbs	mustard
4 slices bacon, partially cooked	6 slices bread
and cut into small pieces	Salt
4 tablespoons butter	Parsley
1 tablespoon minced chives	
1 cup ground, cooked	
ham	

■ Cut stem end from each tomato, leaving a small cup. Add salt, chives, bits of bacon, and bread crumbs. Bake at 350°F (moderate oven) until tomatoes are hot and crumbs brown. Serve on slices of hot buttered toast, spread with ground ham mixed with mustard. Garnish with parsley.

REUBEN SANDWICHES

Corned beef slices   Rye bread
Swiss cheese slices
Sauerkraut, heated and
  drained

■ Place corned beef, Swiss cheese, and drained sauerkraut on plain or toasted rye bread. Serve with mustard, horseradish, and dill pickles. These sandwiches may be grilled if desired.

GRILLED CHEESE SANDWICHES

2 slices bread
1 slice cheese, ⅜-inch
  thick

■ Butter bread, place cheese between slices of bread. Preheat a heavy cast iron or aluminum skillet. Butter outside of sandwich, place in skillet and cover. Cook 5 minutes on each side or until sandwich is golden brown and cheese is melted. Cut in half.

CANAPÉS

Canapés are individual appetizers that may be served hot or cold. They generally are used as an hors d'oeuvre for the first course of a meal. They are eaten with the fingers unless a sauce makes this impractical.

Preparation. Use a ¼-inch slice of day-old bread for a foundation. Cut into any desired shape. Toast on 1 side. Spread untoasted side of bread with a uniform layer of highly seasoned savory paste. Garnish in an all-over design or with a border and central decoration as desired.

Large crisp potato chips or assorted crackers may be substituted for bread. Sometimes a slice of tomato or cooked beet or an artichoke bottom is marinated and used as a foundation. Such canapés are eaten with a fork. Raw carrot slices spread with peanut butter are appetizing. Slices of raw apple or pear are delicious spread with cream cheese.

Pastes. Combinations for pastes are largely a matter of taste. Some suggestions are:

Anchovy or sardine paste, hard-cooked eggs, and mayonnaise to moisten.

Caviar, lemon juice, and cayenne.

Soft cream cheese and anchovy paste.

Cream cheese, butter, cayenne, and salt to taste.

Cheese and pimientos.

Chopped ham, chicken or crab meat, creamed butter, highly seasoned with curry powder or chutney.

Equal amounts of chopped lobster and sieved hard-cooked egg yolks moistened with melted butter or heavy cream. Season to taste, garnish with lobster coral and rings of egg white.

Garnishes. Suitable garnishes are:

Hard-cooked eggs, cut into wedges or chopped. White and yolk may be separated and arranged in a pattern.

Olives, sliced or chopped fine.

Green pepper or cooked beets cut into fancy shapes or minced.

Cucumbers sliced thin or chopped.

Pickles and pimentos minced or cut into fancy shapes.

Softened cream cheese applied with pastry decorator.

Soups

SOUPS may be classified according to their liquid base into the following groups:

Stock or broth—the liquid resulting from the extraction of meat, fish, and/or vegetables with water. Brown stock is prepared from beef, white stock, from chicken or veal.

Cream soups—a mixture of thin white sauce and mashed or strained vegetables, meat, or fish. Some stock may be used in sauce.

Bisques—a mixture of chopped shellfish, broth, milk, and seasonings. They are usually thickened.

Purées—a thick soup made by pressing cooked vegetables or fish through a sieve into their own stock. Those made with milk are similar to cream soups but are much thicker.

Chowders—an unstrained stew made of meat, fish, or vegetables with milk, salt pork, and various seasonings. Crackers generally are added just before serving.

MEAT STOCK OR BROTH

BROWN STOCK

6 pounds beef shank	4 cloves
3 quarts water	¼ bay leaf
⅓ cup chopped carrots	2 sprigs parsley
⅓ cup chopped celery	Salt
⅓ cup chopped onions	Thyme, marjoram, and
¼ teaspoon peppercorns	other herbs as desired

Yield: Three quarts
Follow directions for preparation (p. 72) and clearing (p. 72).

WHITE STOCK

4 pounds knuckle of veal	1 sliced lemon
2 quarts water	1 blade mace or ¼ bay
1 chopped onion	leaf
¼ cup chopped celery	Salt
¼ teaspoon peppercorns	

Yield: Two quarts

Preparation

Select a less tender cut of meat. If brown stock is desired, brown the meat in fat. Allow 1 pint or more of water for each pound of meat and bone. Add seasonings. Simmer (185 to 200°F) 4 to 6 hours, replacing water as needed. (Pressure cookers or pressure saucepans often are used for the extraction step to save time). Add vegetables and cook until tender. Season. Strain, if desired. For later use, place in refrigerator within ½ hour.

Clearing

If stock is cold, remove fat as a solid cake; if warm, remove by skimming with a spoon. Add 1 slightly beaten egg white and 1 crushed egg shell per quart of cool soup. The egg albumen coagulates with heating, and meat particles are caught in the coagulum. Heat to boiling, stirring constantly. Boil vigorously 5 minutes. Add ½ cup cold water and allow to settle. Strain through 2 thicknesses of cheesecloth placed over a sieve.

BOUILLON

Make as for Brown Soup Stock (p. 71). Decrease cloves to 2 and each vegetable to ¼ cup. Omit bay leaf. Bouillon may or may not be cleared. Three quarts.

EGG BOUILLON. Add 1 slightly beaten egg to 1 cup cleared hot bouillon. Pour bouillon gradually into egg. Stir constantly while adding, to avoid overcooking egg.

TOMATO BOUILLON. Add 1 cup tomato juice and any desired seasonings to 1 quart uncleared bouillon. Clear and serve.

NOODLE SOUP. Add 1 cup cooked noodles to 1 quart bouillon. Season to taste. Cooked macaroni, spaghetti, or rice may be substituted for noodles.

CONSOMMÉ

3 pounds lean beef	⅓ cup chopped onions
1 pound marrowbone	⅓ cup chopped carrots
3 pounds knuckle of veal	⅓ cup chopped celery
2 pounds chicken	2 sprigs parsley
5 quarts water	Salt
8 peppercorns	

■ Follow directions for preparation of Meat Stock (p. 72), browning the beef. Consommés are always cleared. Five quarts.

VEGETABLE CONSOMMÉ. Serve consommé with cooked mixed vegetables cut into small pieces. Allow ½ cup vegetables to 1 quart consommé.

CREAM SOUPS

2 cups Very Thin or Thin   1 cup cooked vegetable,
White Sauce (p. 95)   meat, or fish

Preparation. Prepare white sauce using milk or a combination of milk and liquid in which the vegetable, meat, or fish was cooked. If desired, vegetables may be diced or puréed. Add vegetable, meat, or fish and seasonings to hot white sauce and mix. If soup must stand before serving, cover and hold over hot water. Just before serving, shredded or finely chopped raw vegetables may be added for texture and flavor contrast or garnish. Four cups.

Variations

KIND	AMOUNT, CUPS	WHITE SAUCE, CUPS	SUGGESTED SEASONINGS	SUGGESTED GARNISHES
Asparagus	1, purée	2, thin	Grated lemon peel	Paprika
Carrot	1, purée or diced	2, thin	Minced parsley	Ripe olive rings
Celery	1, diced	2, thin	Onion juice	Minced green celery leaves, toasted almonds
Chicken	1, shredded or diced	2, thin	Onion juice	Minced pimiento and green pepper
Corn	1, whole	2, thin	Onion juice	Minced green pepper
Mushroom	1, sliced	2, thin	Worcestershire sauce	Whipped cream, browned crumbs, or minced olives
Onion	1, chopped and browned	2, thin	Grated cheese	Croutons
Pea	1, purée	2, very thin	Mint	Pimiento riced in whipped cream
Potato	1, mashed or diced	2, very thin	Minced onion	Caraway seed, minced parsley or chives, paprika
Spinach	1, purée	2, thin	Minced onion, nutmeg	Sieved hard-cooked egg yolk

CREAM OF TOMATO SOUP

2 cups tomato juice	2 tablespoons flour
1 tablespoon chopped onion	Salt
2 tablespoons butter or	2 cups milk
margarine	

■ Simmer tomato juice and onion for 5 minutes. Melt butter or margarine, add flour and salt. Stir until smooth. Add tomato juice, and cook with constant stirring until thickened. Slowly add tomato mixture to cold milk with constant stirring. Heat and serve immediately. Four cups.

CLAM CHOWDER

1 to 2 cups clams	½ tablespoon flour
1-inch cube salt pork, minced	1 cup boiling water
½ medium onion, sliced	2 cups cubed potatoes
1 tablespoon chopped celery	2 cups scalded milk
½ green pepper, chopped, if	Salt and pepper
desired	4 crackers

■ Clean clams. Heat in their own liquor to boiling point. Remove from liquor and chop. (Chopped clams may be purchased in their own liquor.) Strain liquor. Brown pork lightly. Add onion, celery, and green pepper, and cook until tender. Stir in flour. Add potatoes and boiling water and continue cooking. Add clams and liquor when the potatoes are tender. Add scalded milk and crackers. Serve immediately. Six cups.

CORN CHOWDER

1-inch cube salt pork, minced	2 cups boiling water
½ medium onion, sliced	3 cups milk
2 cups diced or sliced potatoes	Salt and pepper
1 cup corn	Crackers

■ Brown pork lightly. Add onion, cook until transparent. Add potatoes, corn, and enough boiling water to cover. Cook until tender. Add milk and seasonings. Heat. Pour over crackers before serving. Six cups.

MISCELLANEOUS SOUPS

CHICKEN GUMBO

1 chopped onion	1 cup cooked okra chunks
¼ cup fat	1 small green pepper,
1 quart chicken stock or	chopped
3 cups chicken stock and	Salt
1 cup tomatoes	Pepper
1 cup shredded chicken, if	
desired	

■   Cook onion with fat until soft and transparent. Add remaining ingredients. Simmer 15 minutes. Add water if needed to maintain volume. Five cups.

CHILI

1 pound hamburger	1 cup water
2 small onions, chopped	2½ cups canned tomatoes
2 tablespoons chili powder	2½ cups canned kidney
Salt	beans

■   Cook hamburger, onion, chili powder, and salt until brown. Add tomatoes, beans, and water. Cook slowly 1 hour. Approximately 7 cups.

OYSTER SOUP (OYSTER STEW)

1 cup oysters	Salt
2 cups milk, scalded	Pepper
2 tablespoons butter or margarine	

■   Melt butter, add oysters, and simmer in their liquor just until the edges curl. Add scalded milk, salt, and pepper. Hold just a few minutes to blend flavors. Oyster stew is apt to curdle upon standing. Three cups.

SPLIT PEA SOUP

2 cups split peas	½ cup sliced celery and celery leaves
1 ham bone with or without meat	½ cup sliced carrots
6 cups water	1 bay leaf
¼ pound salt pork	⅛ teaspoon thyme
½ cup sliced onion	Salt
½ clove garlic, crushed	Pepper

■   Cover peas with water and bring to boil. Cover with lid and remove from heat and allow to stand for 1 hour. Sauté the salt pork until crisp and brown. Remove salt pork and save. To fat add chopped onions, and garlic; sauté until golden. Add split peas, ham bone, celery, and carrots. Season with bay leaf, thyme, salt, and pepper. Simmer for 2 hours until peas are tender. Remove meat from bone; cut into small pieces and return salt pork and ham to soup. Thin with water to desired serving consistency. Approximately eight cups.

VEGETABLE SOUP

⅓ cup sliced carrots
½ cup sliced celery
½ medium onion, sliced
5 tablespoons butter or margarine (part beef suet may be used)
1½ cups cubed potatoes

2 cups water
2 cups canned tomatoes
½ tablespoon chopped parsley
Salt
Pepper

■   Slowly cook carrots, celery, and onions for 10 minutes in 4 tablespoons of fat. Add potatoes, cover, cook 2 minutes longer, add water. Boil gently until vegetables are soft. More water may be necessary to maintain volume. Add tomatoes, remaining butter, and parsley. Season, and heat to serving temperature. Vegetables may be varied to suit taste. Six cups.

SOUP ACCOMPANIMENTS

CRISP CRACKERS

Spread crackers lightly with butter allowing ¼ teaspoon to each cracker. Bake at 375°F until delicately brown.

CROUTONS

Sliced bread   Butter or margarine

■   Trim crusts from bread. Spread slices lightly with butter. Cut into ⅓-inch cubes. Brown in (300°F) oven. Serve on top of cream soups or as an accompaniment to other soups. Garlic may be added to butter if desired.

TOAST STRIPS

Prepare as for Croutons (p. 76) making long strips instead of cubes. If desired, sprinkle with grated cheese and paprika before toasting.

MELBA TOAST (p. 61)

NOODLES

1 egg or 2 egg yolks, slightly beaten
½ teaspoon salt

Flour to make a very stiff dough

■   Add salt to egg. Stir in flour. Knead until smooth. Roll paper thin. Cover with towel. Let stand ½ hour to dry. Cut into ⅛-inch strips. Cook as for Boiled Macaroni (p. 28). Noodles may be dried and kept for some time before using. One cup, uncooked.

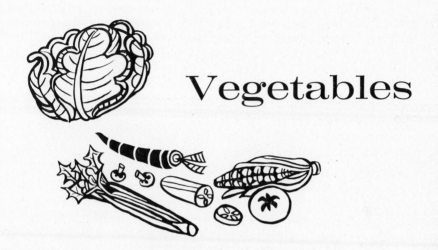

Vegetables

Selection, Storage, and Preparation

Selection. Vegetables of high quality are fresh, crisp, and firm. Peas and corn, particularly, should be obtained as fresh as possible as they are less sweet after standing. Fresh vegetables have a bright color and show no signs of spoilage. Such vegetables as cauliflower, cabbage, and lettuce should be heavy in proportion to size and solid to the touch.

Storage. Proper storage of fresh vegetables helps conserve their food values. The length of time raw vegetables are stored, storage temperature, and humidity affect nutrient retention. Green vegetables are best stored at refrigerator temperature in the vegetable crisper or in moisture proof bags. Green peas and green lima beans may be stored in the pod. If they are shelled, place in a polyethylene bag before refrigeration. Ripe, firm tomatoes should be held in the refrigerator or at a low room temperature. Roots and tubers should be kept cool and moist enough to prevent withering.

Preparation. Wash vegetables thoroughly before cooking. Food nutrients are retained when vegetables such as potatoes and carrots are cooked whole with skin. Water in which vegetables have been cooked may be utilized in soups, thus saving valuable nutrients.

General Directions for Cooking

Vegetables are cooked to soften the cellulose or fiber, to cook the starch, and in many cases, to increase palatability. Boiling, steaming, and baking are methods of cooking commonly used. Steaming and baking are often

77

preferable, particularly for young vegetables, as they conserve more nutrients. Boiled vegetables should be cooked as quickly as possible to insure best flavor, texture, and appearance. Volatile acids are released from vegetables during cooking. They may have harmful effects on the quality of strong-flavored and green colored vegetables.

Strong-Flavored Vegetables. Volatile substances, such as hydrogen sulfide, may be formed in cooking strong-flavored vegetables because of the decomposition of certain compounds by heat. If these materials are retained in cooking, they give a strong odor and flavor to the vegetable. Vegetables should be cooked quickly to prevent undesirable flavor changes. Experiments indicate that good products are obtained with careful cooking in a small amount of water.

Mild-Flavored Vegetables. Cook mild-flavored vegetables, as carrots and corn, in a small amount of water and as quickly as possible.

Green Vegetables. It is desirable to retain the color of green vegetables in cooking. Anything that shortens the cooking time has this effect. Chlorophyll of green vegetables is readily destroyed by acid. The volatile acids formed in cooking, unless diluted or neutralized, are often sufficient to destroy the green color. The water in many localities may contain enough alkalies to neutralize the acids liberated from the vegetables in cooking and thus help retain color. Green vegetables should be cooked quickly to preserve color and may be uncovered, at least during the early part of the cooking period, to allow acids to volatilize. Covering after the first few minutes of cooking shortens cooking time. The amount of water for cooking green vegetables is stated in different ways. Small quantities are more satisfactory because of greater nutrient and flavor retention.

Green vegetables, as a rule, lose color if cooked in a steamer. However, there is excellent retention of green color when the pressure saucepan is used properly.

Yellow Vegetables. The yellow pigments of vegetables are stable and are not injured by any ordinary method of cooking.

Red Vegetables. Generally red vegetables retain their color best in an acid medium. Red cabbage, for example, requires addition of acid to cooking water to retain a red color. Acid should be added late in cooking period to avoid toughening. If vinegar is used, allow 1 tablespoon to 1 cup water. Beets ordinarily contain enough acid to protect their color during cooking.

White Vegetables. White vegetables should be cooked only until tender as they darken when overcooked.

Frozen Vegetables. Any suitable method of cooking or serving fresh vegetables may be used for frozen ones. Most frozen vegetables are not defrosted before cooking. However, corn-on-the-cob is best completely defrosted in order to make sure that the cob is not still cold when the kernels are tender. Leafy vegetables such as spinach or greens will cook more evenly if defrosted enough to separate the leaves before cooking.

Frozen vegetables may be cooked in a small amount of water in a covered saucepan. The amount of water depends on the vegetable and the size of the package; as little as possible should be used. When partially defrosted, the vegetable should be broken up with a fork for more uniform cooking.

The cooking time for frozen vegetables is only about ½ as long as for fresh ones, because scalding and freezing have softened the tissues. Time of cooking is counted from the time the water returns to a boil after the vegetable has been added. When done, it should be seasoned and served immediately.

Methods of Cooking Vegetables

Baking. Cook in oven with dry heat. Use temperature and length of time suitable for individual vegetables.

Boiling. Allow ½ teaspoon salt to 1 pound of vegetable. Heat (required amount) water to boiling point. Add vegetable, cover if desired, heat quickly to boiling and cook until vegetable is tender. See Time Table For Boiling Vegetables (p. 80).

Deep-Fat Frying (French Frying). Fry in enough fat to cover food entirely, but do not fill fryer more than ¾ full. Heat to desired temperature (350 to 400°F). The temperature should be below the smoking point of the fat. Cooked foods need only heating and browning, whereas uncooked foods must be cooked as well as browned. The uncooked foods, therefore, require a lower temperature. Foods to be fried should be dry on surface, as moisture causes fat to splatter.

Deep-fat fryers may be purchased with thermostatic heat controls. If not available, use a thermometer to obtain the correct temperature of the fat. Another test of the fat may be made by dropping a 1-inch cube of soft bread into the fat. The bread should brown in 40 seconds at 375 to 400°F or 60 seconds at 350 to 375°F. If fat is too cool, foods will soak up fat; if too hot, they either will be too brown or not thoroughly cooked. Overheating also decomposes fat.

Do not cook too much food at one time, because pieces of food that touch each other tend to brown unevenly. After cooking, remove food from fat and drain. Reheat fat after each lot of food is removed. Strain fat through cheesecloth after use. Store in cool, dark place.

Panning. Use 2 to 4 tablespoons of fat to 1 pound of vegetable, or fry bits of bacon or salt pork until crisp and use the drippings. Add vegetable, salt, and other seasonings and 1 to 2 tablespoons of water, if necessary. Cover tightly, reduce heat, and cook slowly, retaining steam. Stir as needed to prevent burning. Cook just until done. As a rule, the vegetable is shredded or cut into very small pieces so that cooking time may be the same or less than that given for boiling. Little or no liquid should remain so that there is no loss of nutrients in discarded cooking liquid.

Pan-Frying. Dip sliced vegetable in flour or egg and crumb (p. 98) and fry in small amount of fat on griddle or in frying pan until nicely browned and cooked through.

Pressure Cooking. Follow directions given by the manufacturer for use of the saucepan.

Scalloping. Bake seasoned vegetable in a sauce in an uncovered casserole. Liquid from the vegetable or milk may be used to make the sauce.

Time Table for Boiling Vegetables

VEGETABLES	BOILING TIME (MIN)	VEGETABLES	BOILING TIME (MIN)
Asparagus tips *	5 to 15	Chard, Swiss *	10 to 20
Asparagus butts *	10 to 20	Corn-on-the-cob	6 to 10
Beans, green * and wax,		Cucumbers	5 to 6
whole or 1-inch pieces	15 to 30	Eggplant, diced	8 to 12
Beans, lima, green	20 to 25	Kohlrabi	20 to 30
Beet greens *	5 to 15	Onions, whole *	20 to 35
Beets, whole, young	30 to 45	Parsnips, quartered	10 to 15
Broccoli *	8 to 15	Peas	8 to 20
Brussels sprouts *	6 to 15	Potatoes, white, medium	25 to 40
Cabbage, Chinese	8 to 10	Potatoes, sweet, medium	20 to 35
Cabbage, green, shredded	3 to 8	Pumpkin, diced	20 to 30
Carrots, young, whole, or		Rutabaga, diced	20 to 30
halves	15 to 25	Salsify, sliced	15 to 20
Carrots, mature, diced	15 to 20	Spinach	3 to 10
Cauliflower, flowerets	8 to 10	Squash, summer, sliced	5 to 15
Cauliflower, whole, me-		Squash, winter, diced	15 to 25
dium	15 to 20	Tomatoes, whole	5 to 15
Celery, ½-inch pieces	15 to 20	Turnips, diced	10 to 20

* Strong-flavored or green vegetables may be cooked uncovered for the first few minutes.

General Suggestions for Serving Vegetables

BUTTERED VEGETABLES

1 tablespoon butter (other fats such as bacon or ham drippings may be used)
1 cup cooked salted vegetable

■ Melt fat. Add to vegetable. Mix lightly. Serve hot. Add horseradish, garlic, lemon juice, celery seed, chopped parsley, chives, paprika, or other seasoning.

Other foods may be lightly cooked or browned in the fat before they are added to the vegetable. They include chopped onion, shredded almonds, pecans, and poppy seed. Two servings.

CREAMED VEGETABLES

2 cups cooked vegetable   1 cup Medium White Sauce
                                                          (p. 94)

■   Leave vegetable whole or cut into pieces. Combine with white sauce, mixing lightly, taking care that vegetable is not broken. Four to 6 servings.

SCALLOPED VEGETABLES

Prepare sauce and food materials as for Creamed Vegetables (p. 81). Combine by either of the following methods.
METHOD I. Combine sauce and prepared vegetable. Pour into oiled baking dish. Cover top with Buttered Crumbs (p. 60). Bake at 400°F until sauce bubbles and crumbs are brown.
METHOD II. Arrange prepared vegetable and sauce in alternate layers in oiled baking dish, making top layer of sauce. Cover with Buttered Crumbs (p. 60), and bake as above. Four to 6 servings.

Specific Directions for Cooking Vegetables

FRENCH ARTICHOKE

Wash artichoke and cut off stem to about ½-inch. If desired, cut off thorny leaf tips (use kitchen scissors). Cook uncovered in 1½-inches boiling, salted water 30 to 45 minutes, until a leaf pulls away easily. Remove from kettle and trim off stem. Serve upright on plate with Hollandaise Sauce (p. 100) or with ¼ cup melted butter mixed with 1 tablespoon lemon juice. Place sauce or butter in a small container and serve beside the artichoke. One artichoke per serving.

ASPARAGUS

Break off lower stalks at point at which they are tender. Wash. Cook in boiling salted water for 5 to 20 minutes. Drain and serve buttered, creamed, or with Hollandaise Sauce (p. 100).

SNAP BEANS

Wash either green or wax beans. Cut or break off stem end and blossom tip. Leave whole, cut into 1-inch lengths, or cut in long narrow strips with knife or special cutter (Frenched). Cook 15 to 30 minutes. Drain, and serve buttered, buttered with browned almonds or sautéed mushrooms, creamed, or with sour cream.

SWEET-SOUR BEANS

2 strips bacon, diced
½ cup minced onion
1 tablespoon flour
¼ cup vinegar
2 tablespoons sugar

¾ cup bean liquid
1 teaspoon salt
¼ teaspoon pepper
2 cups cooked green or
   wax beans

■ Cook bacon until crisp. Remove bacon. Add onion to fat and cook until yellow. Stir in flour. Add other ingredients except beans. Bring to rolling boil. Add beans and stir until heated through. Serve with the crisp bacon sprinkled over top. Four servings.

GREEN LIMA BEANS

Shell the beans. Wash. Cook 20 to 25 minutes. Drain, and serve buttered.

BOSTON BAKED BEANS

2 cups navy beans
¼ to ½ pound salt pork
1 teaspoon salt

1 teaspoon prepared mustard
1 tablespoon molasses
1 tablespoon sugar

■ Wash beans, cover with water, and boil 2 minutes. Remove from heat and allow to stand 1 hour. Cover and cook slowly, in water in which beans were soaked, until tender. Drain, and save cooking liquid. Fill bean pot ½ full, add pork, rind of which has been scored. Place remaining beans in pot, pour over them mustard, salt, sugar, and molasses dissolved in hot water. Add enough of the cooking liquid to cover beans. Cover, and bake 8 or more hours at 275°F. Replace water as needed. Draw pork to surface during last hour of baking. Remove cover to brown beans and pork. Six servings.

BEET GREENS

Wash. Discard tough stems and leaves. Cook in a small amount of water 5 to 15 minutes. Drain, and serve with butter or bacon drippings.

BEETS

Cut tops from beets leaving 1½-inch stems. Retain roots. Wash. Cook 30 to 45 minutes. Drain, and remove skins, stems, and roots. Dice, slice, or leave whole.

Beets may be pared and diced, shredded, or thinly sliced before cooking. The tendency to "bleed" is increased by this method and they should be cooked in the minimum amount of water until tender. A little vinegar added to cooking water helps to prevent fading of color. Serve buttered, in Harvard sauce, in orange sauce (p. 83) or pickled (p. 240).

HARVARD BEETS

½ cup vinegar
½ cup water
1⅓ tablespoons cornstarch

2 tablespoons sugar
A few grains salt

■ Make as for Starch Sauces (Method III, p. 94). Add cooked beets, heat, and serve. Eight servings.

BEETS WITH ORANGE SAUCE

Water to make 1 cup liquid
2 tablespoons cornstarch
1 to 2 tablespoons frozen
concentrated lemonade

¼ cup frozen concentrated
orange juice

■ Mix cornstarch with cold liquid. Cook all ingredients over low heat with constant stirring until thickened and clear. Add cooked beets. Heat thoroughly, and serve.

BROCCOLI

Cut off heads or blossoms at point where easily cut with sharp knife. Stalks below that point may be peeled and cooked with heads. Wash thoroughly, preferably in running water. Look carefully for insects. Cut into serving-size pieces by cutting from bottom of stalk up toward blossom. The blossom part may be divided, leaving buds attached to a portion of the stalk. Cook 8 to 15 minutes. Drain and serve with butter, almonds browned in butter, Hollandaise Sauce (p. 100), or Cheese Sauce (p. 94).

BRUSSELS SPROUTS

Remove wilted and discolored leaves. Wash carefully, and cut away any insect damage. If sprouts are large, make a cross cut in the stem end about ⅓ the depth of the head to hasten cooking. Cook 6 to 15 minutes. Drain, and serve buttered.

CABBAGE

Wash. Remove coarse, outside leaves; shred or cut into wedges. Remove tough stalk. Cook 3 to 8 minutes if shredded or 8 to 15 minutes for wedges. Drain, and serve buttered, buttered with caraway seeds, scalloped, or with Cheese Sauce (p. 94).

PENNSYLVANIA DUTCH RED CABBAGE

1 tablespoon salad oil or bacon drippings
2 cups shredded red cabbage
1 cup cubed unpared apple
(1 medium apple)

2 tablespoons vinegar
2 tablespoons water
½ teaspoon salt
¼ teaspoon caraway seed

■ Heat oil in sauce pan. Add remaining ingredients. Cover tightly. Cook 12 to 15 minutes over low heat, stirring occasionally. Four to 5 servings.

CELERY CABBAGE (CHINESE CABBAGE)

Wash, remove discolored leaves. Slice in 1-inch slices. Cook 8 to 10 minutes. Drain, and serve buttered or creamed.

CARROTS

Select small new carrots. Wash and scrape. Leave whole or slice, dice, or cut into strips as desired. Cook 15 to 25 minutes. Drain, and serve buttered, buttered with minced parsley or grated onion or both, creamed, pan fried, or glazed.

GLAZED CARROTS

3 tablespoons fat
12 small carrots, slightly undercooked

6 tablespoons brown or white sugar

■ Melt fat, add carrots, sprinkle with sugar, and cook until they begin to brown. Add a small amount of water. Cook until well glazed, turning as necessary. If preferred, the carrots may be baked at 375°F. Four or 5 sprigs of fresh mint may be chopped fine and added either at the beginning or the end of the glazing process. Four servings.

ZESTY CARROTS

6 to 8 carrots cut in lengthwise strips
¼ cup water or liquid from cooking carrots

1 tablespoon grated onion
2 tablespoons horseradish
½ cup salad dressing
½ teaspoon salt

■ Cook carrots. Place cooked carrots in a shallow baking dish. Mix remaining ingredients and pour over carrots. Top with Buttered Crumbs (p. 60) and bake at 375°F for 15 to 20 minutes. Garnish with minced parsley. Six servings.

CAULIFLOWER

Remove leaves. Wash carefully. Break into flowerets and cook 8 to 10 minutes. If left whole, cook 15 to 20 minutes. Drain. Serve buttered, creamed, scalloped, scalloped with cheese, with Hollandaise Sauce (p. 100), or with Cheese Sauce (p. 94).

CELERY

Use the outside stalks. Wash and cut into pieces either straight across or on the diagonal. Cook 15 to 20 minutes. Drain. Serve buttered, creamed, scalloped, or with Cheese Sauce (p. 94).

CHARD, SWISS

Wash carefully, removing discolored parts. Arrange leaves in a bunch. Cut crosswise into 1½ to 2-inch pieces. Cook 10 to 20 minutes. Drain. Serve buttered or with bacon drippings, bacon drippings in which chopped onion has been cooked until lightly browned, Soubise Sauce (p. 94), Mushroom Sauce or creamed with a dash of nutmeg.

CORN-ON-THE-COB

Remove husks and silks. A vegetable brush is helpful in removing the silks. Cut out any discolored or worm-eaten spots. Wash. Add water to cover. Cook 6 to 10 minutes. Drain, and serve with butter.

CORN CUSTARD

2 cups cooked whole kernel corn	3 tablespoons butter or margarine
2 or 3 eggs, slightly beaten	1 teaspoon salt
2 cups milk	
1 tablespoon chopped green pepper and/or pimiento	

■ Combine corn, eggs, milk, and pepper and/or pimiento. Add melted fat and salt. Pour into oiled baking dish. Bake as for Custard (p. 154). Six servings.

CUCUMBERS

Wash. Pare. Cut into strips, removing seeds unless they are very small. Cook 5 to 6 minutes. Drain, and serve creamed, scalloped, or with Cheese Sauce (p. 94).

EGGPLANT

Wash, peel, and dice. Cook 8 to 12 minutes. Drain, and serve with Cheese Sauce (p. 94) or with Tomato Sauce (p. 99).

FRIED EGGPLANT

Wash. Pare if desired. Cut in ⅓-inch slices or fingerlike sticks. Sprinkle with salt, then egg and crumb (p. 98) or coat with flour. Cook slowly in small amount of fat until crisp and brown, or fry in deep fat until golden brown. Serve plain or with Tomato Sauce (p. 99).

SPANISH EGGPLANT

1 large eggplant	⅛ teaspoon pepper
4 slices bacon, diced	1 (6-ounce) can tomato purée plus 1 can water
1 medium onion, finely chopped	½ cup grated cheese
1 green pepper, finely chopped	Buttered bread crumbs
1 teaspoon salt	

■ Peel eggplant and cut into ½-inch cubes. Fry bacon until crisp and add onion and green pepper. Cook about 5 minutes, add eggplant, salt, pepper, tomato purée and water. Cook until egg plant is tender. Place mixture into a buttered 1½ quart casserole. Sprinkle with grated cheese and top with Buttered Bread Crumbs (p. 60). Bake at 350°F, 35 to 45 minutes. Six to 8 servings.

KOHLRABI

Wash and pare, being sure to remove all the outer fiber. Cut into cubes or slices. Cook 20 to 30 minutes. Drain, and serve buttered or creamed.

MUSHROOMS

Wash mushrooms carefully, and trim off tough end of stalk. Caps should be drained with gill side down. Peeling is not necessary for small tender mushrooms. If mushrooms are of a variety that darkens after peeling, they should be prepared immediately before using. Otherwise, add a little acid to prevent discoloration.

Mushrooms are best if cooked and seasoned simply. As a rule, they may be served in the same ways as oysters. They may be left whole or sliced according to size. Broiling, frying, creaming, and scalloping are good methods of cooking. Mushrooms add variety and flavor to such dishes as creamed chicken, sweetbreads, and sauces. Mushrooms broiled with steak will cook in 5 to 10 minutes and will be toughened if cooked longer.

SAUTÉED MUSHROOMS

Put whole, halved, or sliced mushrooms in butter in a frying pan. Cover pan, and let mushrooms cook slowly for about 10 minutes. Juices cook from the mushrooms so that a relatively small amount of butter need be used. Serve creamed on toast or with buttered vegetables such as fresh lima beans, carrots, green beans, or peas.

CREAMED MUSHROOMS

Add a small amount of cream to the sautéed mushrooms. Heat, and serve on toast. If desired, more cream may be used and flour added to thicken.

ONIONS

Peel onions. If small, leave whole or cut into halves. If large, cut into quarters. Cook 20 to 35 minutes. Drain. Serve buttered, creamed, or scalloped.

FRENCH FRIED ONION RINGS

Wash and peel large sweet onions. Use a sharp knife with a long blade. Cut the slices no more than ¼-inch thick and preferably a little thinner. Separate slices into rings. Dip rings in flour. Make a batter of 1 beaten egg, ½ cup milk, ½ cup flour, and 1 teaspoon salt. Dip floured rings in batter and fry a few at a time in deep fat heated to 375°F. Remove when golden brown. Drain on soft crumpled paper and sprinkle with salt.

PARSNIPS

Wash and scrape parsnips. Cut into quarters lengthwise, removing woody centers if necessary. Cook 10 to 15 minutes. Drain, and serve buttered, creamed, or pan-fried.

PEAS

Shell peas. Discard those that are too mature. Wash. Cook 8 to 20 minutes. Drain, and serve buttered, buttered with carrots or mushrooms, or creamed.

STUFFED PEPPERS

6 green peppers	⅓ cup milk
2 cups cooked, ground meat	1 tablespoon chopped parsley
1 small onion, finely chopped	1 teaspoon salt
1 tablespoon fat	½ cup bread crumbs
1 egg, slightly beaten	1 cup hot water

■ Cut cap from stem end of each pepper. Remove seeds. Parboil peppers 10 minutes. Chop cap. Cook with onion in fat until lightly browned. Add remaining ingredients except water. Fill peppers with mixture, stand them in baking dish, and pour water around them. Bake at 375°F about ½ hour, basting often. Tops may be covered with Buttered Crumbs (p. 60). Six servings.

BAKED POTATOES

Scrub potatoes of uniform size. Bake at 400°F until tender. Allow about 60 minutes for potatoes of medium size. When done, cut a small cross in skin of potato. Then press potato in clean cloth until contents are mealy. Insert butter and seasoning. Garnish with parsley. Serve immediately. To make a tender, glossy skin, oil potatoes before baking. The washed potatoes may be wrapped in aluminum foil before baking.

STUFFED POTATOES (POTATOES IN THE HALF SHELL)

Cut hot, baked potatoes into halves lengthwise, or if potatoes are small, cut a slice from 1 side. Scoop out contents. Mash; season with salt, pepper, butter, and hot milk. Pile lightly into shells, leaving tops rough. Bake until tops are delicately browned. Small bits of pimiento, stuffed olive, or grated cheese may be added to potato or sprinkled over top. Garnish with parsley.

BOILED POTATOES

Scrub potatoes of uniform size, peel if desired. Cook 25 to 40 minutes. Drain at once, and dry by shaking pan gently over fire. Serve in an open dish to prevent sogginess due to condensation of steam. If served with "jackets" on, skin should be broken immediately after cooking, to allow steam to escape. Serve buttered, creamed, scalloped, or with Cheese Sauce (p. 94).

RICED POTATOES. Force boiled potatoes through ricer into hot serving dish. Sprinkle with salt and pepper. Dot with bits of butter.

MASHED POTATOES

3 cups hot, mashed or riced potatoes (4 to 5 medium-sized potatoes)	4 to 6 tablespoons hot milk or cream
3 tablespoons butter or margarine	1½ teaspoons salt
	⅛ teaspoon pepper

■ Add butter, milk or cream, and salt to mashed potatoes. Beat until light and creamy. Pile lightly into a hot dish, sprinkle with pepper, dot with bits of butter, and serve immediately from uncovered dish. Six servings.

DUCHESS POTATOES

3 cups hot, mashed or riced potatoes	1½ teaspoons salt
3 tablespoons butter or margarine	⅛ teaspoon pepper
	3 egg yolks, slightly beaten
6 tablespoons milk or cream	3 egg whites, beaten stiff

■ Mix thoroughly all ingredients except egg whites. Fold egg whites in carefully. Pile mixture lightly into oiled baking dish. Set in pan of hot water. Bake at 400°F until set. Serve at once. Six servings.

POTATO ROSES. Force unbaked Duchess Potatoes through pastry tube (p. 6) forming fancy shapes. Brown lightly in a 400°F oven. These make a suitable garnish for Planked Steak (p. 110).

POTATO CAKES

Prepare Mashed Potatoes (p. 88), omitting milk and adding 1 beaten egg yolk and 1 teaspoon finely chopped parsley. Leftover mashed potatoes may be used. Shape into balls, egg and crumb (p. 98), fry (p. 79), and drain. If preferred, the mixture may be shaped into flat cakes, rolled in flour, and browned in a small amount of fat.

LYONNAISE POTATOES

1 tablespoon minced onion	Salt
2 to 3 tablespoons fat	Pepper
2 cups boiled, diced potatoes	1 tablespoon chopped parsley

■ Cook onion slowly in fat 5 minutes without browning. Add seasoned potatoes. Cook until fat is absorbed. Shake pan occasionally, but do not stir, to avoid breaking potato cubes. Add parsley, and serve. Four servings.

OLD FASHIONED SCALLOPED POTATOES

Potatoes   Chopped onion or onion juice,
Milk   if desired
Salt   Butter or margarine
Pepper   Flour
                                   Chopped parsley, if desired

■   Cut pared potatoes into thin slices. Arrange in layers in oiled baking dish. Sprinkle each layer with salt, pepp , onion, parsley, and flour. Dot with butter or margarine. Add milk to cover. Baking dish should be no more than ¾ full. Bake uncovered at 375°F until potatoes are tender.

FRANCONIA POTATOES

Scrub potatoes, pare, and place in pan in which meat is roasting. Bake until tender, basting with fat in pan. Potatoes may be parboiled 10 minutes before putting in with meat. They will be less crusty if so treated.

FRIED POTATOES

Wash and pare potatoes. Cut into desired shape. Potato chips and lattice potatoes are cut most successfully with special vegetable slicers. A knife is satisfactory for cutting French fried potatoes if a regular cutter is not available.

Prepared potatoes may be wiped dry with a clean towel and fried at once, or they first may be soaked in salted cold water (1 teaspoon of salt per quart of water, for 1 hour). This last process is thought to improve crispness, but some food value is lost in the water. Fry in deep fat, following directions (p. 79), cooking only a small quantity at a time. Drain on soft, crumpled paper. Sprinkle with salt. Serve at once.

PUMPKIN

Wash pumpkin, and cut it into pieces that can be easily handled. Peel and cut into 1-inch cubes. Cook 20 to 30 minutes. More flavor is retained if pumpkin is cooked until water is evaporated and pumpkin is quite dry. Mash, or run through a sieve or food mill. Serve buttered or in pie.

RUTABAGA

Wash, pare, dice, or slice. Cook 20 to 30 minutes. Drain, and serve buttered or mashed.

SALSIFY

Wash, pare, and slice. Cook 15 to 20 minutes. Drain, and serve buttered or in creamed soup.

SPINACH

Remove roots, wilted leaves, and coarse stems; wash several times until free from sand, lifting from water each time rather than draining. If spinach is young and tender, cook it without the addition of water other than that clinging to leaves. Cover to hasten cooking. Heat gradually, and boil 3 to 10 minutes until tender. Drain, and season with butter or bacon fat.

SPINACH TIMBALES

2 cups cooked, chopped spinach	¼ teaspoon white pepper
½ teaspoon salt	¼ teaspoon nutmeg, if desired
½ teaspoon sugar	3 egg yolks, slightly beaten
	1 hard-cooked egg, sliced

■ Combine ingredients except the hard-cooked egg. Heat slowly, stirring until eggs are cooked. Avoid overcooking. Oil custard cups. Place slice of hard-cooked egg in bottom of each. Fill with spinach mixture. Set molds in pan of hot water. Bake at 375°F about 10 minutes or until set. Serve with Medium Brown Sauce (p. 95) or White Sauce (p. 94). Six servings.

SUMMER SQUASH

Wash, and cook whole, or slice. Do not pare or remove seeds unless squash is quite mature. Cook 5 to 15 minutes. Drain, and serve buttered or with Tomato Sauce (p. 99).

WINTER SQUASH

Wash and cut into pieces. Peel. Remove seeds and stringy portion. Cut into 1-inch cubes. Cook 15 to 25 minutes. Squash is better if cooked until water is evaporated and squash is quite dry. Serve with cream or butter. Brown sugar may be added.

BAKED SQUASH

Wash, and cut into pieces of suitable size for serving. Remove seeds and stringy portion. Bake at 375°F until tender, about 1 hour. Season with salt, pepper, and butter. Serve in shell.

Baked squash may be scraped from shell, run through vegetable ricer, and seasoned. Reheat, and serve.

BAKED ACORN SQUASH

Cut acorn squash in ½ lengthwise. Place in baking dish cut side down. Add a little water. Cover and bake at 375°F until tender. Place cut side up. Season with salt, butter, and a little brown sugar. Leave in oven uncovered until sugar melts.

FRIED SQUASH

Cut squash into thin slices. Season with salt and pepper, egg and crumb (p. 98), then fry in deep fat (p. 79) or in shallow fat until brown.

ZUCCHINI (SQUASH)

Wash and cut zucchini into ¼-inch slices. Sauté in a small amount of fat with salt, pepper, chopped chives or minced onion to taste. Cook over low heat until lightly browned and tender.

SWEET POTATOES

Wash thoroughly. Sweet potatoes are usually cooked with skins on. If very large, they may be cut in halves or quarters. Cook 20 to 35 minutes. Drain and peel. Serve plain; mashed with cream and butter; mashed with orange juice, grated orange rind, and butter; or pan fried.

GLAZED SWEET POTATOES

4 boiled sweet potatoes	¼ cup melted butter or margarine
½ cup brown or white sugar	

■ Cut peeled potatoes into halves lengthwise. Put into baking dish. Spread with sugar and butter or margarine that have been mixed together. Add a little water, and glaze at 375°F (moderate oven) or in a broiling oven, or cook slowly in a shallow pan on top of stove. Four servings.

ORANGE SWEET POTATOES

2 or 3 medium-sized sweet potatoes	2 teaspoons cornstarch
½ cup strained orange juice	1½ tablespoons butter
1 teaspoon grated orange rind	3 tablespoons brown sugar
	3 tablespoons white sugar

■ Wash potatoes and cook in boiling water until tender. Peel potatoes, cut in halves, and arrange in baking dish. Combine remaining ingredients and cook until thickened to make a sauce. Pour sauce over potatoes. Cover and bake at 350°F for 20 minutes. Uncover and bake 10 minutes longer. Four servings.

BAKED SWEET POTATOES

Prepare as for Baked Potatoes (p. 87).

BAKED TOMATOES

Wash tomatoes of medium size. Remove hard part of stem end. Cut into halves crosswise. Place in oiled baking dish, cut side up. Sprinkle with salt, pepper, and grated cheese. Cover with Buttered Crumbs (p. 60). Bake at 375°F until tender.

FRIED TOMATOES (SAUTÉED)

Wash tomatoes. Cut out hard part of stem end. Cut into ½-inch slices. Sprinkle with salt and pepper. Egg and crumb (p. 98), or dredge with flour or bread crumbs. Brown in small amount of fat. Place on hot platter. Pour sauce or gravy over tomatoes if desired.

SCALLOPED TOMATOES

6 medium-sized tomatoes	Soft bread crumbs
3 tablespoons butter or marga-	Salt
rine	Pepper

■   Peel tomatoes. Cut into pieces. Place layer of tomatoes in oiled baking dish. Add fat, salt, pepper, and bread crumbs. Repeat until dish is filled, making last layer of crumbs. Dot with bits of butter or margarine. Bake at 375°F about 30 minutes. Serve from baking dish. Canned tomatoes may be used. Six servings.

STEWED TOMATOES

6 medium-sized tomatoes	Soft bread crumbs
2 tablespoons butter or	Salt
margarine	Pepper

■   Peel tomatoes and cut into pieces. Cook in their own juice until tender. Add fat, salt, pepper, and enough pieces of bread or crumbs to thicken. Bread may be omitted if preferred. Chopped green pepper and onion may be cooked with tomatoes. Canned tomatoes may be used. Six servings.

TOMATO JUICE COCKTAIL

2 cups tomato juice	½ teaspoon Worcestershire
½ teaspoon celery salt	sauce
1½ teaspoons lemon juice or	3 drops Tabasco sauce
vinegar	

■   Mix ingredients and chill. Six servings.

BOILED TURNIPS

Wash. Pare. Leave whole, dice, or slice. Cook 10 to 20 minutes. Drain, and serve buttered, creamed, or mashed. Season with pepper and butter or hot cream.

Sauces

A SAUCE serves as an accompaniment to meat, fish, vegetables or dessert. The quantity of sauce used should be small in proportion to the amount of food. Certain sauces are associated with particular foods: Soubise and Tomato with omelet; Fruit sauces, Horseradish, Béchamel, and Mint with meat, fish, and poultry; Hollandaise and Mousseline with vegetables; and Hard Sauce and other Sweet sauces with desserts. Sauces may be classified as starch (contain starch as the thickening agent) and non-starch sauces.

STARCH SAUCES

Thickening agents commonly used in sauces include starch from wheat, corn, potato, and rice. Different starch materials have different thickening values. Starch is insoluble in cold water; however, moist heat causes the starch granules to swell and gelatinize. Large granules such as those in potato starch appear to gelatinize at lower temperatures than small ones, such as those in corn. Starch mixtures should be heated sufficiently to insure maximum swelling. Prolonged cooking may cause starch paste to become thin, because some of the starch is converted to dextrins. In the presence of acid, such as lemon juice or vinegar, conversion is more rapid. For this reason, it may be advisable to add acids at the end of the cooking period.

At 127°F starch begins to dextrinize (and change) resulting in decreased thickening power. This occurs when flour is browned. A sauce made with browned flour requires a greater amount of thickening agent to obtain the same consistency as one made with white flour.

BROWNED FLOUR

Spread flour in thin layer on flat surface. Bake at 400 to 450°F (hot oven), stirring often until evenly browned throughout. This may be made in quantity and used as needed for Brown Sauce (p. 95). The color may be light or dark as preferred. Thickening power will vary accordingly, being greater for light-colored flour.

Methods of Making Starch Sauces

When liquids are thickened with starch, the starch granules should be separated before heating by mixing with cold liquid, creamed or melted fat, or sugar. Otherwise lumps enclosing uncooked starch are formed. An instantized flour is on the market, which does not lump when added to liquid. Proportions of ingredients for selected sauces are listed on p. 95.

I. COLD LIQUID. Mix starch material gradually with twice its volume of cold liquid to form a smooth paste. Add slowly to heated liquid while stirring. Cook with continued stirring until sauce is thickened. After mixture has thickened, continue cooking for approximately 5 minutes over direct heat or 10 to 15 minutes in a double boiler. Add fat and seasonings before serving.

II. MELTED FAT. Melt fat, add starch material, and stir until smooth. Add cold liquid and cook as for Method I.

III. SUGAR. (When making sweet sauces.) Mix starch material with sugar, add liquid, and cook as for Method I. Flavor.

MEDIUM WHITE SAUCE

2 tablespoons fat	½ teaspoon salt
2 tablespoons flour	1 cup milk

■ Melt fat in double boiler, add flour and salt, and stir until smooth. Add milk and cook until thickened.

BÉCHAMEL. Substitute seasoned meat stock for ½ the milk.

CHEESE. Add ½ to 1 cup grated cheese and stir until cheese melts.

CURRY. Add 1 teaspoon curry powder. Sautéed onion also may be added. Meat stock may be substituted for part or all of the milk.

DRAWN BUTTER. Substitute water or stock for milk. Add 1 to 2 tablespoons butter and 1 teaspoon lemon juice just before serving.

EGG. Add 1 sliced hard-cooked egg to Medium White Sauce or Drawn Butter Sauce.

PARSLEY. Add 2 teaspoons finely chopped parsley.

SOUBISE. Add ½ cup sautéed onion.

Starch Sauces

KINDS	PROPORTIONS FOR MAKING				USES	PROPORTIONS FOR USE
	LIQUID	THICKENING AGENT	FAT *	SEASONING OR FLAVORING		
White sauce, Very thin	1 cup milk	½ tablespoon flour	1 tablespoon	½ teaspoon salt	Cream soups made from starch foods	Allow ¾ to 1 cup cooked, strained vegetable or other pulp to 1 cup sauce. The average amount is ½ cup (p. 73).
Thin	1 cup milk	1 tablespoon flour	1 tablespoon	½ teaspoon salt	Cream soups made from non-starch foods	
Medium	1 cup milk	2 tablespoons flour	2 tablespoons	½ teaspoon salt	Creamed dishes, scalloped dishes, gravies	Allow 2 to 3 cups vegetable, meat, or fish—cut into suitable pieces—to 1 cup sauce for creamed or scalloped dishes (p. 96).
Thick	1 cup milk	3 to 4 tablespoons flour	2 tablespoons	½ teaspoon salt	Soufflés	Allow 3 eggs and from ¾ to 1 cup other ingredients to 1 cup sauce (p. 96).
Very thick	1 cup milk	4 to 5 tablespoons flour	2½ tablespoons	½ teaspoon salt	Croquettes	Allow 1 to 3 cups finely divided ingredients to 1 cup sauce (p. 98).
Brown sauce	1 cup liquid, such as: water, meat stock, vegetable stock, milk	1½ tablespoons light brown flour or 3 tablespoons dark brown flour	2 tablespoons (meat fats much used)	½ teaspoon salt Pepper Bay leaf Cloves	Meat sauces, gravies	According to taste.
Sweet sauce	1 cup liquid, such as: water, fruit juice, milk, cream	1 to 2 tablespoons flour or ⅔ to 1½ tablespoons cornstarch	Varies	A few grains salt Sugar Extracts	Pudding sauces	According to taste.

* Butter or margarine is preferable for many sauces.

Products Using White Sauce

MEDIUM WHITE SAUCE

CREAMED FOODS

1 cup Medium White Sauce (p. 94).

2 to 3 cups prepared foods

■ Leave food whole, or cut into pieces. Combine with white sauce, mixing lightly, taking care that pieces are not broken. Four to 6 servings.

SCALLOPED FOODS

Prepare sauce and food materials as for Creamed Foods (p. 96). Combine sauce and prepared food material or arrange food and sauce in alternate layers in oiled baking dish, making last layer of sauce. Cover with Buttered Crumbs (p. 60). Bake at 400°F until sauce bubbles and crumbs are brown.

AU GRATIN FOODS

Prepare as for Scalloped Foods (p. 96). Sprinkle each layer with grated cheese.

THICK WHITE SAUCE

SOUFFLÉ

2 tablespoons fat
3 to 4 tablespoons flour
½ teaspoon salt
1 cup liquid (milk, meat, or vegetable stock)

½ to 1 cup prepared food (see Soufflé Combinations p. 97)
3 egg yolks, beaten
3 egg whites, stiffly beaten

■ Melt fat in double boiler. Add flour and salt and stir until smooth. Add liquid and cook until thick.

Add prepared food to hot white sauce. Stir in egg yolks. Remove from heat and fold in egg whites. Pour into unoiled 1½-quart casserole. Set in pan of hot water, and bake at 350°F until firm and when inserted, a sharp pointed knife comes out clean (45 to 60 minutes). *Serve at once.* Four servings.

Soufflé Combinations

TYPE OF SOUFFLÉ	TO 1 CUP OF THICK WHITE SAUCE ADD	OPTIONAL ADDITIONS
Cheese	½ cup grated	Paprika, cayenne
Fish: crab, haddock, halibut, lobster, oyster, salmon, tuna	¾ to 1 cup cooked, shredded or flaked, except oysters which may be added raw, whole, or cut in fourths.	Chopped parsley, lemon juice, curry powder, olives
Meat: beef, ham, lamb, fresh pork	1 cup cooked, ground, or chopped	Grated carrots, celery, onions, chopped parsley, celery salt, paprika, Worcestershire sauce, catsup, curry powder
Poultry: chicken, turkey	1 cup cooked, ground, or chopped	Nutmeg, paprika, capers, parsley, nuts
Nut	½ cup chopped or ground	
Chocolate	½ to 2 squares melted unsweetened chocolate, ½ cup sugar, 1 teaspoon vanilla	Whipped cream, nuts
Fruit: dried apricots, dates, prunes	½ to 1 cup chopped fruit, ¼ cup sugar. Apricots and prunes may be raw or cooked	Whipped cream, thin custard
Vegetables: cooked asparagus, carrots, cauliflower, celery, eggplant, mushrooms, salsify, spinach	1 cup minced or sieved, alone or in combination	Paprika, nutmeg, chopped parsley
Celery Cheese	1 cup minced celery, ½ cup grated cheese	
Corn	¾ cup well drained	2 tablespoons pimiento and/or 2 tablespoons chopped green pepper
Vegetables: raw carrots, celery, onion, spinach	1 cup minced or grated, alone or in combination	

VERY THICK WHITE SAUCE

CROQUETTES

2½ tablespoons fat
4 to 5 tablespoons flour
½ teaspoon salt
1 cup milk

1 to 3 cups prepared foods
(see Croquette Combina-
tions, p. 98)

■ Melt fat in double boiler. Add flour and salt and stir until smooth. Add milk and cook until thickened. Add prepared food to hot white sauce.

To Shape. Allow ¼ cup mixture for each croquette. Roll into ball then on board into a cylinder 2 to 3 inches long and 1 inch in diameter. Flatten ends with spatula. Other shapes, such as cones or balls may be used.

To Egg and Crumb. Beat egg slightly. Mix with equal amount of cold water. Put prepared Bread Crumbs (p. 60) on a shallow plate and egg mixture on another. Roll food in crumbs or flour; dip into egg, and again roll in crumbs. Care should be taken to have all parts completely covered.

To Fry. Lower carefully into deep fat heated to 385°F or hot enough to brown a 1-inch bread cube in 40 seconds. Fry until golden brown, about 1 minute. Remove from fat and drain on absorbent paper.

Croquette Combinations

TYPE OF CROQUETTE	TO 1 CUP VERY THICK WHITE SAUCE ADD	OPTIONAL ADDITIONS
Cheese	3 cups grated	Beat 4 egg whites until stiff. Fold into mixture. Dip in fine bread crumbs
Eggs	6 hard cooked, cut into small pieces	1 tablespoon chopped parsley or other herb
Fish: salmon, haddock, lobster	2 cups cooked, flaked	Parsley, lemon juice, Worcestershire sauce
Meat and Poultry: beef, lamb, ham, fresh pork, chicken, turkey	1 to 2 cups cooked, ground, or chopped	1 tablespoon grated onion or chopped parsley, cayenne
Nut	1 to 2 cups chopped	

TYPE OF CROQUETTE	TO 1 CUP VERY THICK WHITE SAUCE ADD	OPTIONAL ADDITIONS
Sweetbreads	2 cups cooked, chopped sweetbreads or 1 cup sweetbreads and 1 cup sautéed mushrooms	Cayenne
Carrot	1 to 2 cups cooked, well-drained, finely chopped	1 tablespoon grated onion, 2 tablespoons chopped parsley, nutmeg, paprika

PAN GRAVY

2 tablespoons flour
2 tablespoons fat from pan in which meat was cooked

½ teaspoon salt
1 cup liquid (milk, water, or vegetable stock)

■ Cook flour in fat until brown, stirring constantly. Add salt and liquid. Cook with continued stirring until gravy boils. One cup.

GIBLET GRAVY

Simmer giblets slowly in small amount of water until tender. Chop. Make Pan Gravy (p. 99) using giblet stock for liquid. Add giblets.

TOMATO SAUCE I

1 slice onion
1 slice carrot
1 sprig parsley
2 cups tomato juice or pulp

4 tablespoons fat
4 tablespoons flour
Salt
Pepper

■ Cook onion, carrot, and parsley in tomato juice or pulp until tender. Strain. Add water to seasoned tomato juice to make 2 cups of liquid. Melt fat in double boiler. Add flour and stir until smooth. Add seasoned tomato juice and cook with continued stirring until sauce is thick. Add salt and pepper. Two cups.

TOMATO SAUCE II

1 slice onion or shallot
1 tablespoon fat
½ tablespoon flour
2 cups canned tomatoes
½ green pepper, diced
1 clove
A bit of bay leaf

1 teaspoon sugar
½ teaspoon salt
A few peppercorns
1 sprig parsley
A little chopped celery
   with leaves or celery salt
   or seed

■ Brown onion in fat. Add flour, cook until smooth. Add other ingredients. Simmer until vegetables are tender. One cup.

MAÎTRE D'HÔTEL SAUCE

Add lemon juice and parsley to Drawn Butter Sauce (p. 94). Cool slightly and add to beaten egg yolk, stirring to prevent curdling. Reheat. Season to taste. Do not boil after egg is added. One cup.

VANILLA SAUCE

1 cup boiling water	½ cup sugar
1 tablespoon cornstarch	1 teaspoon vanilla
2 tablespoons butter	A few grains of salt

■ Combine as for Starch Sauces, following Method III (p. 94). One cup.
BUTTERSCOTCH SAUCE. Substitute brown sugar for ½ or more of white sugar.
CARAMEL SAUCE. Add sufficient Caramel Syrup (p. 103) to color and flavor Vanilla Sauce. Decrease vanilla if desired.
CHOCOLATE SAUCE. Decrease cornstarch to 2 teaspoons. Add 1 square unsweetened chocolate at beginning of cooking process.
LEMON SAUCE. Decrease butter to 1 tablespoon and omit vanilla. Cool slightly and add ¼ cup lemon juice and a little grated lemon rind.

ORANGE SAUCE

⅔ cup sugar	1½ tablespoons grated orange
1 tablespoon cornstarch	rind
½ teaspoon salt	1 cup orange juice
½ teaspoon cinnamon	8 unpeeled orange slices
20 whole cloves	

■ Mix sugar, cornstarch, salt, cinnamon, cloves, and orange rind. Stir in orange juice. Cook with continued stirring until thickened and clear. Remove cloves. Add orange slices cut in halves. Cover pan and remove from heat. One cup.

NON-STARCH SAUCES

HOLLANDAISE SAUCE

2 egg yolks	½ cup butter or margarine,
1 tablespoon lemon juice	divided into 3 portions
1 speck of cayenne	⅛ teaspoon salt

■ Place egg yolks in top of double boiler. Add lemon juice and ⅓ of butter. Cook over hot, *not boiling*, water, stirring constantly until thickening begins. Add second portion of butter. Allow mixture to thicken again. Then add third portion of butter and seasonings. Serve as soon as thickened. If sauce separates, cream may be beaten into it. One-half cup.

MODIFIED HOLLANDAISE SAUCE

¾ cup boiling water
Juice of 1 lemon
¼ cup butter or margarine

1 tablespoon cornstarch
2 egg yolks, slightly beaten

■ Put water, lemon juice, and butter in top of double boiler. Mix cornstarch with eggs. Add hot mixture to egg mixture a little at a time, stirring constantly. Return to double boiler. Cook until thickened, stirring constantly. Three-fourths cup.

MOUSSELINE SAUCE

½ cup thin cream
½ cup butter or margarine
3 egg yolks, beaten thick
½ tablespoon lemon juice

1 tablespoon sugar
A few grains of salt
1 speck cayenne

■ Add cream and butter to egg yolks, cook over hot, *not boiling,* water, stirring constantly until mixture thickens. Remove from heat at once to avoid curdling. Add lemon juice, sugar, salt, and cayenne. One cup.

TARTARE SAUCE

1 cup Mayonnaise Dressing
   (p. 148)
½ tablespoon capers
½ tablespoon finely chopped
   pickle

½ tablespoon finely chopped
   parsley
½ tablespoon finely chopped
   onion

■ Mix ingredients lightly. Chill. One cup.

HORSERADISH SAUCE

½ cup heavy sweet or sour
   cream

¼ cup prepared horseradish
Soft bread crumbs

■ Whip cream. Fold in horseradish with sufficient bread crumbs to give it body. Serve at once. Thick applesauce may be substituted for bread crumbs. Three-fourths cup.

BARBECUE SAUCE

3 tablespoons meat stock
3 tablespoons chili sauce
3 tablespoons catsup
1½ teaspoons salt
¼ teaspoon red or black
   pepper

½ teaspoon Worcestershire
   sauce
2 tablespoons vinegar
½ small onion, minced
1 tablespoon (or more to taste)
   brown sugar

■ Combine ingredients. Three-fourths cup.

COCKTAIL SAUCE

6 tablespoons catsup
1 to 3 tablespoons lemon juice
  or vinegar
12 drops Tabasco sauce
1 tablespoon Worcestershire
  sauce
2 tablespoons chopped celery

½ teaspoon salt
1 tablespoon minced onion
2 tablespoons grated horseradish
1½ teaspoons minced green
  pepper

■ Combine ingredients. Chill. Three-fourths cup.

FOAMY EGG SAUCE

½ cup powdered sugar
1 egg white, beaten stiff
½ teaspoon vanilla

1 egg yolk, well beaten
½ cup cream, whipped

■ Gradually add powdered sugar to egg white while beating. When mixture is smooth and light, add vanilla and egg yolk. Fold in cream. Serve at once. Three-fourths cup.

HARD SAUCE

4 tablespoons butter or margarine

1 cup powdered sugar
Flavoring to taste

■ Cream butter, gradually add sugar, then flavoring. Continue creaming until light. Chopped nuts or shredded coconut may be added for variety. Three-fourths cup.

STERLING SAUCE

½ cup butter or margarine
1 cup brown sugar

4 tablespoons thin cream
Flavoring

■ Cream butter, gradually add sugar, slowly add cream, and flavor to taste. Beat until very light. Three-fourths cup.

LEMON SAUCE

1 cup sugar
Juice of 1 lemon

Grated rind of ¼ lemon
1 cup heavy cream, whipped

■ Mix sugar, lemon juice, and lemon rind together. Allow to stand 2 to 3 hours, then add cream, mixing lightly. Serve at once. Two cups.

MINT SAUCE

1 tablespoon sugar
½ cup vinegar

¼ cup finely chopped mint
  leaves

■ Dissolve sugar in vinegar. Add mint. Steep 30 minutes at room temperature. One-half cup.

CHOCOLATE SAUCE

2½ squares unsweetened chocolate
⅓ cup water

¾ cup sugar
1 cup cream, whipped

■ Cook chocolate with water until thick, stirring as necessary to prevent sticking. Add sugar and bring to boiling point. Remove from heat and cool. Fold in whipped cream. Use for French Chocolate or as sauce for ice cream. Two and ½ cups.

HOT CHOCOLATE SAUCE

½ cup butter or margarine,
melted
5½ cups powdered sugar

1¼ cups evaporated milk
8 squares unsweetened chocolate, cut fine

■ Mix butter and sugar in upper part of double boiler. Add milk and chocolate. Mix well. Cook 30 minutes in double boiler stirring occasionally. Two and ½ cups.

BUTTERSCOTCH SAUCE

1½ cups sugar
4 tablespoons white corn syrup
¾ cup boiling water
6 tablespoons boiling water

1¼ tablespoons butter or margarine
¾ teaspoon vanilla

■ Combine the sugar, syrup, and ¾ cup water. Cook to soft-crack stage (p. 218) 270°F. Remove from heat. Beat in remaining ingredients. Color light yellow with food coloring, if desired. Serve hot. One and ½ cups.

CARAMEL SYRUP

1 cup sugar

1 cup boiling water

■ Place sugar in heavy saucepan over low heat. Stir constantly until sugar melts and forms a brown syrup. Avoid burning. Add boiling water and cook slowly to form a thick syrup. One cup.

HONEY BUTTER

½ cup butter

1 cup honey

■ Butter and honey should be at room temperature. Cream butter, gradually add honey, beating until light. One cup.

PARSLEY BUTTER

6 tablespoons butter
6 tablespoons chopped parsley

¾ teaspoon salt
6 teaspoons lemon juice

■ Cream butter, add parsley and salt, then slowly add lemon juice. Spread on hot steak, chops, or fish. Lemon juice may be omitted.

WHIPPED CREAM

1 cup heavy cream   Flavoring to taste
1 tablespoon sugar

■   Thoroughly chill cream in deep bowl. Add sugar and flavoring. Whip with rotary beater until stiff as desired. Increase speed of beating as cream begins to thicken. For ease in whipping, use cream that is thick, cold, and at least 24 hours old.

WHIPPED EVAPORATED MILK

Thoroughly chill undiluted evaporated milk in deep bowl. Whip with cold beater. Milk whips more readily if partially frozen when beating begins. If milk fails to whip it is not cold enough.

Meat

THE word meat usually refers to the flesh of beef, veal, lamb, and pork. It presents special problems in care and storage as compared to fruits and vegetables because the natural coverings are removed in slaughter. Meat can be purchased in a number of processed forms and each requires special consideration in its care. Meat cookery methods are determined by the muscle structure, weight and thickness of the cut, and the degree of doneness desired.

Storage

Meat is a most perishable food. At the time of slaughter the nutrients of the cells are exposed to permit the growth of microorganisms. Enzymes inherent in tissues may bring about desirable or undesirable changes. Any further treatments applied to meat may inhibit or destroy microorganisms and/or enzymes. The care of meat in the home involves the control of causes of spoilage. Sterile canned meat may be recontaminated with microorganisms after the seal is broken and the microorganisms may cause secondary spoilage.

Fresh and cured meats:
    1. Cover loosely with wax paper.
    2. Place in coldest part of the refrigerator (36 to 40°F).
Frozen:
    1. Wrap in moisture-proof packaging.
    2. Store immediately at 0°F.

Cooked:

1. May be cooled at room temperature for ½ hour before placing in the refrigerator.

2. Cover or wrap tightly to prevent drying.

3. Place in the coldest part of the refrigerator.

Canned:

1. Unopened—store in a cool, dark place.

2. Opened—store as cooked meat.

Dehydrofrozen or freeze dried:

1. Do not break the seal on the moisture-proof wrap.

2. Store in a cool place.

Storage Time of Fresh or Cured Meat

CUT	STORAGE TIME (DAYS)
Thick pieces	5–8
Chops and steaks	3–4
Stew meat	2–3
Ground meats	1–2
Variety meat	1–2

Cooking Methods

Meat is cooked either by dry heat (roasting, broiling, pan-broiling, frying) or by moist heat (braising, cooking in liquid). The transfer of heat, which does the actual cooking, varies with the method of meat cookery. There are 3 methods of heat transfer: convection, conduction, and radiation. Most of the methods of meat cookery involve a combination of heat transfer methods. Roasting, modified broiling, frying in deep fat, braising, and cooking in liquid use a combination of convection currents of a liquid or air to heat the surface of the cut, and conduction to transfer the heat to the center of the cut. Pan-broiling and frying in a small amount of fat uses conduction. Broiling uses radiation. It is important with any form of heat transfer used to cook meat that not only must the temperature be correct but that sufficient time be allowed for the transfer of heat to take place. With any 1 of the 3 methods of heat transfer the surface of the meat could be overcooked and the interior raw if the temperature is too high and the time too short. Tender cuts of meat are roasted, broiled, pan-broiled, or fried whereas less tender cuts are braised or cooked in liquid. The following cooking methods generally are recommended for various cuts.

MEAT	CUTS	COOKING METHODS
Beef	Loin, Rib	Roast, Broil, or Pan-broil
	Round, Rump,	Braise or Stew
	Flank, Chuck,	
	Plate, Brisket,	
	Shank	
Veal	Thick	Roast or Braise
	Thin	Braise
Lamb	All except	Roast, Broil, or Pan-broil
	Breast, Shank	
	Breast, Shank	Braise
Pork, Fresh	Thick cuts	Roast
	Thin cuts	Braise, Broil, or Pan-broil
Pork, Cured	Thick cuts	Roast, Broil, or Pan-broil

The degree of doneness to which meat is cooked can best be determined with a meat thermometer. Cooking time in minutes per pound is an approximate guide but internal temperature of the meat as measured with a meat thermometer is a more accurate guide. The thermometer should be inserted so that the bulb rests in the center of the lean portion of the cut and is not in contact with bone. It is difficult to determine doneness of thin steaks and chops with a thermometer.

Roasting. Season meat either before or after cooking. Salt will not penetrate more than ½ inch below the surface of the meat during cooking. Place meat, fat side up on a rack in a shallow roasting pan. Insert meat thermometer parallel to cut surface. Roast beef, veal, lamb, and cured pork at 300 to 325°F and fresh pork at 325 to 350°F to the desired degree of doneness. In roasting, meat is cooked without water in an uncovered pan.

Broiling. Turn the oven regulator to broil. The broiler may or may not be preheated. The temperature is regulated by the distance the meat is placed from the source of the heat. Insert thermometer parallel to the surface and place meat on rack of broiler pan. The top surface of the meat should be 2- to 3-inches from the heat. Steaks or chops 1½ to 2 inches thick should be at least 3 inches from the heat; those 1 inch or less, about 2 inches. Broil until top side is brown or when meat is approximately half done. Season top side, turn with tongs and brown the other side. Season and serve at once on a hot platter.

Pan-broiling. Steaks or chops less than 1 inch thick may be prepared satisfactorily by pan-broiling. Place meat in a heavy skillet or on a griddle that may or may not be preheated. Cook meat slowly and turn occasionally with tongs. Pour off fat as it accumulates in pan. In pan-broiling, meat is cooked without added fat or water in an uncovered pan. When meat is done, season and serve at once.

Modified Broiling. Insert thermometer in center of meat. Place meat on a rack that stands at least 4 inches above the surface of the broiler pan. Cook meat in the oven at 400°F with oven door closed. Meat so cooked will brown evenly on both sides and will not need to be turned during cooking.

Pan-frying. Use a heavy skillet and brown meat on both sides. If meat contains moderate amount of fat, shortening will not be needed. A small amount of additional fat will be needed if meat is low in fat or has a coating of flour, meal, eggs, or crumbs. Cook at moderate temperature until meat is done, turn occasionally. In pan-frying the meat is cooked without added water in an uncovered pan. Thin meat cuts often are pan-fried.

Braising. Brown meat slowly in heavy skillet or roaster. A small amount of fat will be needed if a coating agent is used or if meat is lean. After browning, season meat and place on a rack. Add a small amount of liquid if desired. It is not necessary to add water if meat is cooked slowly. Cover tightly and cook until tender in a 300 to 325°F oven or at a low temperature on top of the range. When pressure saucepan is used, brown meat and cook at 10 pounds pressure for 15 minutes per pound for thick cuts or 10 minutes per pound for thin cuts. When done, remove meat, thicken liquid for gravy using 2 tablespoons flour for each cup of broth.

Pot-roasting is cooking large less tender cuts by the braising method.

Cooking in Liquid (Stews). Cut meat into uniform pieces, usually 1- to 2-inch cubes. If a brown stew is desired, dredge cubes in flour and brown in a small amount of fat. Add water, vegetable juices, or soup stock to cover the meat. Season as desired with salt, pepper, herbs, and spices. Some seasonings that may be used are bay leaves, parsley, thyme, marjoram, cloves, peppercorn, allspice, onion, and celery. Cover tightly and simmer (do not boil) until meat is tender. Add vegetables to the meat at the proper time but do not overcook. Vegetables may be left whole, quartered, or cut into uniform pieces. When done, remove meat and vegetables and keep hot. Thicken the stock using 2 tablespoons flour for each cup of stock. Pour hot gravy over the meat and vegetables or serve separately. If desired, make meat pie from the stew by topping with pastry, biscuits, or mashed potatoes.

Frozen Meat. Frozen meat may be prepared by the same methods used for fresh meat. Meat may be defrosted at room or refrigerator temperatures. Roasts may be cooked without being defrosted, but the cooking time will be approximately doubled. If rare or medium cooked steaks are desired, these should be defrosted prior to cooking.

Meat Tenderizers. Commercial meat tenderizers are available and are intended for the less tender cuts. After the tenderizer is applied according to the directions of the manufacturer, it may be possible to broil or pan-broil the treated steaks.

Some beef is injected with a proteolytic enzyme solution prior to slaughter. Cuts so treated generally may be roasted, broiled, or pan-broiled. Variety meats from these animals will need shorter cooking times.

Time Table for Broiling Meat [1]

	APPROXIMATE THICKNESS (IN)	APPROXIMATE TOTAL COOKING TIME (MIN)		
		RARE [2]	MEDIUM [3]	WELL DONE [4]
Beef steaks	¾	10	14	18
	1	15 to 20	20 to 30	
	1½	25 to 35	35 to 50	
	2	30 to 40	50 to 70	
Beef patties	¾		12	14
	1	12 to 15	18 to 20	
Lamb chops	¾		12	14
	1		15	18
	1½		18	22
	2		22	28
Cured ham slice	1			20
Liver, calf, young beef, lamb	½			12

[1] Pan-broiling requires approximately ½ the time for broiling.
[2] 140°F
[3] 160°F
[4] 176°F

Time Table for Roasting Meats [1,2]

	DEGREE OF DONENESS	END POINT TEMPERATURE (°F)	TIME (MIN/LB)
Beef [3]	Rare	140	18 to 20
	Medium	160	22 to 25
	Well done	170	27 to 30
Lamb [3]	Well done	175 to 180	30 to 35
Pork			
Fresh [4]	Medium	165	
	Well done	185	35 to 40
Cured [3]		160	15 to 25
Veal [3]	Well done	170	25 to 35

[1] See p. 107 for cuts commonly roasted.
[2] For boned rolled roasts add approximately 10 to 15 min/lb.
[3] Oven temperature of 300 to 325°F.
[4] Oven temperature of 325 to 350°F.

BEEF

PLANKED STEAK

Use tender steak, such as porterhouse, cut 1¾ inches thick. Remove excess fat, and broil, until about half done. Oil plank, which has been soaked in cold water and then warmed. Arrange steak on plank. The plank should be enough larger than the steak to permit additions and yet be completely covered when the steak is served. Make nests or a border of Duchess Potatoes (p. 88) using pastry bag and tube. Place in broiler to complete cooking of steak and browning of potatoes. A variety of vegetables may be prepared with the planked steak, such as cooked peas, carrots, green beans and onions, or raw mushrooms and tomatoes.

FLANK STEAK EN CASSEROLE

1 2-pound flank steak, well scored	2 cups stuffing (p. 129) Salt Pepper

■ Season steak with salt and pepper, spread with stuffing. Roll steak with grain of meat. Skewer or tie. Brown in a small amount of fat. Place in casserole and add a small quantity of water. Cover, bake at 300°F about 2 hours or until tender. Remove to serving dish, thicken stock, and pour over meat. If desired, tomatoes may be used for part of liquid and carrots, turnips, and celery added for last 30 minutes of cooking. Eight servings.

SWISS STEAK

2 pounds steak, ¾- to 1-inch thick from round or chuck ½ cup flour Suet or other fat	1 cup water or other liquid Salt Pepper

■ Rub salt and pepper into meat. Pound in flour. Brown meat in fat, place on rack in heavy pan. Add liquid and cover. Bake at 300°F or simmer on top of stove one hour or until tender. Add more liquid if needed. Chopped green pepper, onion, and tomatoes may be added. Six servings.

BRAISED BEEF

3 pounds round, chuck, or brisket Salt Pepper Flour	1 cup water or other liquid Vegetables—onions, carrots, turnips, etc.— cut into wedges, halves, or quarters

■ Season meat with salt and pepper, dredge with flour, and brown in fat. Place in a casserole, add water, cover, and bake slowly at 300°F until tender, approximately 2 hours. Add vegetables for last 30 minutes of cooking. Eight servings.

BEEF STROGANOFF

1½ pounds top round steak,
  ½-inch thick
5 tablespoons flour
3 tablespoons fat
1 medium onion, thinly sliced
1½ cups sliced fresh
  mushrooms

1 cup bouillon or consommé
1 teaspoon lemon juice
½ teaspoon salt
¼ teaspoon pepper
⅛ teaspoon dry mustard
1 cup sour cream
Hot noodles or rice

■ Cut meat in strips 1 by 2 inches; dredge in 3 tablespoons flour and brown in fat. Push meat to one side of pan, add onion; cook until soft. Add mushrooms, ½ cup consommé, lemon juice, salt, pepper, and mustard to meat and onion mixture. Cover pan; cook over low heat 45 to 60 minutes or until meat is tender. Blend remaining 2 tablespoons flour with remaining consommé, add to hot mixture; cook over low heat until sauce is smooth and thickened, stirring constantly. Blend in sour cream and heat; do not boil. Serve over hot noodles or rice. Six servings.

BEEF STEW WITH DUMPLINGS

2½ pounds beef, shoulder or
  other less tender cut
Salt
Pepper

Flour
2 cups diced potatoes
⅓ cup diced carrots
½ cup sliced onions

■ Cut meat into 1½-inch cubes. Season with salt and pepper, dredge with flour, and brown in fat. Cover with water. Simmer 1½ to 2½ hours or until tender. Add vegetables for last 20 minutes of cooking. Add more water if needed. Thicken liquid with flour, and season to taste. Serve with Dumplings (p. 51). Other meats and vegetables may be substituted. Ten servings.

GROUND BEEF PATTIES

1 pound ground beef
1 egg, slightly beaten
½ teaspoon onion juice or
  minced onion

Salt
Pepper

■ Mix ingredients lightly. Shape into flat cakes. Broil or pan-broil. Four servings.

BROILED GROUND BEEF PATTIES ON ONION RINGS. Place ½-inch slices of onion in shallow, oiled baking dish. Pour 2 tablespoons melted fat over them. Sprinkle with salt and pepper. Add 1 tablespoon water, cover, bake at 325 to 350°F, 15 to 20 minutes or until almost tender. Shape Ground Beef Patty mixture into flat cakes. Skewer a slice of bacon around edge of each. Place on onion slices. Broil patties 5 minutes on each side, basting occasionally with drippings in pan.

MEAT CAKES. Season ground beef with salt and pepper. Shape into small cakes. Roll in flour, or egg and crumb (p. 98). Cook in small amount of fat.

MEAT LOAF

1 pound ground beef	¼ small onion, chopped
1 egg, slightly beaten	1 teaspoon salt
½ cup bread crumbs or dry cereal	⅓ teaspoon pepper
½ cup milk or tomato juice	¹⁄₁₆ teaspoon sage

■ Mix ingredients lightly. Shape into a loaf. Place on rack in pan. Bake at 325°F, 45 to 60 minutes, basting as needed with drippings in pan. Six servings.

GROUND BEEF AND MACARONI

1 pound ground beef	1 tablespoon chopped parsley
1 small onion, sliced	1 cup macaroni or spaghetti
2 cups canned tomatoes	½ cup mushrooms
1 teaspoon salt	½ cup grated cheese

■ Cook macaroni or spaghetti (p. 28). Brown meat in fat. Add tomatoes, parsley, onion, and macaroni. Season. Cook slowly until well blended. Add cheese and mushrooms. Continue cooking, and stir until cheese is melted. Six servings.

VEAL

VEAL BIRDS

Use 3-inch squares of veal round cut ⅓-inch thick. Season with salt. Spread each piece with Stuffing (p. 129), keeping it away from edges. Roll, skewer, dredge in flour, and brown in fat. Place in a casserole and add a small amount of water.

BREADED VEAL CUTLETS

Cut veal round into ½-inch thick slices. Season with salt and pepper, roll in flour, or egg and crumb (p. 98). Brown in a small amount of fat. Add water and cook approximately 45 minutes or until tender. A Thin Brown Sauce (p. 95) may be used instead of water.

LAMB

LAMB CURRY

1 pound lamb stew meat
1 slice from a clove of garlic
1 large onion
½ cup celery, cut in 1-inch
  pieces
¼ cup chopped green pepper
½ tablespoon curry powder

1 tart apple, diced or
  sliced thin
1 large carrot, sliced
½ teaspoon salt
Water enough to keep
  the mixture moist

■ Brown meat. Push meat to one side of frying pan. Add garlic, onion, celery, and green pepper and cook slowly for 2 or 3 minutes. Add curry powder, and cook a few minutes longer. Add other ingredients, and mix with meat. Cover, and simmer until the meat is tender. Six servings.

SHISH KABOB

2 pounds boned sirloin end
  leg of lamb
2 tablespoons oil
Juice of 1 lemon
½ teaspoon salt
⅛ teaspoon pepper
1 medium onion, sliced in
  rings
2 bay leaves
1 large green pepper

½ cup boiling water
9 small, equal-sized
  onions
½ cup boiling water
9 mushroom caps, 1½
  inches in diameter
3 medium tomatoes,
  sliced
Parsley
Hot fluffy rice

■ Cut meat in 9 cubes about 2 inches square. Mix oil and lemon juice to make marinade. Dip meat cubes in marinade. Place in casserole. Sprinkle with seasonings and add onion rings, bay leaves, and 1 tablespoon marinade. Cover. Chill 4 to 5 hours.

Cut green pepper lengthwise in thirds; remove seeds. Cook in ½ cup water 1 minute. Cook onions in ½ cup water 5 minutes. Cut each green pepper third in thirds crosswise. Alternate meat, green pepper, onions, and mushroom caps on rotisserie spits placing spits lengthwise through onions and stem sections of mushroom caps. Brush with marinade. Place in rotisserie compartment of range. Cook 20 minutes with medium heat, then 10 minutes with high heat, or until meat is browned. Serve on platter with hot fluffy rice. Garnish with tomatoes and parsley. Four to 6 servings.

PORK

BREADED PORK CHOPS

4 pork chops   ½ cup fine bread crumbs
1 egg, slightly beaten   ½ cup water

■ Season chops with salt and pepper. Dredge with flour; dip into slightly beaten egg and roll in bread crumbs. Brown in fat. Place in casserole. Add water. Cover and bake at 350°F about 45 minutes, or until tender. Four servings.

BAKED PORK CHOPS WITH STUFFING

4 pork chops   2 cups Stuffing (p. 129)

■ Season chops with salt and pepper. Brown in fat. Place browned chops in casserole with a mound of stuffing on each chop. Add a small amount of water and bake at 350°F about 45 minutes or until tender. Cover for the first part of the baking period. Uncover to finish baking and to brown stuffing. Four servings.

CRANBERRY PORK CHOPS

4 pork chops   1 cup sugar
2 cups cranberries   ¼ cup water

■ Season chops with salt and pepper. Dredge with flour. Brown chops in a small amount of fat and place in a baking dish. Wash cranberries and mix with sugar and water. Cover chops with cranberry mixture. Cover baking dish, and bake at 350°F approximately 45 minutes, or until tender. Four servings.

BARBECUED SPARERIBS

2 pounds spareribs   ¾ cup Barbecue Sauce
                                (p. 101)

■ Simmer spareribs in a small amount of water until tender. Place spareribs in a single layer in a baking pan. Add barbecue sauce and bake at 350°F until brown. Spareribs may be basted during baking.

SWEET-SOUR PORK

1 pound pork shoulder,
  cut in strips
½ cup water
⅓ cup vinegar
¼ cup brown sugar
½ teaspoon salt
1 tablespoon soy sauce
½ cup pineapple juice

2 tablespoons cornstarch
½ cup water
¼ cup thinly sliced green
  pepper
½ cup thinly sliced onion
1½ cups pineapple chunks
Hot fluffy rice

■ Brown meat. Add vinegar, brown sugar, salt, soy sauce, and pine-apple juice. Cover and cook over low heat 30 minutes or until meat is tender. Blend cornstarch with water, stir into meat mixture and cook until clear and thickened, approximately 2 minutes. Add green peppers, onions, and pineapple chunks. Cook 2 minutes. Serve with hot fluffy rice. Four servings.

CHOW MEIN

1½ pounds pork, thinly sliced
¼ cup soy sauce
2 cups water
½ teaspoon monosodium
  glutamate
1½ cups sliced celery
1 cup chopped or sliced
  onions
¼ cup cornstarch
1 tablespoon molasses

1 (8 ounce) can water
  chestnuts, sliced
2 cups bean sprouts
1 (4 ounce) can sliced
  mushrooms, drained
Salt and pepper
Toasted whole blanched
  almonds
Chow Mein noodles

■ Cut meat into thin strips and brown. Add soy sauce, 1½ cups water, and monosodium glutamate and simmer 30 minutes. Add celery and onion and simmer 10 to 15 minutes. Blend cornstarch and ½ cup water; stir into meat mixture. Add molasses, water chestnuts, bean sprouts, and mush-rooms; heat thoroughly. Season with salt and pepper. Garnish with toasted whole almonds. Serve with Chow Mein noodles. Six to 8 servings.

BAKED HAM WITH GLACÉED PINEAPPLE

½ teaspoon prepared mustard
½ cup brown sugar
1 cured ham slice, 1 inch
  thick

6 cloves
1 cup pineapple juice
Pineapple rings

■ Combine mustard with brown sugar and spread on ham. Insert cloves and place in casserole. Add pineapple juice. Bake at 325°F until heated through. Arrange pineapple rings on ham. Bake until pineapple is delicately brown, basting often with syrup in pan.

GLAZED HAM LOAF

1 pound ground ham	2 eggs, slightly beaten
1½ pounds ground pork	1 cup brown sugar
1 cup soft bread crumbs	½ teaspoon dry mustard
1 cup milk	½ cup vinegar

■ Combine ground meat with bread crumbs. Add milk and eggs. Shape into a loaf. Place in shallow pan. Mix sugar, mustard, and vinegar together. Pour over loaf. Bake at 350°F about 1½ hours, basting often with vinegar mixture. One cup crushed pineapple may be substituted for vinegar. Ten to 12 servings.

ITALIAN MACARONI

1 cup macaroni	½ pound cheese, grated
2 cups Tomato Sauce I	½ pound ground ham
(p. 99)	Salt
1 green pepper, chopped	Pepper
1 small onion, chopped	

■ Cook macaroni (p. 28). Combine ingredients. Place in oiled casserole. Bake at 325°F 1 hour. Six servings.

VARIETY MEATS

BREADED CALVES' BRAINS

½ pound calves' brains	Salt
1 egg	Pepper
1 cup fine bread crumbs	Flour

■ Wash brains in cold water. Divide into serving portions. Cover with water and add ¼ teaspoon salt and 1 teaspoon lemon juice or vinegar. Simmer 10 minutes. Drain. Plunge into cold water. Drain when cool. Dip in flour, then in beaten egg. Season with salt and pepper, then roll in fine bread crumbs. Fry (p. 79) in deep fat (365°F). Four servings.

STUFFED HEART

1 pork or veal heart	2 cups Stuffing (p. 129)

■ Remove veins and arteries from heart and wash. Cover with water and simmer 1 hour or cook in pressure saucepan according to manufacturer's directions. Drain and stuff. Place in baking dish. Add stock, in which heart was cooked, to ½ the depth of the meat. Cover. Bake at 325°F 2 hours or until tender. Vegetables such as onions, carrots, and celery may be added for the last 30 minutes of cooking.

KIDNEY CASSEROLE

3 beef kidneys
8 carrots
3 tablespoons flour, lightly
  browned
¼ cup fat

1½ cups stock
3 teaspoons salt
¼ teaspoon pepper
Bread crumbs

■ Soak kidneys in salt water ½ hour, remove and simmer 20 minutes in unsalted water. Then cook in fresh water about 1 hour or until tender. Cut into small pieces. Make a sauce using browned flour, fat, stock, salt, and pepper. Mix carrots, kidneys, and brown sauce. Place in oiled casserole. Cover top with Buttered Bread Crumbs (p. 60). Bake uncovered at 325°F until mixture is hot and crumbs are brown. Ten to 12 servings.

LIVER AND BACON

8 slices bacon

¾ pound liver

■ Pan-fry bacon. Season liver with salt and pepper. Dredge with flour. Cook slowly in bacon fat. Do not overcook. Serve with crisp bacon. Four servings.

LIVER LOAF

1½ pounds beef liver
1 tablespoon diced onion
1 tablespoon diced celery
½ green pepper
¼ pound pork sausage
1½ cups bread crumbs

1 cup milk
2 eggs, beaten
1½ teaspoons salt
⅛ teaspoon pepper
1 tablespoon parsley

■ Simmer liver 5 minutes. Grind liver and vegetables. Add other ingredients. Pour into oiled baking dish. Set in pan of hot water. Bake 1 hour at 325°F. To brown, remove cover during last 15 minutes of baking. Serve hot or cold with catsup, chili, or tomato sauce. Ground beef may be substituted for ½ of the liver. Eight to 10 servings.

LIVER BUTTER (FOR SANDWICHES)

1 pound calves' liver
½ cup melted butter or
  margarine
2 tablespoons prepared
  mustard

½ teaspoon salt
⅛ teaspoon pepper

■ Simmer liver 5 minutes. Grind liver and combine with other ingredients. Use as sandwich spread.

PRECOOKED SWEETBREADS

Wash 1 pair sweetbreads in cold water. Cover with water and add ¼ teaspoon salt and 1 teaspoon lemon juice or vinegar. Simmer 15 minutes. Drain. Plunge into cold water and drain when cool. Precooking is preliminary to using sweetbreads in any way.

CREAMED SWEETBREADS

½ pound sweetbreads

1 cup Medium White Sauce (p. 94)

■ Precook Sweetbreads (p. 118). Chop and add to sauce. Reheat. Serve on toast, in patty cases, or in Swedish Timbale Cases. Six servings.

SWEETBREAD CUTLETS

Precook Sweetbreads (p. 118). Cut into halves and season. Egg and crumb (p. 98) and fry in deep or shallow fat. Serve with Tomato Sauce (p. 99). One sweetbread, 2 servings.

TONGUE

1½ pounds tongue
4 cloves
1 teaspoon salt for each quart of water

4 peppercorns
1 tablespoon vinegar
⅛ teaspoon pepper

■ Place tongue in water to cover and add seasonings. Simmer until tender, 3 to 4 hours, or cook in pressure saucepan according to manufacturer's directions. Cool tongue, remove skin and roots. Chill and slice. Serve with Tomato Sauce (p. 99) or Horseradish Sauce (p. 101). Six servings.

TONGUE CREOLE

1 slice onion, finely chopped
1 clove garlic
1 tablespoon chopped green pepper
½ teaspoon flour
1 tablespoon fat

2 cups tomatoes
1 teaspoon sugar
1 teaspoon paprika
1 teaspoon salt
1½ pounds cooked tongue

■ Cook onion, garlic, peppers, and flour in fat 3 to 5 minutes. Add tomatoes, sugar, and seasonings and mix well. Place tongue in casserole. Add sauce. Bake at 350°F, ½ hour or until tender. Six to 8 servings.

MIXED GRILLS

A broiled meal, known as a "mixed grill" often is used as the main dish for a luncheon or dinner. Some fruits and almost any preferred combinations of meat and vegetables, may be prepared in this way. Vegetables usually are precooked, or leftovers may be used. If they are brushed with melted fat, they dry less and brown better in cooking. Mushrooms should be marinated with French dressing before grilling to retard darkening; place in broiling pan, cap-side up with a small amount of butter in each. Several combinations are suggested and details of preparation are given for one. In general, the principles are the same for all combinations, but the time for cooking will vary according to foods used.

1. For each serving allow 1 lamb chop, ½ tomato, ½ precooked potato, 1 slice pineapple, and mushrooms. Place chops and potatoes on broiler rack. Cook until half done. Add remaining foods, and broil 5 minutes.
2. Pork sausage, small whole potatoes, whole green beans, and apple rings.
3. Ground meat patty, potato halves, small onions, and sliced tomatoes.
4. Filet mignon (beef tenderloin), precooked potato halves, small tomatoes, mushrooms, and summer squash.
5. Ham, sweet potatoes, whole green beans, and pineapple.
6. Oysters, clams or white fish, asparagus spears, and small whole beets.
7. Liver, sliced onions, and small tomatoes.
8. Beef steak, precooked sliced potatoes, whole green beans, and apricot halves.

PRECOOKED MEATS

MEAT PIE

Combine equal amounts of cooked, cubed meat, cooked vegetables such as carrots, peas, and celery, and Pan Gravy (p. 99) or Medium White Sauce (p. 94). Place ingredients in baking dish. Cover with Baking Powder Biscuits (p. 50) or a crust of the same mixture. Chopped parsley and/or minced pimiento added to biscuit mixture add color and flavor. Bake at 425°F.

MEAT AND MACARONI CASSEROLE

½ cup macaroni	⅓ to ½ cup Buttered Crumbs
1 cup Medium Cheese Sauce	(p. 60)
1 cup cooked, cubed meat	Seasonings

■ Cook macaroni (p. 28). Prepare Medium Cheese Sauce (p. 94). Combine macaroni, meat, seasonings, and cheese sauce. Place in casserole. Cover with buttered crumbs. Bake at 325°F until brown. Six servings.

CREAMED MEAT ON TOAST

1¼ cups cooked, cubed meat	6 slices toast, buttered
1 cup Medium Brown Sauce	
(p. 95)	

■ Reheat meat in sauce. Serve on toast. Six servings.

MEAT SOUFFLÉ (p. 96)

MEAT CROQUETTES (p. 98)

JELLIED MEAT LOAF (p. 160)

2 cups cooked, chopped meat	½ bay leaf
1 cup stock	1 clove
1 tablespoon gelatin, softened in ¼ cup cold water	½ teaspoon celery salt
	Salt
1 tablespoon catsup	Pepper

■ Add seasonings to stock. Bring to boiling point. Add gelatin. Stir until dispersed. Strain. Add meat, mold and chill. Six servings.

Fish

FORMS of fish commonly available in the market, either fresh or frozen, are vertebrate or fin fish and shellfish. Vertebrate fish may be marketed whole (undrawn), drawn (entrails removed), dressed (scaled and eviscerated), steaks (cross-sectional slices), fillets (boneless lengthwise slices), butterfly fillets (two single fillets joined by uncut flesh), and sticks (uniform pieces of fillets). Both shellfish and fin fish are available as well in breaded portion-ready form.

Cleaning and Storage

If fish is obtained whole or drawn, it should be cleaned and excess moisture removed immediately. It should then be placed on ice until ready to use.

To scale a fish, draw a blunt knife, inclined toward the worker, over fish, working from tail to head. Wipe fish and knife occasionally to remove loosened scale. Non-scaly fish, such as catfish usually are skinned. Remove fins; cut off a narrow strip of skin down full length of back; cut and loosen skin around gills. Remove this skin one side at a time, by pulling gently with one hand while pushing with back of knife held in the other hand. Avoid tearing flesh. Remove head unless fish is to be served whole. Make an incision on ventral side and remove internal organs. Wash, drain, and wipe dry.

Large fish such as haddock, halibut, cod, and white fish are easily boned. After cleaning run a sharp knife close to backbone beginning at tail and continuing length of fish. Remove flesh carefully from bones with knife and fingers.

Fish deteriorate rapidly at temperatures above freezing; therefore, cook immediately or wrap in moisture-proof paper and store at 0°F.

Preparation

Methods of cooking fish include baking, broiling, steaming, sautéing, and deep-fat frying. Fish may be combined with other ingredients to make scalloped dishes, loaves, and casseroles. Fish, such as salmon, bluefish, and mackerel, that contain a high percentage of fat may be cooked by methods that do not require the addition of fat. Lean fish, such as haddock, cod, and halibut, are best cooked by methods that include the addition of some fat. Fresh fish is cooked until well done, but requires less time than most other types of meat because the connective tissue holding fibers together softens readily.

Frozen fish is easier to handle in cooking processes if it is defrosted partially. Defrosting should be done shortly before cooking by placing the fish in the lower part of the refrigerator. A 1-pound package of fish will be partially defrosted in 3 to 4 hours.

STEAMED FISH

Leave small fish whole; cut large ones into thick pieces. Place in kettle. Special fish kettles have racks on which to lay the fish that are useful. Alternative procedures include laying fish in wire frying basket or tying in cheesecloth and placing in appropriate sized pan. Cover with warm water. Add 1 teaspoon salt and 1 tablespoon vinegar or lemon juice per 2 quarts of water. These ingredients add flavor and keep the fish white and firm. Bring the water to the boiling point quickly, then reduce heat to simmer. Cook until fish separates readily from bone, about 5 to 8 minutes per pound of fish. Overcooking destroys flavor. Stock may be reserved for soup.

BROILED FISH

Split small, cleaned, fat fish down back, and wipe as dry as possible. Sprinkle with salt and pepper; place skin side down, on well-oiled, preheated broiler. Cook until nicely browned, about 10 minutes. Turn skin side up long enough to brown and crisp. Serve with melted butter and chopped parsley or Parsley Butter (p. 103). A large fish should be sliced, and its surface brushed with melted butter before broiling.

FRIED FISH (SAUTÉED)

Leave small fish whole. Cut large ones into individual servings. Sprinkle with salt and pepper, roll in flour, cornmeal, or fine bread crumbs. Cook in a small amount of fat.

FRIED FISH (DEEP FAT)

Cut large fish into individual servings and leave small fish whole. Sprinkle with salt and pepper. Egg and crumb (p. 98). Fry in deep fat heated to 350°F (p. 79).

PLANKED FISH

Select any white fish (whitefish or shad are preferable). Clean, wipe dry, and bone, season with salt and pepper. Fold one side over other bringing 2 halves together. Place on hot, oiled plank previously soaked in water. Lay strips of bacon or thin slices of salt pork over top of fish. Bake fish of medium size approximately 30 minutes at 400°F. Serve on plank garnished with lemon, parsley, or Duchess Potatoes (p. 88). The potatoes should be added before fish is done so that they will brown as fish finishes cooking. Sections of tomato and slices of cucumber marinated in French Dressing (p. 147) make attractive garnishes. The bacon or salt pork may be omitted, and fish may be basted with melted fat while baking.

BAKED FISH FILLET WITH OYSTER DRESSING

1 3 to 4 pound fresh fish	1 egg, well beaten, mixed with
Salt	1 tablespoon milk
Pepper	1 pint oysters
Lemon juice	

■ Clean, skin, and bone fish. Season fillets with salt and pepper, then brush with lemon juice and egg diluted with milk. Lay 1 fillet in shallow pan. Cover with oysters that have been seasoned and rolled in crumbs. Lay other fillets on them. Brush with egg mixture. Cover thickly with Buttered Crumbs (p. 60). Bake at 375°F until tender, approximately 1 hour. Serve with Hollandaise Sauce (p. 100). Six to 8 servings.

BAKED FISH

Clean fish, bone, stuff, sew up opening, and truss. Scatter minced bacon on bottom of baking dish. Place fish on it. An oven dish in which fish may be served without moving is ideal. If not available, place fish on piece of cheesecloth for baking so it may be moved without breaking. Dredge with salt, pepper, and flour. If fish is lean make 3 slanting gashes in back. Insert thin slices of bacon or salt pork. Bake at 400°F, allowing 10 to 15 minutes per pound. Baste frequently. A little water may be added if needed.

CREAMED FISH

Follow directions for Creamed Dishes (p. 96). Use cooked fish, either shredded or flaked. Minced parsley, pimiento, green pepper, or celery may be added to give variety in color and flavor.

SCALLOPED FISH

Follow directions for Scalloped Dishes (p. 96). Use cooked fish, either shredded or flaked.

FISH SOUFFLÉ

Follow directions for Soufflés (p. 96). Use cooked fish, either shredded or flaked.

SALMON LOAF

2 cups canned salmon	⅛ teaspoon pepper
2 egg yolks, well beaten	1 tablespoon chopped parsley
½ cup soft bread crumbs	2 tablespoons lemon juice
1 tablespoon fat, melted	2 egg whites, beaten stiff
½ teaspoon salt	

■ Combine ingredients, folding in egg whites last. Put into oiled loaf pan. Set in pan of hot water. Bake at 375°F until firm. Six servings.

TUNA NOODLE CASSEROLE

1 7-oz can tuna (⅞ cup, drained and packed)	½ cup small or sliced mushrooms
2 cups cooked egg noodles	Salt
3 hard-cooked eggs, sliced	Pepper
2 chopped pimientos	Buttered Crumbs (p. 60)
2 cups Medium Cheese Sauce (p. 94)	

■ Combine ingredients. Season rather highly. Pour into oiled casserole. Cover with buttered crumbs. Bake at 375°F until sauce bubbles and crumbs are brown. Ten servings.

SHELLFISH

COOKED SHRIMP

Drop shrimp, fresh or frozen, into salted boiling water. Add spices, such as bay leaf, caraway seed, or commercially prepared mixed spices. Simmer 5 to 8 minutes. Remove from water and cool. Break shells on under side and remove. Make a slit down center back and remove dark sand vein. One pound of green (fresh) shrimp will yield approximately 1 cup after shells are removed.

SHRIMP COCKTAIL

Arrange cooked shrimp in cocktail glasses. Place on cracked ice. Serve with Cocktail Sauce (p. 102).

SHRIMP CREOLE

1 tablespoon minced onion	½ teaspoon chili powder
1 tablespoon minced green pepper	or pepper
	½ teaspoon salt
4 to 6 mushrooms or okra pods, sliced	Monosodium glutamate
	¾ pound husked shrimp
2 tablespoons fat	½ cup rice
2 cups canned tomatoes	

■ Cook onion, green pepper, and mushrooms in fat over low heat. Add tomatoes, (okra if used) chili powder, and salt. Simmer until sauce thickens. Add shrimp and simmer 8 to 10 minutes. Serve with steamed rice.

SHRIMP GUMBO

¼ cup fat	2½ cups canned tomatoes
¼ cup flour	2 6-ounce cans tomato sauce
1 stalk celery, chopped	1 bag Crab Boil
1 green pepper, chopped	2 pounds husked shrimp
2 medium onions, chopped	3 cups water, more if desired
2 cloves garlic, chopped	to thin
1 pound okra, sliced	

■ Melt fat. Add flour and brown until very dark. Add celery, pepper, onions, and garlic. Simmer until ingredients are tender. Add okra, tomatoes, tomato sauce, Crab Boil, and water to desired consistency. Simmer 15 minutes. Remove Crab Boil and add shrimp. Simmer at least 1 hour. Serve over steamed rice. Eight servings.

OYSTER COCKTAIL

Clean oysters, arrange in cocktail glasses and place on cracked ice. Top with Cocktail Sauce (p. 102).

OYSTERS ON THE HALF SHELL

Use deeper half of shells. Place a single raw, cleaned oyster in each. Arrange, radiating from center, on bed of cracked ice on a deep plate. Garnish with ¼ lemon. Serve with horseradish or Tabasco sauce and small crackers or thin slices of buttered graham or brown bread. Hardshell clams may be served in same way. One serving. Five oysters.

FRIED OYSTERS

Clean and dry oysters. Season with salt and pepper. Egg and crumb (p. 98), and fry in shallow or deep fat heated to 350°F (p. 79). Serve with Tomato Sauce (p. 99). One serving. Four oysters.

CREAMED OYSTERS

Follow directions for Creamed Dishes (p. 96). Add cleaned oysters to sauce. Cook only until edges curl. Serve at once, preferably on toast.

Some of oyster liquor, which has been scalded and strained, may be substituted for part of milk in sauce. One serving. One-third cup.

SCALLOPED OYSTERS

Clean and drain oysters. Put a layer in an oiled baking dish. Season with salt and pepper. Add thin layer of cracker crumbs, and dot with bits of butter or margarine. Repeat until all are used, making last layer of crumbs. Add milk to moisten well. Bake at 425°F approximately 20 to 30 minutes. One serving. One-half cup.

LOBSTER COCKTAIL

Arrange ⅓ cup lobster meat in cocktail glass. Place in cracked ice. Serve with Cocktail Sauce (p. 102).

LOBSTER À LA NEWBURG

4 tablespoons butter or margarine	1 speck pepper
1 tablespoon flour	A few grains cayenne
2 cups fresh or canned, chopped lobster meat	½ cup thin cream
½ teaspoon salt	2 egg yolks, beaten
	½ cup milk
	¾ teaspoon lemon juice

■   Melt fat, add flour, stir until smooth. Add lobster, salt, pepper, cayenne, and cream. When mixture is smooth and thickened, gradually add the egg yolks that have been combined with the milk. Stir constantly. Add lemon juice. Serve on toast or crackers. Six servings.

LOBSTER À LA KING

1½ cups fresh or canned lobster meat	2 teaspoons minced pimiento
2 teaspoons minced green pepper	1 hard-cooked egg, minced
	1½ cups Medium White Sauce (p. 94)

■   Add lobster, pepper, pimiento, and egg to white sauce. Mix gently, reheat, and serve on toast or in Croustades of Bread (p. 61). Six servings.

CRAB SUSY

1 egg	1 cup crab meat
½ cup flour	1 cup chicken stock
½ cup milk	½ cup tomato paste
⅛ teaspoon salt	¼ cup grated cheese

■   Mix egg, flour, milk, and salt. Beat thoroughly. Make very thin pancakes about 6 inches in diameter. Wrap crab meat in each pancake and place in individual casseroles. Make sauce of chicken stock and tomato paste. Cover each "susy" with sauce. Sprinkle generously with cheese. Place in 425°F oven until cheese is melted and sauce is bubbling.

Poultry

POULTRY is a perishable food and should be kept refrigerated or frozen. Fresh chickens, turkeys, and ducklings should be loosely wrapped and stored not longer than 2 days in the refrigerator (36 to 40°F). Cooked, cooled poultry should be stored in a covered container not longer than 3 to 4 days in the refrigerator.

For roasted, stuffed poultry, the dressing should be removed from the bird immediately following the meal at which it is served and cooled separately from the meat. This allows for more rapid cooling of both the meat and the dressing. Poultry may be cooled at room temperature for 30 minutes but should be refrigerated after that time. Cooked poultry should not be covered until cool. A covered dish, aluminum foil, or other wrappings retard cooling. When cooled, cooked meats may be covered to prevent excess drying.

Frozen Poultry

Fresh-killed poultry should be chilled in ice-slush (36 to 40°F) for 10 to 12 hours following slaughter to assure maximum tenderness. Birds to be frozen should be wrapped in moisture-proof packaging material, frozen and stored at 0°F or below. Poultry should not be stuffed prior to freezing in the home.

Frozen poultry is cooked by the same methods used for fresh poultry. Commercially frozen stuffed poultry should not be defrosted prior to roasting. Other frozen poultry may be defrosted at refrigerator or room temperature. If defrosted at room temperature, the internal temperature of the bird should not be allowed to reach a higher than refrigerator temperature. A 10 to 12 pound turkey will defrost at room temperature in approximately 18 hours whereas in the refrigerator, 2 to 3 days will be required.

Cleaning and Cutting

Cleaning Ready-to-Cook. Ready-to-cook poultry should need little cleaning but the interior cavity should be inspected and any lung tissue removed. The bird should be thoroughly washed.

Cleaning New York Dressed. Cut off head and feet and cut out oil sac which is on top of tail. Remove pinfeathers and singe off hair. Slit skin lengthwise at back of neck, slip down and remove crop and windpipe. Cut circle around vent below tail. Make a crosswise cut large enough for drawing between circle and end of breast bone. Remove internal organs and the vent. Wash inside and outside of bird. In cleaning giblets, wash clotted blood out of heart and cut away the intact, green gall sac from liver, being careful not to break sac. Cut through thickest part of gizzard to inner lining, remove and discard lining and contents. Wash giblets.

Cutting. To cut up whole, drawn poultry, separate legs by cutting skin next to body, bending leg back to separate joints and then cutting flesh. Separate thigh or second joint from leg or drumstick. Remove wings by cutting skin and flesh on under side and separating joint. Separate breast from back by cutting skin and flesh just below breast bone and following ribs to shoulder; bend back portion to break and separate back from breast by cutting. To facilitate cooking back may be broken crosswise or divided lengthwise. Breast may be divided into two portions by cutting crosswise at the tip of the keel bone or cutting lengthwise along the keel bone.

Stuffing and Roasting

Stuffing. In preparation for stuffing, salt inside of bird. Fill neck cavity loosely with stuffing, fold neck skin to back, and fasten with skewer. Fold wing tips over neck skin and fill body cavity with stuffing. Place small skewers across opening of body cavity and lace across skewers with string. Wrap string around legs and tail and tie.

Approximately 1 cup stuffing is needed for each pound of ready-to-cook weight. A 1-pound loaf of bread yields about 2 quarts of ½-inch bread cubes. Stuffing may be baked separately to shorten cooking time. Poultry should be stuffed just prior to roasting.

Roasting. Insert thermometer in mid-point of breast of stuffed or unstuffed bird. Place bird on rack and cook at 325°F to an end point temperature of 195°F. If the bird is stuffed, the center of the dressing should not be less than 165°F. Baste with drippings approximately every 30 minutes. If desired a piece of thin cloth moistened with fat may be placed over the breast of the bird.

A double cooking period in which turkeys are partially roasted 1 day and the cooking completed the following day is not recommended. Cooking time is doubled, cooking losses increased, and a microbiological problem is introduced by the double cooking period.

Time Table for Roasting Poultry *

KIND OF POULTRY	READY-TO-COOK WEIGHT (POUNDS)	APPROXIMATE TIME FOR ROASTING (HOURS) STUFFED BIRDS	UNSTUFFED BIRDS
Chicken			
Roasters	2½ to 4½	2 to 3½	
Capons	4 to 8	3 to 5	
Duck	3 to 5	2½ to 3	
Goose	4 to 8	2¾ to 3½	
Turkey	8 to 12	3½ to 5	
Fryer-roasters	4 to 8	3 to 4½	2 to 2¾
Roasters	6 to 12	3½ to 5	2½ to 3½
	12 to 16	5 to 6	3½ to 4½
	16 to 20	6 to 7½	4½ to 6
	20 to 24	7½ to 9	6 to 7
Halves and			
quarters	3½ to 5	3 to 3½	
	5 to 8	3½ to 4	
	8 to 12	4 to 5	
Boned light and dark meat rolls	8 to 10		4 to 5

* Roasting in an uncovered pan at 325°F.

STUFFING OR DRESSING (POULTRY OR MEAT)

4 cups ½-inch cubed dry bread
1 to 1½ cups boiling water, stock, or hot milk
¼ cup fat
1 teaspoon salt
Pepper
¼ to ½ teaspoon sage
¼ cup chopped celery
1 tablespoon finely chopped onion
1 tablespoon finely chopped parsley
1 egg, slightly beaten

■ Add seasoning to bread and mix. Melt fat in hot liquid, add bread and mix lightly. Add egg. Stuffing may be cooked apart from bird or meat in an oiled pan. In that case, baste with stock. Stuffing for 3½ to 4 pound bird.

DRIED CORN STUFFING

¼ cup chopped onion
¼ cup chopped green pepper
⅜ cup fat
4 cups cracker crumbs (25 to 30 crackers, coarsely crumbled)
2½ cups cooked dried corn or drained whole-kernel canned corn

1 egg, slightly beaten
⅔ cup thin cream, scalded
1 teaspoon celery salt
½ teaspoon savory seasoning
½ teaspoon salt
⅛ teaspoon pepper

■ Slowly cook onion and pepper in fat for 5 minutes. Add cracker crumbs, corn, and seasonings. Slowly beat cream into egg. Add to crumb mixture. Stuffing for 10 to 12 pound turkey.

BROILED CHICKEN

1 chicken broiler, 1½ to 2 pounds
¼ cup margarine or butter, melted

Salt
Pepper

■ Split in half lengthwise. Brush halves with fat and season with salt and pepper. Place skin side down on rack in shallow pan. Place chicken in broiler 6 inches below heat and broil slowly about 20 minutes, then turn skin side up and broil 10 to 15 minutes. Brush with fat as needed. Two servings.

MODIFIED BROILING. Prepare as for Broiled Chicken. Place chicken skin side down on rack that stands 4 inches above the bottom of a shallow pan. Cook chicken in a preheated oven at 425°F for 30 minutes per pound. Chicken so cooked will not need to be turned as it browns evenly during cooking. Two servings.

FRIED CHICKEN

1 chicken fryer, 2 to 3 pounds
Fat
Flour or

1 egg and crushed flaked cereal or potato chips
Salt
Pepper

■ Roll chicken pieces in seasoned flour or dip in slightly beaten egg and roll in crushed flaked cereal or potato chips. Brown in fat and turn as needed. Cook slowly about 30 to 45 minutes or until tender. If a crisp crust is desired, cook uncovered. Four to 6 servings.

OVEN-FRIED. Prepare as for Fried Chicken. Arrange single layer of floured pieces in shallow pan. Dot generously with margarine or butter. Bake in uncovered pan at 375°F for approximately 1 hour. Turn pieces with tongs once or twice to assure even browning.

CHICKEN FRICASSEE

1 chicken, 3 to 4 pounds	1 cup cream or milk
Fat	Salt
Flour	Pepper

■ Roll chicken in seasoned flour. Brown in fat and turn as needed. Add cream or milk and cook covered until chicken is tender. If desired, sauce may be thickened with browned flour. Six servings.

CHICKEN RÉCHAUFFÉ

1½ cups cooked, diced chicken	Salt
3 egg yolks, well beaten	Pepper
½ cup heavy cream	3 egg whites, stiffly beaten
2 tablespoons lemon juice	

■ Mix ingredients in order listed and fold in egg white. Pour into oiled ring mold and set in pan of hot water. Bake at 350°F until firm. Six servings.

CHCKEN FONDUE

1½ cups cooked, diced chicken	Pepper
1 cup milk or chicken broth	1 teaspoon lemon juice
½ cup soft bread crumbs	½ teaspoon paprika
2 tablespoons fat	4 egg yolks, well beaten
1 teaspoon salt	4 egg whites, well beaten

■ Cook crumbs in milk with fat to form a thick paste. Add chicken, seasonings, and egg yolks, cool and fold in egg whites. Pour into casserole, set in pan of hot water and bake at 350°F until firm. Six to 8 servings.

CHICKEN AND RICE CASSEROLE

1 cup uncooked rice	4 cups cooked, cubed (1-inch) chicken
2 tablespoons butter or margarine	1 cup blanched almonds, chopped or
2 tablespoons flour	1 cup chopped celery
2 cups chicken broth or milk	1 large pimiento, diced
Salt	1 cup sliced, canned mushrooms
Pepper	

■ Cook rice (p. 27). Prepare White Sauce (p. 94). Season to taste. Oil casserole. Add chicken, mushrooms, almonds, and pimientos to sauce. Place layer of rice in bottom, add chicken mixture, and top with thin layer of rice. Dot with butter. Bake 1 hour at 350°F. Eight servings.

JELLIED CHICKEN

2 cups cooked, diced chicken
2 cups chicken broth
4 hard-cooked eggs, sliced
2 tablespoons gelatin, softened
in
½ cup cold water
¼ cup sliced olives

¼ cup chopped pickles
½ cup chopped celery
2 tablespoons chopped
pimiento
Salt
Pepper

■   Combine chicken, broth, eggs, celery, olives, pickles, pimientos, and softened gelatin that has been dispersed over hot water. Pour into wet molds. Chill. Twelve servings.

CHICKEN À LA KING

1½ cups mushrooms
¼ cup fat
2 cups cooked, diced chicken
3 tablespoons chopped pimiento
½ teaspoon salt
¼ cup chopped green pepper

Paprika
3 cups liquid (broth, cream,
or milk)
3 tablespoons flour
2 egg yolks, slightly beaten

■   Cook mushrooms 5 minutes in 2 tablespoons fat. Combine with chicken, pimiento, green pepper, salt, and paprika. Prepare White Sauce (p. 94) from remaining fat, flour, and liquid. When cooked, pour slowly over egg while stirring. Add chicken mixture. Reheat and serve on toast. Six to 8 servings.

SINGAPORE CURRY

½ cup uncooked rice
¼ cup margarine or butter
¼ cup flour
2 cups liquid (broth or milk)
⅓ to 1 tablespoon curry
½ teaspoon salt
2 cups cooked, diced
turkey

Chutney
¼ cup flaked coconut
½ cup peanuts
½ cup pineapple chunks
1 tomato, wedged

■   Cook rice (p. 27). Prepare White Sauce (p. 94) from fat, flour, milk, and seasonings. Add turkey and heat to serving temperature. Serve curried turkey on rice. Place pineapple, tomato wedges, peanuts, and coconut on curried turkey and top with chutney. Four servings.

Cheese

NATURAL cheese is a curd prepared from milk. During processing, water and some water soluble nutrients are removed. The removal of water makes cheese a concentrated food. Generally, natural cheese is said to contain approximately equal amounts of fat, protein, and water. Most meats do not contain as much protein as cheese. Some cheeses, such as cottage cheese, made from skim milk are very low in fat. The high protein level of cheese requires low cooking temperatures.

A great number of aged natural cheeses take their name from the place where they were first made; such as Cheddar cheese from the village of Cheddar in Somersetshire, England, and Swiss from Switzerland. Most of the natural cheese made and used in the United States is domestic. Therefore it is often referred to as American Cheddar or simply American cheese. The word Cheddar can also refer to the shape of Cheddar cheese.

The aging of natural cheese refers to a ripening or curing process which utilizes microbial growth. The growth of bacteria or molds changes the texture and flavor of the original curd. Different environmental conditions of temperature, humidity, and salt determine which microorganism is used for the production of a particular cheese.

In addition to natural cheeses there are pasteurized and coldpack ones. Pasteurized process cheese is a blend of fresh and aged natural cheeses which have been shredded, mixed, and heated to prevent further ripening. It melts easily when reheated. Pasteurized process cheese food is prepared much as process cheese but contains less cheese, with nonfat dry milk or whey solids and water added. Pasteurized process cheese spread resembles cheese food but contains less milk fat and more water. Coldpack cheese is like process cheese but is not heated. Coldpack cheese food is coldpack cheese but has other ingredients added as process cheese food.

Storage. To keep cheese from drying, cover tightly in the original package, plastic bag, or aluminum foil, and store in the refrigerator. Keep strong cheeses in a tightly covered jar away from food that may absorb odors. Some cheese may develop surface mold with storage; this should be cut away before using the cheese. Hard cheeses may be kept for months. Soft cheeses keep only a short time because of their high water content. The additional moisture in soft cheeses permits many kinds of microorganisms to grow other than the desired ones that give the cheese its characteristic flavor.

Preparation. The preparation of any protein food usually requires low temperatures, that is below the boiling point of water, or protection from heat. Slices of bread or bread crumbs often are used for the latter. High temperatures toughen cheese. To combine cheese with other ingredients, cheese can be sliced, shredded, grated, ground, or forced through a sieve.

Classification and Uses of Cheese

CLASSIFICATION	USES
Soft, unripened	
Cottage and Cream	Salads, dips, sandwiches, cheese cake, and desserts
Firm, unripened	
Mozzarella	Snacks, casseroles, lasagne, and pizza
Soft, ripened	
Camembert and Limburger	Snacks—crackers and fruit, dark breads, and desserts
Semisoft, ripened	
Brick and Muenster	Sandwiches, snacks, and desserts
Port du Salut	Snacks—fruit and desserts
Firm, ripened	
Cheddar, Edam, Gouda, and Swiss	Snacks, sandwiches, sauces, and desserts
Provolone	Snacks, macaroni, spaghetti, and pizza
Very hard, ripened	
Parmesan, Romano, and Sap Sago	Grated for seasoning soups, vegetables, spaghetti, and breads
Blue-vein mold, ripened	
Blue (American made)	Snacks, dips, salads, and desserts
Bleu (Imported)	
Gorgonzola, Roquefort and Stilton	

CHEESE BALLS

3 cups grated cheese
2 tablespoons flour
½ teaspoon salt

1 speck cayenne
4 egg whites, beaten stiff
Cracker crumbs

■   Mix cheese, flour, and seasonings. Fold in egg whites. Shape into balls from 1 to 1¼ inches in diameter. Roll in cracker crumbs. Fry (p. 79) until golden brown. Serve with soup or salad. Eighteen balls.

CHEESE FONDUE

1 cup milk, scalded
1 cup soft, stale bread crumbs
1 cup diced cheese
1 tablespoon butter or
   margarine, melted

½ teaspoon salt
1 speck cayenne
3 egg yolks, beaten thick
3 egg whites, beaten stiff

■   Mix milk, crumbs, cheese, fat, salt, and cayenne. Add egg yolks. Fold in egg whites. Pour into unoiled baking dish. Set in pan of hot water. Bake at 350°F until firm and a sharp-pointed knife comes out clean, approximately 45 minutes. Three cups.

CHEESE PUDDING

8 slices thin, buttered bread
1½ cups grated cheese
4 eggs, slightly beaten

2 cups milk
½ teaspoon salt
Pepper

■   Place ½ of the bread on the bottom of an oiled baking dish. Add cheese, cover with remainder of bread. Mix eggs, milk, salt, and pepper. Pour over bread and cheese. Set in pan of hot water, and bake at 375°F for about 45 minutes or until firm. Four cups.

CHEESE SOUFFLÉ (p. 97)

CHEESE THINS

Cut circular pieces from ¼-inch slices of bread. Butter lightly. Toast to a golden brown. Cover with thick layer of grated cheese seasoned with salt and cayenne. Bake at 350°F until cheese melts. Serve at once with soup or salad. Crackers may be used instead of toast for a foundation.

LASAGNE

1 pound ground beef
2 tablespoons olive oil
2 cloves garlic, crushed
1 cup tomato sauce
2½ cups canned tomatoes
1½ teaspoons salt
½ teaspoon orégano

¼ teaspoon pepper
½ pound lasagne noodles
¼ pound sliced Mozza-
   rella cheese
¾ pound cottage cheese
½ cup grated Parmesan
   cheese

■   Brown beef in a skillet with olive oil and garlic. Add tomato sauce, tomatoes, salt, orégano, and pepper. Cover and simmer 15 to 20 minutes.

Cook noodles in boiling, salted water until tender, approximately 15 minutes. Drain.

Fill a rectangular casserole with alternate layers of the noodles, Mozzarella cheese, cottage cheese, tomato, meat sauce, and grated Parmesan cheese, ending with a layer of sauce and topping with some Parmesan cheese. Bake at 375°F (moderately hot oven) for 15 to 20 minutes until bubbling. Four to 5 servings.

PIZZA

1 recipe White Bread (p. 55)
 or
1 package hot roll mix
½ cup minced onion
1 tablespoon olive oil
1 cup tomato sauce
¾ cup tomato paste
1 teaspoon salt
¼ teaspoon orégano
⅛ teaspoon garlic salt
⅛ teaspoon pepper
1½ cups grated sharp Cheddar cheese or

Thin slices Mozzarella cheese (about ½ pound)
¼ cup finely cut parsley
Parmesan cheese
Additional toppings:
 1 cup chopped or sliced mushrooms
12 to 14 anchovies, whole or pieces
1 cup diced or thinly sliced pepperoni
1 cup cooked pork sausage

■ Prepare White Bread (p. 55) according to recipe or hot roll mix as directed on package. Sauté minced onion in olive oil until golden brown. Add tomato sauce, tomato paste, salt, orégano, garlic salt, and pepper.

Divide dough into 4 parts. Flatten each piece and pat into bottoms of four 9- or 10-inch pie pans. Or divide dough in half, roll out and place on ungreased baking sheets. Brush with additional olive oil or salad oil.

Arrange ½ of the Cheddar or Mozzarella cheese on top of dough. Cover with tomato sauce. Top with remaining cheese and additional topping as desired. Sprinkle with parsley and Parmesan cheese. Bake immediately at 450°F (hot oven), 15 to 20 minutes. Six to 8 servings.

WELSH RAREBIT I

1 cup milk
1 egg
¼ teaspoon salt
¼ teaspoon dry mustard

⅛ teaspoon Tabasco sauce
¼ teaspoon paprika
1 cup grated Cheddar cheese
Toast slices or crackers

■ Combine milk and egg. Cook in a double boiler until the mixture coats the spoon. Stir constantly. Add seasonings and cheese and stir until the cheese is blended. Serve over toast slices or crackers. Four servings.

WELSH RAREBIT II

1 tablespoon butter or
 margarine
1 tablespoon flour
1 cup milk
1 cup grated cheese

⅛ teaspoon salt
⅛ teaspoon dry mustard
1 speck cayenne
Crackers or buttered toast

■   Melt fat in top of double boiler. Stir in flour. Remove from heat. Add liquid all at once, stirring constantly. Cook over boiling water, stirring until thick. Add cheese and seasonings. Continue heating over hot, *not boiling* water, stirring until cheese melts. Pour over crackers or toast for serving. If desired, slightly beaten egg may be added just before serving, by adding 1 to 2 tablespoons of hot sauce to the egg, then adding the egg to the sauce with stirring. Tomato juice may be used instead of milk. Four servings.

TOMATO RAREBIT

1 No. 1 can tomato soup

2 cups grated cheese
Saltines or toast

■   Heat soup, add cheese, cook over hot water, stirring until melted. Serve on toast or saltines. Ten servings.

Salads,
Salad Dressings,
and Relishes

SALADS usually consist of cold foods, cooked or uncooked, served with a dressing. They are made from meat, fish, poultry, vegetables, eggs, fruit, nuts, or any combination of foods having harmonious flavors.

Salads may be served as a first course, with the main course, as a separate salad course following the main one, or as a dessert. The place in the meal largely determines the nature of the salad. It should be light and crisp when served as an accompaniment to a heavy meal, more substantial when intended as the main dish, and light and delicate if it takes the place of dessert. A dessert salad usually has a fruit foundation and is more or less sweet.

General Suggestions

Preparation. Work for an attractive product, choosing raw or cooked foods as desired. Have fresh vegetables clean, cold, and crisp. Dry in a towel or shake in a wire basket. Cut main ingredients into pieces of uniform size large enough to be eaten easily and to retain identity. Remove skin, bone, and gristle from meat. To give flavor to such cooked foods as meat, fish, or vegetables, marinate for an hour or more. To retard darkening of apples, bananas, and fresh pears dip in acid fruit juice such as lemon or pineapple juice or treat with an ascorbic acid preparation.

Marinade is a well-seasoned French Dressing. To marinate, coat food with marinade. Marinate different kinds of food separately, combining them just before serving.

Mixing. Use a salad bowl sufficiently large for mixing. Add only enough dressing to coat the ingredients. Mix lightly by tossing with 2 forks just before serving. The flavor of potato salad is improved if allowed to chill a few hours before serving.

Storage. Salads that are high in protein and starch should be held at refrigerator temperature to prevent food infections or poisonings.

Service. The type of salad determines the service. A tossed green salad may be served from a large serving bowl at the table. Others may be arranged in individual bowls or on plates. As a rule, individual salads are served in a cup made of one or more leaves of head lettuce or on a bed of endive, water cress, or leaf lettuce.

Garnishes. The garnish contributes to the attractiveness and palatability of a salad. The best effects are produced by a few ingredients that contrast pleasantly in color or by 2 or 3 shades of the same color. As a rule, a garnish should be edible. Chopped parsley, chives, or like garnishes may be sprinkled over a green salad. Small strips of pimiento or green pepper add a bright touch to many salads.

Accompaniments. When salad forms a separate course it may be served with plain or toasted crackers, melba toast, cinnamon toast, toast strips, cheese straws, bread sticks, small buttered rolls, or sandwiches. Cheese often is served with a green salad.

Preparation of Head Lettuce for Salad

Cut out core; remove coarse outer leaves. Then hold head, cut part up, under cold running water to open up leaves. Separate and wash each leaf thoroughly, and drain on a towel. Place in a moist cloth, plastic bag, or vegetable crisper. Refrigerate until ready to use.

Salad Combinations

The following combinations are suggested and may be varied according to taste and food available. Serve in a lettuce cup or on a bed of lettuce or other salad greens.

CHEESE

Cream or cottage cheese balls with a dash of paprika.

Cottage cheese with pineapple, chopped nuts, onion, chives, olives, pickles, or pimiento.

Green or red pepper stuffed with cheese, seasoned to taste, chilled, and cut into thin slices.

Prunes or dates stuffed with cheese.

Cream or cottage cheese balls with sliced pineapple, halves of peaches, pears, or apricots.

Edam or Roquefort cheese, broken coarsely and scattered over lettuce.

EGGS (HARD-COOKED)

Cut into quarters lengthwise or into thin slices.

Chopped, hard-cooked egg whites mixed with shredded lettuce or celery and salad dressing, garnished with hard-cooked egg yolks pressed through a sieve.

Deviled eggs (p. 32) and lettuce.

Slices or sections of hard-cooked egg, tomato sections, lettuce hearts, and garnish of water cress.

FRUITS

Apples diced with celery and chopped English walnuts (Waldorf Salad); apples need not be pared if skin is attractive.

Apples diced with celery and halves of seeded grapes or cherries.

Apples diced with chopped celery and dates.

Apples diced with raisins, shredded carrots, and nuts.

Avocado, cut in half, peeled and sliced, or cut in wedges.

Alternate sections of avocado with sliced cucumber, tomato, orange, or grapefruit sections.

Avocado halves stuffed with diced orange or grapefruit, chicken or sea food salad.

Avocado with melon balls.

Banana chunks rolled in chopped nuts.

Banana slices with cubed pineapple and orange or tangerine sections. Marshmallows may be added if desired.

Cantaloupe, watermelon, honeydew melon wedges, or balls.

Cantaloupe cubes, Bing cherries, sweet green or Tokay grapes.

Cantaloupe ring filled with melon balls, pineapple wedges, and seeded Tokay grapes.

Grapefruit sections, orange sections, grapes, and pecans.

Grapefruit sections, sliced pineapple, and tomato wedges.

Grapefruit sections with alternate slices of unpeeled red apple.

Orange sections with alternate sections of grapefruit.

Orange sections, grapefruit sections, and avocado wedges sprinkled with pomegranate seeds.

Pineapple chunks, sweet green grapes, sliced banana, raspberries, or strawberries.

Pineapple chunks, nuts, and bits of candied ginger.

MEAT, POULTRY, AND SEA FOOD SALADS

Chicken, hard-cooked egg, and pickles.

Chicken, celery, diced pineapple, halved green grapes, and salted almonds.

Chicken, celery, diced apple, and nuts.

Ham, diced, with celery, and pickles.

Meat, diced, with carrots, celery, and pickles.

Meat, diced, with celery, peas, and hard-cooked egg.

Sea food, diced celery, lettuce hearts, and lemon juice or onion juice.

Sea food, diced celery, cucumbers and capers.

Sea food, diced celery, hard-cooked eggs, and pickles.

Sea food, diced celery, tart apple, chopped green pepper, and olives.

Sweetbreads with cucumber.

VEGETABLE SALADS

Asparagus with rings of pimiento.

Asparagus and slices of tomato sprinkled with grated cheese.

Beans (kidney or lima) with celery, dill or sweet pickles, minced onion, and hard-cooked egg.

Beans (string) with celery, onion, diced cooked bacon, and pimiento.

Beets, cooked and diced, with celery, peas, onion, and diced American cheese.

Cabbage, shredded, with banana, and peanuts.

Cabbage and carrots, shredded, with chopped nuts or raisins.

Cabbage, shredded, with diced apple or pineapple, and celery.

Cabbage, shredded, with diced celery, green or red pepper, and onion.

Cabbage, shredded, with diced cucumber, tomato, and green pepper.

Carrots, shredded, with raisins and celery.

Carrots, shredded, with chopped peanuts.

Carrots, shredded, with coconut, and diced orange.

Cauliflower, raw or cooked, shredded carrots, chopped green pepper, and lettuce.

Cauliflower, raw or cooked, tomato sections, water cress, parsley, or lettuce.

Cucumber, tomato, celery, onion, and green pepper.

Lettuce, coarsely broken, with cucumber and radishes.

Potatoes, cooked and diced, with crisp bacon, hard-cooked egg, pickles, and onion.

Potatoes, cooked and diced, with onion, pickle, hard-cooked egg, and celery or cucumber.

Spinach, raw and coarsely cut, with onion, diced celery, and hard-cooked egg.

Spinach, raw and coarsely cut, with hard-cooked egg, tomato, or radishes.

Tomatoes, diced, with cucumber, onion, or green pepper.

Tomatoes, sliced, with cottage or cream cheese balls.

Tomatoes, sliced, with green pepper, hard-cooked egg, and olives.

FRESH VEGETABLE SALADS

HEAD LETTUCE SALAD

I. Wash lettuce, remove coarse outside leaves, cut lengthwise or crosswise into sections in size suitable to serve. Loosen leaves or cut to some extent for ease in eating. Serve with French, Russian, or Thousand Island Dressing (pp. 147, 148).

II. Pile leaves of crisp lettuce lightly on salad plate. Serve with French Dressing (p. 147), plain or modified.

TOSSED SALADS

Any variety of coarsely shredded or torn green vegetables, such as head and leaf lettuce, spinach, chicory, endive, cabbage, and water cress form the base of these salads. Add other vegetables such as sliced raw carrots, radishes, cucumbers, tomato wedges, pepper and onion rings, chopped chives, and parsley. Combinations of this type are sometimes known as Chef's Salad. For a main dish salad include meat, chicken, cheese, or fish. Chill vegetables. Pile lightly into bowl. Just before serving add some variety of French Dressing (p. 147). Toss with 2 forks or a fork and spoon.

SPINACH SALAD

Wash and shred spinach. Add finely chopped onion and diced tomato. Serve with Bacon Dressing (p. 147). Garnish with hard-cooked egg.

POINSETTIA TOMATO SALAD

Peel medium size tomato (p. 6). Chill. Cut lengthwise into eighths to ½-inch from bottom so tomato will spread but not fall apart. Sprinkle with salt. Serve on lettuce leaf with spoonful of dressing in center, or fill center with cottage cheese, meat, fish, chicken, or chopped vegetable salad.

GELATIN SALADS

JELLIED FRUIT OR VEGETABLE SALADS

Prepare Lemon Jelly (p. 161) using 1½ tablespoons gelatin. Pour small amount into bottom of mold. When nearly set, put in a layer of fruit or vegetables. These may be arranged in a design if desired. Allow this to set firmly, then cover with jelly mixture. Repeat until all is used. Chill. Unmold when ready to serve. Cut into squares, diamonds, or slices according to mold used. Individual molds may be preferred. Vegetable or fruit juices may be substituted for part of liquid in Lemon Jelly.

JELLIED MEAT OR FISH SALAD. Make Lemon Jelly (p. 161), omitting sugar. Substitute cooked meat or fish for fruit. Add chopped celery or pickles as desired. Finish as for Jellied Fruit or Vegetable Salad.

PERFECTION SALAD

½ cup vinegar
2 tablespoons lemon juice
2 cups boiling water
1 teaspoon salt
½ cup sugar
2 tablespoons gelatin,
    softened in

½ cup cold water
2 cups diced celery
1 cup shredded cabbage
2 pimientos, chopped

■ Add vinegar, lemon juice, boiling water, salt, and sugar to softened gelatin. Strain and chill. When mixture begins to set, add remaining ingredients. Mold. Remove from mold and serve on salad greens with Mayonnaise (p. 148). Any desired combination of vegetables may be used. Twelve servings.

JELLIED TOMATO SALAD

2½ cups tomato juice
4 teaspoons gelatin
½ teaspoon salt
2 tablespoons sugar, if desired

2 tablespoons vinegar
3 cloves
Parsley, chopped

■ Soften gelatin in ½ cup cold tomato juice. Boil remainder of juice 1 minute with salt, sugar, vinegar, and cloves. Remove from heat, add gelatin. Stir until dispersed. Strain, add parsley, pour into molds. Chill. When firm, unmold on lettuce. Serve with Mayonnaise (p. 148). A sprig of parsley may be placed in each mold before filling if desired. Six servings.

CRANBERRY SALAD

2 cups sugar
1 cup water
2½ tablespoons gelatin,
    softened in
½ cup cold water
4 cups raw cranberries,
    ground

1 medium-size orange with
    rind, ground
1 cup chopped celery
1 cup nuts, chopped

■ Cook sugar and water to make thin syrup. Add softened gelatin. Stir until dispersed. Cool. Add remaining ingredients. Pour into mold. Chill. Sixteen servings.

CUCUMBER AND PINEAPPLE SALAD

Add equal parts of diced cucumber and pineapple to Lemon Jelly (p. 161) in which pineapple juice has been substituted for part of liquid.

When partially set, fold in ½ cup each of Mayonnaise (p. 148) and whipped cream. Chill. Cut into squares for serving.

PINEAPPLE HORSERADISH MOLDS

1 package lemon flavored
  gelatin
2 cups hot liquid (syrup drained
  from canned pineapple and
  water)

2 tablespoons horseradish
1 cup crushed pineapple,
  well-drained
½ cup Mayonnaise (p. 148)

■ Disperse gelatin in hot liquid. Chill until gelatin begins to thicken. Add horseradish and pineapple. Fold in mayonnaise. Pour into molds. Chill until firm. Unmold on lettuce and serve. Six servings.

MISCELLANEOUS SALADS

HOT POTATO SALAD

6 medium potatoes
6 slices bacon
¾ cup chopped onion
2 tablespoons flour
1 to 2 tablespoons sugar

1½ teaspoons salt
½ teaspoon celery seeds
Dash of pepper
¾ cup water
⅓ cup vinegar

■ Boil potatoes in their jackets until tender. Peel and slice thinly. Pan-fry bacon slowly in skillet, then drain on paper. Sauté chopped onion in bacon fat until golden brown. Blend in flour, sugar, salt, celery seeds, and pepper. Cook over low heat, stirring until smooth. Remove from heat. Stir in water and vinegar. Bring to boil, stirring constantly. Boil 1 minute. Carefully stir in the potatoes and crumbled bits of bacon. Remove from heat. Cover and let stand until ready to serve. Six to 8 servings.

HOT CHICKEN SALAD

2 cups cooked, diced chicken
2 cups diced celery
½ cup blanched, chopped
  almonds
2 tablespoons chopped pimiento
2 tablespoons minced onion
½ teaspoon salt

2 tablespoons lemon juice
½ cup Mayonnaise (p. 148) or
  Salad Dressing (p. 146)
⅓ cup shredded cheese
2 cups coarsely broken potato
  chips

■ Mix ingredients together except cheese and potato chips. Place in oiled baking dish. Sprinkle cheese, then potato chips on top. Bake at 350°F until hot. Six to 8 servings.

FROZEN FRUIT SALAD

2 teaspoons gelatin, softened in
3 tablespoons cold water
1 cup Mayonnaise (p. 148)
1 cup cream, whipped

3 cups fruit, mixed and cut
into pieces (1 cup each
of oranges, bananas, and
shredded pineapple is a
good mixture)

■   Disperse softened gelatin by placing over hot water. Add to dressing. Mix dressing and cream with fruit. Pour mixture into refrigerator tray or mold and freeze. Twelve servings.

FROZEN FRUIT AND CHEESE SALAD

1 cup crushed pineapple,
drained
1 tablespoon lemon juice
¼ teaspoon salt
6 ounces cream cheese

1 cup Mayonnaise (p. 148)
1 cup cream, whipped
⅓ cup maraschino cherries,
cut into strips or halves

■   Mix pineapple, lemon juice, and salt. Mash cheese with fork. Work in mayonnaise gradually. Fold in whipped cream. Combine with pineapple mixture, and add cherries. Pour into refrigerator tray or mold. Freeze without stirring. Eight servings.

SALAD DRESSINGS

Cooked Salad Dressings, French, and Mayonnaise are the 3 commonly recognized classes of salad dressings. In general, slightly sweeter dressings are recommended for fruit salads. Salad greens are best with a sharp tangy dressing.

COOKED SALAD DRESSING

¾ teaspoon salt
1 teaspoon mustard
1½ tablespoons sugar
2 tablespoons flour
1 speck cayenne

2 egg yolks, slightly beaten
or
1 egg
¾ cup milk or water
¼ cup mild vinegar
2 tablespoons fat

■   Mix dry ingredients. Add to egg yolks, mixing well. Add milk gradually, then vinegar very slowly. Cook over hot water, stirring until mixture thickens. Add fat. Cool. Serve plain, or fold in an equal volume of whipped cream just before using. One and ⅛ cups, without cream.

PEANUT BUTTER SALAD DRESSING. Add ¼ cup peanut butter to Cooked Salad Dressing. Serve with carrot, banana, or any desired salad combination.

FRUIT SALAD DRESSING

½ cup sugar
1 pinch salt
2 eggs, beaten

¾ cup hot fruit juice (equal
    parts orange, lemon, and
    pineapple)
½ cup cream, whipped

■   Combine sugar, salt, and eggs. Add fruit juice gradually. Cook over hot water, stirring constantly until mixture thickens. Cool. Fold in cream just before serving. Other acid fruit juices may be used. Two and ¼ cups.

BACON DRESSING

1 to 2 strips raw bacon, diced
½ cup water
⅛ to ¼ cup vinegar

1 to 2 tablespoons sugar
1 pinch salt
1 speck cayenne

■   Cook bacon slowly until brown. Add remaining ingredients, heat to boiling point. Serve at once on leaf lettuce, shredded spinach, dandelion greens, potatoes, or cooked string beans. Chopped hard-cooked eggs, chili sauce, or chopped green onions may be added. Two-thirds cup.

FRENCH DRESSING I

½ teaspoon salt
⅛ teaspoon white pepper
1 speck cayenne
Paprika, if desired

3 tablespoons salad oil
1 tablespoon vinegar or
    lemon juice

METHOD I. Mix dry ingredients. Add oil and vinegar or lemon juice alternately, beating until thick. Do this just before serving, as emulsion is temporary.

METHOD II. Pour ingredients into a bottle or jar. Close tightly, and shake vigorously just before using. A bottle marked for amounts of acid and oil simplifies measuring.

Vinegar is used more commonly for acid when dressing is to be served with meat or vegetables. Lemon juice is more suitable for fruits. Half vinegar and half lemon juice may be used. If a more tangy dressing is desired increase the acid by 1 teaspoon. For a sweeter dressing 1 to 4 tablespoons or more of sugar may be added. The larger amount helps to stabilize the emulsion and imparts a pleasing flavor. Mustard, Worcestershire sauce, onion juice or chopped onion, Roquefort cheese, chopped olives, and pickles or pimientos may be added for variety. One-fourth cup.

FRENCH DRESSING II (SUITABLE FOR FRUIT SALADS)

½ cup sugar
1 teaspoon dry mustard
¼ teaspoon salt
1 teaspoon paprika

⅓ cup vinegar
1 teaspoon onion juice
1 cup salad oil

■   Mix dry ingredients. Stir in vinegar and onion juice. Gradually add oil while beating with an electric beater. One and ½ cups.

POPPY SEED DRESSING. Omit paprika and add 1½ tablespoons of poppy seed to French Dressing II.

TOMATO DRESSING

1½ cups salad oil
½ cup vinegar
1 10½-ounce can tomato soup
2 tablespoons sugar
1 teaspoon dry mustard
1 teaspoon salt

1 teaspoon paprika
1 tablespoon Worcestershire sauce
½ small onion, minced
¼ clove garlic, minced
¼ green pepper, minced

■ Place all ingredients in bowl in order indicated. Beat with rotary beater until thoroughly blended. Three cups.

HONEY DRESSING

⅔ cup sugar
1 teaspoon dry mustard
1 teaspoon paprika
1 teaspoon celery seed
¼ teaspoon salt

⅓ cup honey
⅓ cup vinegar
3 tablespoons lemon juice
1 teaspoon grated onion
1 cup salad oil

■ Mix dry ingredients. Blend in honey, vinegar, lemon juice, and onion. Add oil slowly while beating with an electric beater. One and ⅔ cups.

MAYONNAISE

½ teaspoon sugar, if desired
1 speck cayenne
½ teaspoon salt
¼ teaspoon mustard, if de- sired

1 egg yolk, beaten
1 tablespoon vinegar
1 tablespoon lemon juice
1 cup salad oil

■ Mix dry ingredients. Add to egg yolk. Beat well. Add vinegar and lemon juice gradually while beating. Add oil, drop by drop at first, beating well between each addition. After about ½ the oil has been added, remainder may be added more rapidly. Mixture should be thick and smooth when finished.

If dressing curdles start with another egg yolk or 1 tablespoon of water or vinegar. Add curdled mixture a small amount at a time, beating well after each addition. One cup.

CUCUMBER MAYONNAISE. Add ¼ to ½ cup fresh cucumbers cut into ¼-inch cubes to 1 cup Mayonnaise just before serving. Serve with jellied salmon or other fish salads.

RUSSIAN DRESSING. Just before serving, add 2 tablespoons chili sauce, 2 tablespoons whipped cream, and 1 tablespoon chopped, green pepper to ¼ cup Mayonnaise. Serve on crisp, green salad.

THOUSAND ISLAND DRESSING. Just before serving, add 1 tablespoon chili sauce, ½ teaspoon tomato catsup, ½ teaspoon chopped green pepper, ½ tablespoon chopped pimiento, ½ teaspoon chopped chives or minced onion, and ¼ teaspoon paprika to ¼ cup Mayonnaise. Serve with crisp, green salad. WHIPPED CREAM MAYONNAISE. Add equal amount of whipped cream to Mayonnaise just before serving. Use with fruit salads.

SALAD DRESSING (STARCH BASE)

1 egg	¼ cup vinegar
2 tablespoons sugar	¾ cup salad oil
1½ teaspoons salt	¼ cup cornstarch
2 teaspoons dry mustard	½ cup cold water
⅛ teaspoon paprika	½ cup hot water

■   Place egg, sugar, seasonings, vinegar, and oil in mixing bowl, but *do not stir*. Make a paste by mixing cornstarch with cold water, then stir in hot water. Cook, stirring constantly, over a low heat until clear. Add hot mixture to ingredients in mixing bowl. Beat briskly with a rotary beater. Cool. Serve as desired. Two cups.

CREAMY ROQUEFORT OR BLUE CHEESE DRESSING

1 cup Mayonnaise (p. 148)	½ pound Roquefort or Blue
or	cheese
Cooked Salad Dressing (p. 146)	1 cup light cream
1 tablespoon lemon juice	

■   Combine Mayonnaise, lemon juice, and cream. Crumble the Roquefort or Blue cheese into the mixture. Mix thoroughly until the dressing has a uniform creamy consistency. Three and ½ cups.

CREAM SALAD DRESSING (FOR COLESLAW)

1 to 2 tablespoons sugar	½ teaspoon chopped green
¼ teaspoon salt	pepper
⅛ teaspoon pepper	3 tablespoons sweet or sour
¼ teaspoon paprika	cream
1 speck cayenne	1 to 2 tablespoons vinegar
½ teaspoon chopped onion	

■   Mix dry ingrdients, onion, and green pepper. Add cream, then vinegar gradually. Beat until thickened. Serve on shredded cabbage or leaf lettuce. One-third cup.

RELISHES

CARROT CURLS

Cut paper-thin, lengthwise slices from peeled, large carrots that have been warmed to room temperature. Carrots taken directly from the refrigerator tend to break when cut. A vegetable peeler is the ideal tool for slicing.

Roll each slice around finger, fasten with a toothpick, and chill in crushed ice until crisp.

CARROT FRINGES

Peel large carrots warmed to room temperature. Cut lengthwise into thin, even slices. Cut a ½-inch diagonal fringe along both lengthwise edges. Place in crushed ice until edges curl and fringe is crisp.

CARROT FRILLS

Peel large carrots. Make 6 to 8 lengthwise cuts down each carrot, about ⅛-inch deep. Cut carrot crosswise into paper-thin slices. Arrange several slices on a toothpick, and place in crushed ice until edges curl and frills are crisp. Drain on a clean towel, and slip a ripe or green olive on each end of toothpick. Radish slices may be used instead of carrots.

CELERY CURLS

Wash celery, and cut into 3-inch lengths. Slash both ends into fringe-like cuts within ½-inch of center. Chill in crushed ice until fringes curl.

CELERY PINWHEELS

Select a fresh, crisp bunch of celery. Trim, cut all stalks same length. Remove bottom end, wash, and dry stalks. Lay each stalk out in same order that it came from the bunch. Fill centers with cheese or other desired spread. Beginning with center stalks, press back together to resemble original bunch of celery. Wrap in wax paper or aluminum foil, and fasten with rubber bands. Chill in refrigerator until firm. Remove wrapping, and slice into ½-inch slices. Serve well chilled.

STUFFED CELERY

Choose deep-grooved stalks of celery. Cut into suitable lengths. Fill grooves with cheese, such as cream, grated Cheddar, or Roquefort. Add chopped pimientos, olives, nuts, or similar ingredients to cheese as desired. If stalks are small they need not be cut. A cake decorator or pastry tube is helpful for filling stalks.

RADISH FANS

Use the long slender radishes from the bunch. Trim ends. Cut crosswise thin slices ⅔ of the way through radish. Allow to stand in crushed ice until cuts spread into fan-like shape.

RADISH ROSES

Clean and trim radishes, leaving a small portion of green attached, if desired. Hold radish by stem end, and make several large diagonal cuts into body of radish. Allow to stand in crushed ice until petal-like portions open.

VEGETABLE STICKS

Peel or prepare vegetables. Cut into finger-like sticks. Chill in crushed ice. Such vegetables as carrots, celery, cucumbers, or green pepper are suitable.

RELISH TRAY COMBINATIONS

Unpeeled cucumber slices, tomato wedges, carrot sticks, and green pepper rings.

Carrot curls, green pepper sticks, ripe olives, and radish fans.

Celery pinwheels, radish roses, ripe olives, and carrot sticks.

Stuffed celery, sweet or dill pickles, raw cauliflower, and green onions.

Wedges of fresh pineapple, fresh whole strawberries, and frosted mint leaves.

Frosted grapes, frosted Bing cherries, and celery curls.

Carrot frills with ripe olives, radish roses, and slices of raw turnip, or kohlrabi.

Spiced peaches, apricots or crabapples, celery and green pepper sticks, and cheese-nut balls.

Desserts

CUSTARDS

True custards are combinations of milk and eggs, sweetened, salted and flavored. Custards are classified as soft and firm. *Soft* custards are cooked in a double boiler and stirred while cooking. *Firm* custards may be either steamed or baked. The degree of firmness depends upon proportion of ingredients used.

Proportions

Use a smaller proportion of eggs when a thin soft custard or a very delicate firm custard is desired. For most purposes 1 egg and 2 tablespoons sugar to 1 cup milk is a satisfactory proportion. To make a custard that will hold its shape when turned from individual molds, use 1½ to 2 eggs to 1 cup milk. These proportions are satisfactory for custard pie. Use larger amounts of egg only in large custards that are to be unmolded or in custards to be cut into fancy shapes.

Mixing

Beat egg just enough to mix, as too much beating makes a frothy top. Add salt and sugar, and stir milk into egg mixture. Flavor firm custards before cooking. Soft custards are flavored after cooking to avoid possible loss of flavor.

Cooking

Soft Custards. Cook over hot, *not boiling,* water, stirring constantly until foam disappears and mixture coats spoon. As soon as done remove from hot water and set in cold water to stop cooking. Cool slightly, and flavor. If custard curdles slightly, place in cold water and beat with a rotary beater.

Baked Custards. Set baking dish in pan of hot water. Bake at 350°F until tip of a small, pointed knife comes out clean when inserted near center of custard. Remove at once to avoid overcooking.

Steamed Custards. Set cups of custard in steamer. Cover tops with aluminum foil to keep out moisture, and steam until firm. Remove at once.

FOUNDATION CUSTARD

1 cup milk	⅟₁₆ teaspoon salt
2 tablespoons sugar	¼ to ½ teaspoon flavoring
1 to 2 eggs	

■   Follow general directions for mixing and cooking. Two servings.

BROWN SUGAR CUSTARD. Substitute brown sugar for white in Foundation Custard. Maple sugar may be used in same way.

CAKE CUSTARD. Make as for Foundation Custard. Cook as for Soft Custard and pour over slices of cake.

CHOCOLATE CUSTARD. Make as for Foundation Custard, cooking ½ to 1 square unsweetened chocolate with ½ the sugar and a little water until glossy. Combine with milk, and proceed in usual way.

COCONUT CUSTARD. Add ¼ to ½ cup shredded coconut to Foundation Custard. Chopped nuts may be used in the same way.

FLOATING ISLAND. Make Foundation Custard, substituting 2 to 4 egg yolks, cook as for Soft Custard, and make a meringue (p. 216). Poach meringue by spoonfuls in hot water, turning once. Drain. Place meringue in serving dish, and pour custard over it. Garnish with chopped nuts, coconut, cherries, cubes of jelly, or other desired material.

FRUIT CUSTARD. Make Foundation Custard. Cook as for Soft Custard. Place any desired fruit in serving dish, and pour custard over it. Garnish as desired.

PUDDINGS

A pudding usually contains flour, cornstarch, bread, or some other starch thickening agent. It may be boiled, steamed, or baked. The last 2 methods most commonly are used. A baked pudding may be drier than one that is boiled or steamed.

BREAD PUDDING

4 slices stale bread	6 tablespoons sugar
1 tablespoon butter or margarine	1 pinch salt
	2 cups milk
1 to 2 eggs, slightly beaten	½ teaspoon vanilla

■   Butter bread lightly, and cut in ½-inch cubes. Place in baking dish. Mix egg, sugar, salt, milk, and flavoring. Pour custard mixture over bread cubes. Set in pan of hot water and bake at 350°F (moderate oven) until firm, approximately 40 minutes.

Serve with whipped cream or Hard Sauce (p. 102). Five servings.

BUTTERSCOTCH BREAD PUDDING. Make as for Bread Pudding, substituting brown sugar for white.

CHOCOLATE BREAD PUDDING. Make as for Bread Pudding, using unbuttered bread cubes. Mix 3 tablespoons cocoa, and ¼ teaspoon cinnamon, if desired, with the sugar. More sugar may be preferred.

FRUIT BREAD PUDDING. Make as for Bread Pudding, adding ½ cup chopped raisins, dates, figs, orange marmalade, or nuts.

ORANGE BREAD PUDDING. Make as for Bread Pudding, substituting orange juice for ½ of the milk and adding grated rind of 1 orange instead of vanilla.

QUEEN OF PUDDINGS. Make as for Bread Pudding, reserving egg whites. When baked, spread with a thick layer of jelly or jam, and cover with meringue made from egg whites. Bake according to directions for Soft Meringues (p. 216).

INDIAN PUDDING

2 cups milk, scalded	3 to 4 tablespoons sugar
2 tablespoons cornmeal	½ teaspoon salt
2 to 3 tablespoons molasses	½ teaspoon ginger

■   Pour milk slowly on cornmeal, and cook in double boiler 20 minutes. Add remaining ingredients. Pour into oiled baking dish; bake at 300°F (slow oven) for 2 hours or longer without stirring. Serve warm with Hard Sauce (p. 102). Three to 4 servings.

RICE PUDDING

⅓ cup uncooked rice	½ teaspoon salt
4 cups milk	½ lemon rind, grated
⅓ cup sugar	

■   Wash rice, mix with remaining ingredients, and pour into an oiled baking dish. Bake at 250°F (slow oven) about 3 hours, stirring occasionally during first hour of cooking. Raisins may be added instead of lemon rind. Six to 8 servings.

RICE CUSTARD PUDDING

2 tablespoons sugar
½ teaspoon salt
1 egg, beaten
½ tablespoon butter or
margarine

1 cup milk, scalded
1 cup steamed rice (p. 27)
¼ cup raisins

■ Mix sugar and salt with egg. Melt fat in hot milk, and add slowly to egg mixture. Add rice and raisins. Pour into oiled baking dish. Bake as for Custards (p. 154). Serve with Hard Sauce (p. 102). Four servings.

TAPIOCA CREAM

2 cups milk
6 tablespoons sugar
2⅔ tablespoons granular
tapioca

Speck of salt
2 egg yolks
2 egg whites
½ teaspoon vanilla

■ Combine milk, 4 tablespoons of sugar, tapioca, and salt. Cook in double boiler until slightly thick and tapioca is clear. Carefully add egg yolk and continue cooking until thickened. Remove from heat. Beat egg whites to form soft peaks. Gradually add 2 tablespoons sugar and continue beating to make a meringue. Fold meringue into pudding mixture, cool slightly, and add vanilla.

CHOCOLATE TAPIOCA CREAM. Add 1 square unsweetened chocolate, melted, to Tapioca Cream mixture. More sugar may be desired.

COCONUT TAPIOCA CREAM. Add ⅔ cup dry shredded coconut to Tapioca Cream mixture. Reduce sugar 1 tablespoon.

FRUIT TAPIOCA. Substitute water or fruit juice for milk, and omit egg and vanilla in Tapioca Cream. Increase tapioca to 4 tablespoons. Pour mixture over sliced raw or cooked fruit.

NUT TAPIOCA. Add ¼ cup nuts, chopped, to Tapioca Cream mixture.

TAPIOCA CREAM (PEARL TAPIOCA)

⅓ cup pearl tapioca
2 cups milk
½ cup sugar
¼ teaspoon salt

2 egg yolks, slightly beaten
2 egg whites
1 teaspoon vanilla

■ Soak pearl tapioca overnight in cold water to cover. Drain. Mix milk, ¼ cup sugar, salt, and tapioca in top of double boiler. Cook over hot water until tapioca is transparent, about 1 to 1½ hours. Carefully stir tapioca mixture into beaten yolk. Continue cooking until thickened. Beat egg whites until they hold soft peaks. Add remaining ¼ cup sugar gradually, beating thoroughly after each addition. Fold into tapioca mixture. Add vanilla and chill. Five to 6 servings.

APPLE TAPIOCA

3 tablespoons sugar
2 tablespoons granular tapioca
1 cup boiling water
3 tablespoons red cinnamon
  candies

Juice of ½ lemon
3 cups peeled, sliced apples

■ Mix sugar and tapioca. Add boiling water and cook until clear. Add cinnamon candies and lemon juice. Arrange apples in baking dish. Cover with tapioca mixture and bake at 375°F approximately 30 minutes. Five servings.

CORNSTARCH PUDDING (BLANC MANGE)

2 tablespoons cornstarch
1 pinch salt
¼ cup sugar

2 cups milk
1 teaspoon vanilla

■ Mix cornstarch, salt, and sugar. Add milk gradually, and cook over hot water, stirring until thickened. Cover, and cook about 10 minutes longer, stirring occasionally. Cool slightly, flavor, chill, and serve. Four servings.

CHOCOLATE CORNSTARCH PUDDING. Make as for Cornstarch Pudding. Add ½ square unsweetened chocolate, melted, and increase sugar to 6 tablespoons. Decrease vanilla to ½ teaspoon.

CHOCOLATE CREAM PUDDING. Make Chocolate Cornstarch Pudding. Cool slightly; fold in 2 stiffly beaten egg whites. A portion of the sugar may be beaten into the egg whites.

COCONUT CORNSTARCH PUDDING. Make as for Cornstarch Pudding, adding from ½ to 1 cup dry shredded coconut.

JUNKET PUDDING

¼ to ½ cup sugar, according
  to taste
4 cups milk, heated to lukewarm (98°F)

1 teaspoon vanilla
1 junket tablet, dissolved in
  1 tablespoon cold water

■ The milk must never be allowed to get too hot, or pudding will not set. Dissolve sugar in milk. Add vanilla and dissolve junket to lukewarm milk. Pour into glasses or cups suitable for serving. Keep in a warm place until set, then chill. Avoid jarring, as it is apt to cause pudding to separate. Serve with whipped cream, jelly, nuts, or fruits. Eight servings.

Simple variations in flavor, such as almond, orange, caramel, cinnamon, or grated chocolate are good. Daintily colored junket puddings are attractive.

LEMON CREAM

½ cup sugar	4 egg yolks, slightly beaten
¼ teaspoon salt	4 egg whites, stiffly beaten
6 tablespoons lemon juice	¼ cup sugar

■   Add ½ cup sugar, salt, and lemon juice to egg yolks. Cook over hot water, stirring constantly until slightly thickened. Cool partially. Beat egg whites until they begin to form soft peaks. Add ¼ cup of sugar gradually, and continue beating until stiff. Fold in egg whites carefully. Turn into serving dish. Chill. Four servings.

ORANGE CREAM. Make as for Lemon Cream, using only 2 tablespoons lemon juice and adding 4 tablespoons orange juice.

LEMON SOUFFLÉ. Use proportions and combine as for Lemon Cream. Bake as for Soufflé (p. 96).

FRUIT WHIP OR SOUFFLÉ

¼ cup sugar, more or less as needed	1 egg white, beaten stiff
1 pinch salt	½ tablespoon lemon juice
	¼ to ½ cup fruit pulp

Apricots, prunes, or peaches are a good choice of fruits. Two servings.

FRUIT WHIP. Beat salt and sugar gradually into egg whites, then add lemon juice and fruit pulp in same way. Pile lightly into a glass serving dish. Chill.

FRUIT SOUFFLÉ. Make as for Fruit Whip but bake in unoiled dish set in hot water (350°F) until firm. Serve from baking dish with Soft Custard (p. 154). Two servings.

LEMON SPONGE PUDDING

¼ teaspoon salt	3 tablespoons butter, melted
3 egg whites	4½ tablespoons flour, mixed
¾ cup sugar	with
3 egg yolks	⅓ cup sugar
1 lemon rind, grated	1½ cups milk
4½ tablespoons lemon juice	

■   Add salt to egg white, and beat until they hold soft peaks. Gradually beat in ¾ cup sugar to make a stiff meringue. Use the same beater to beat egg yolks thoroughly with lemon rind, juice, and melted butter. Stir in mixed flour and sugar. Add milk. Fold in meringue. Pour into custard cups. Set in pan of hot water. Bake at 350°F until firm, approximately 30 to 35 minutes. Eight servings.

STEAMED PUDDINGS

To steam a pudding, fill an oiled mold ⅔ full of pudding mixture, and cover tightly with an oiled lid. Cook in a steamer, or place on a rack in a tightly closed kettle surrounded by enough boiling water to cover molds to ⅔ their depth. If the kettle is used, it is well to tie on the lid unless it fits tightly.

PLUM PUDDING

½ cup flour
1 teaspoon salt
2 teaspoons baking powder
½ teaspoon nutmeg
¾ teaspoon cinnamon
½ teaspoon cloves
¼ teaspoon mace
2 cups seeded raisins
¼ pound citron, sliced
2 cups currants

¼ cup blanched almonds, cut into strips
½ cup sugar
5 ounces ground suet
2½ cups soft bread crumbs soaked in
1 cup milk, scalded
½ cup dark corn syrup
3 tablespoons fruit juice
4 eggs, well-beaten

■ Sift together flour, salt, baking powder, and spices. Add fruit and nuts to flour mixture. Mix sugar with suet; add soaked crumbs, syrup, fruit juice, and eggs, then flour mixture. Mix well. Steam 6 hours in oiled molds. This amount fills 2 1-pound coffee cans ⅔ full. Figs or dates cut into strips, and chopped, candied orange peel may replace some of the other fruits. To steam in pressure cooker or pressure saucepan, follow directions provided with cooker. Twelve servings.

STEAMED CHOCOLATE PUFFS

3 tablespoons fat
6 tablespoons sugar
1 egg, well-beaten
⅓ cup milk
1 cup flour

1 pinch salt
1½ teaspoons baking powder
½ teaspoon cinnamon
1 to 1½ squares unsweetened chocolate, melted

■ Mix as for Butter Cake (p. 178). Steam ½ hour in individual oiled molds. Serve hot with any desired sauce. Six servings.

CARROT PUDDING

½ cup fat
1 cup brown sugar
1 cup raw, grated carrots
1 cup chopped apples
1 cup seeded raisins
1½ cups flour

1 teaspoon salt
1 teaspoon cinnamon
½ teaspoon allspice
½ teaspoon nutmeg
2 teaspoons baking powder

■ Cream fat and sugar. Add carrots, apples, and raisins. Sift remaining dry ingredients together. Add to fat mixture. Mix well. Pour into 1 large, well-oiled mold or individual molds, filling ⅔ full. Steam large mold 3 hours or individual molds 1½ hours. Ten to 12 servings.

GELATIN DESSERTS

Gelatin may be obtained in pulverized or granular forms. Gelatin swells in cold water and disperses in hot water. Gelatin thus treated, if added in proper proportions to other liquids, causes them to solidify upon cooling. Boiling and overcooking are to be avoided. A 1-ounce box of ordinary granular gelatin usually contains 4 small envelopes, each holding 1 tablespoon gelatin.

Prepared gelatin desserts are available in a considerable variety and are convenient. Their nutritive value can be improved by substituting fruit juice for part of the water in recipes or by adding fruit before molding. Contents of 1 3-ounce package measures approximately ½ cup.

Proportions. Amount of gelatin to be used for a given amount of liquid depends upon kind of jelly to be made. The usual proportions are:

GELATIN DISH	LIQUID (CUPS)	GELATIN (TABLESPOONS)
Plain jellies	2	1
Whips	2	1
Fruit and vegetable jellies	2	1½
Sponges	2	1½
Creams	2	2

Directions for Making Gelatin Dishes. Soak gelatin in cold liquid until soft. Allow about 4 tablespoons liquid to 1 tablespoon gelatin. Disperse soaked gelatin by adding hot liquid or by placing over hot water, stirring as necessary. Then mix well with remaining ingredients. If the recipe calls for 1 tablespoon or more of sugar, it is not necessary to soften the gelatin in cold liquid. Just mix the gelatin with the sugar and add the hot liquid.

PLAIN JELLIES. Pour into molds.

FRUIT AND VEGETABLE JELLIES. Chill until mixture begins to congeal, then fold in fruit or vegetable, and pour into molds.

SPONGES. Make as for Jelly. When mixture begins to thicken, add unbeaten egg white and beat until mixture holds its shape. Mold if desired.

WHIPS. Chill until mixture begins to congeal, then whip with a rotary beater until light and frothy. Mold if desired.

CREAMS. Chill. When mixture begins to congeal, fold in equal volume of whipped cream. Mold if desired.

General Suggestions

To Unmold. Run tip of sharp-pointed knife around the edge of jelly. Dip mold for a moment into lukewarm water to depth of jelly. Then place serving plate on top, and invert quickly. If this is not sufficient to remove jelly, repeat process. *Water must not be too warm or jelly will melt.*

To Decorate. Pour a thin layer of gelatin mixture into bottom of mold. Chill. When congealed, arrange materials to be used for decoration to form desired design, dipping them first into jelly mixture. Chill until set, then pour in a little more of gelatin mixture to set design. Chill. When firm, add remainder of jelly, a little at a time until danger of disarranging design is past.

To place a design on side of mold, dip pieces to be used for decorating in gelatin mixture and place against sides of chilled mold previously coated with a thin layer of jelly. When set, fill mold gradually to avoid disarrangement.

LEMON JELLY

1 tablespoon gelatin, softened in
4 tablespoons cold water
¾ cup boiling water

⅔ cup cold water
6 tablespoons lemon juice
½ to ¾ cup sugar

■ Disperse softened gelatin in boiling water. Add remaining ingredients, and stir until sugar dissolves. Pour into molds, and chill. Four servings.

COFFEE JELLY. Make as for Lemon Jelly, adding 1 teaspoon instant coffee to boiling water. Omit lemon juice and use 1 cup cold water. Decrease sugar to ⅓ cup.

FRUIT JELLY. Make Lemon Jelly, increasing gelatin to 1½ tablespoons. When almost ready to congeal, add fruit and mold. Whole sections of orange free from membranes, diced cooked pineapple, or slices of banana are suitable.

IVORY JELLY. Make as for Lemon Jelly, substituting milk for all liquid. Decrease sugar to ¼ cup. Flavor with 1 teaspoon vanilla.

ORANGE JELLY. Make Lemon Jelly, using ½ cup sugar, decreasing lemon juice to ¼ cup, and substituting ¾ cup orange juice for the ⅔ cup cold water.

UNCOOKED PLUM PUDDING

1 package orange flavored gelatin
¾ cup grapenuts
¾ cup sugar
1 teaspoon cinnamon
¼ teaspoon cloves

2 cups boiling water
½ cup currants
¾ cup raisins
1 cup dates, chopped
¾ cup nuts, chopped

■ Mix gelatin, grapenuts, spices, and sugar. Add water. Cool. Cook currants and raisins until soft in a very small amount of water. Drain if necessary. Cool. Combine currants, raisins, dates, and nuts with gelatin mixture. Mold. Serve with whipped cream. Twelve to 16 servings.

LEMON SPONGE (SNOW PUDDING)

1½ tablespoons gelatin
¾ cup sugar
1½ cups boiling water

½ cup lemon juice
3 egg whites

■ Mix gelatin and sugar throughly in a small sauce pan. Gradually add the boiling water, stirring constantly until gelatin is dispersed. Add lemon juice and chill until slightly thicker than egg white. Add unbeaten egg white and beat until mixture begins to hold its shape. To speed up beating place mixture over ice water while beating. Spoon into dessert dishes and chill until firm. Eight servings.

ORANGE SPONGE. Make as for Lemon Sponge, using ½ cup orange juice, ¼ cup lemon juice, and 1¼ cups boiling water.

APRICOT SPONGE

1 tablespoon gelatin
½ cup + 1 tablespoon boiling water
½ cup apricot pulp, fresh or canned

½ cup sugar
½ to 1 tablespoon lemon juice
3 egg whites, beaten stiff

■ Make as for Lemon Sponge (p. 162). Garnish with whipped cream and halves of apricots. Five to 6 servings.

STRAWBERRY BAVARIAN CREAM

2 tablespoons gelatin, softened in
½ cup cold water
¼ cup boiling water
¾ cup sugar (less if sweetened frozen fruit is used)

1½ cups crushed strawberries
1½ cups, or more if desired, whipped cream

■ Disperse softened gelatin in boiling water. Add sugar, and stir until dissolved. Add fruit. When mixture begins to stiffen, beat until light, then fold in whipped cream. Pile lightly into serving dish or mold. Serve garnished with whipped cream and whole strawberries. Eight servings.

ORANGE BAVARIAN CREAM. Make as for Strawberry Bavarian Cream, substituting orange juice and pulp for strawberries. Garnish with sections of orange free from membranes.

PINEAPPLE BAVARIAN CREAM. Make as for Strawberry Bavarian Cream, substituting canned crushed pineapple for strawberries. *Fresh pineapple may be used, if heated enough to destroy an enzyme that would otherwise digest gelatin and destroy its ability to congeal.*

SPANISH CREAM

3 egg yolks, slightly beaten
⅓ cup sugar
⅛ teaspoon salt
2½ cups milk, scalded
2 tablespoons gelatin,
   softened in

½ cup cold milk
1 teaspoon vanilla
3 egg whites, beaten stiff
⅔ cup macaroon crumbs

■   Make Foundation Custard (p. 154) of egg yolks, sugar, salt, and milk. Cook as for Soft Custard (p. 154). Disperse softened gelatin in hot custard. Cool, flavor, and as it begins to thicken fold in egg whites and macaroon crumbs. Mold. Chill. Nine servings.

GINGER CREAM

1½ tablespoons gelatin,
   softened in
½ cup cold water
4 eggs, slightly beaten
½ cup sugar
½ teaspoon salt

2 cups milk, scalded
¼ cup preserved ginger,
   cut fine
½ tablespoon ginger syrup
2 cups cream, whipped

■   Make as for Spanish Cream (p. 163), using whole eggs in custard. Substitute ginger and whipped cream for egg whites and macaroons. Nine to 10 servings.

FROZEN DESSERTS

Frozen mixtures require more sugar and flavoring than the usual dessert as taste is less acute when the mouth is chilled. Frozen desserts are crystalline in nature. Size of crystals is affected by ingredients used. Frozen desserts are improved in texture by addition of a stabilizer. In the making of unstirred desserts, one of the best of these stabilizers is cream that can be whipped to incorporate air to give desired smooth texture. The fat is evenly distributed and becomes more solid at lower temperatures, thus adding to smoothness of mixture. It is, however, expensive and too rich for frequent use. Consequently, many recipes have been developed wherein evaporated milk, thin cream, or milk thickened with gelatin, flour, eggs, or marshmallows have been substituted for part or all of the heavy cream. The temperature at which freezing occurs and the rate of freezing also affect the product. Desserts that are stirred while freezing usually are superior if frozen slowly. This allows for separation of crystals as they form. Mixtures that are not stirred while freezing are better if frozen rapidly. The method most often used is to freeze the mixture rather slowly and depend upon agitation by beating to increase the number of ice crystals formed.

Frozen desserts may be classified as follows:

I. *Ices, frappés, granites, punch, sherbets,* and *sorbets.* (Generally stirred while freezing.)

Ice is a diluted fruit juice, sweetened and frozen.

Frappé is an ice frozen to a mushy consistency.

Granite is an ice frozen with little stirring. It is rough and icy in texture.

Punch is an ice containing a highly spiced fruit juice.

Sherbet is an ice to which egg white or gelatin has been added. Milk or cream may be substituted for part of the liquid.

Sorbet is a sherbet containing several kinds of fruit juices.

II. *Ice Creams.* (Stirred while freezing.)

Plain or Philadelphia Ice Cream consists of thin cream, sweetened, flavored, and frozen.

Custard Ice Cream consists of a custard foundation with added cream, frozen.

French Ice Cream consists of a rich custard foundation containing many eggs.

American Ice Cream is less rich and may have cornstarch or flour substituted for part of the eggs.

III. *Parfaits and Mousses.* (Frozen without stirring.)

Parfaits consist of whole beaten eggs or egg whites cooked by pouring hot syrup over them; with whipped cream added and the combination frozen.

Mousses consist of whipped cream, sweetened, flavored, molded, and frozen.

General Suggestions

Freezers for frozen desserts are of 2 main types, those in which a dasher fitted into a can is turned by means of a crank and those in which the *freezing units* are provided by mechanical refrigerators. Mixtures frozen in freezing units need only occasional stirring but require a longer time to freeze than those stirred with a dasher. It is difficult to secure a smooth product with unstirred mixtures.

Before using an ice cream freezer of the dasher type, scald can, cover, and dasher. Fit parts together to be sure they run smoothly before pouring in the mix.

Suggestions for Mixtures Frozen with Salt and Ice

Salt. Use ice cream salt, as it mixes more easily with ice than table salt. Excess salt is apt to cause a granular texture, and too little increases the time required for freezing.

Proportions of Ice to Salt. Commonly used proportions of ice to salt are:

For ordinary mixtures frozen with stirring, such as ice cream—8 parts ice to 1 part salt.

For packing frozen mixtures—4 parts ice to 1 part salt.

Filling. If mixture is to be stirred while freezing, fill container only ⅔ full to allow for increase in volume during freezing.

Packing for Freezing. Place filled can in position, and adjust crank, if used, to see that it turns properly. Place layer of crushed ice in bottom of outer container. Sprinkle with salt. Add remaining ice and salt in alternate layers, or mix them before packing. Ice mixture should extend a little higher than ingredients to be frozen. Refill as ice melts.

Freezing. Freezing is accomplished when melting ice absorbs heat from ingredients to be frozen. Turn crank slowly and steadily to expose as much of mixture as possible to surface of can. Do not drain off salt water until mixture is frozen unless there is a possibility of brine getting into the can. Water causes ice to melt more rapidly and thereby hastens freezing.

Packing for Storage. Ice cream is ready for packing when frozen to a firm, smooth, velvety consistency. Drain off water. Remove dasher, and pack mixture solidly. Lay wax paper over top of can before replacing cover. Repack in ice and salt, using a proportion of 4 parts ice to 1 part salt. Cover can with a layer of this mixture. Cover freezer with newspapers or a heavy burlap bag, and put in cool place. Most frozen mixtures "ripen" or improve in flavor during storage. If desired, the frozen dessert may be placed in home freezer or refrigerator unit for storage.

Molding Frozen Mixtures. Choose a mold with tight cover, and chill. It may be lined with wax paper. Fill to overflowing with partially frozen mixture. Pack solidly to avoid air spaces. Cover, and pack mold in ice and salt in proportion of 4:1. Let stand 3 hours or longer. Follow same procedure for mousses and similar mixtures, using a 1:1 or 2:1 proportion of ice to salt.

Unmolding. Remove mold from freezing mixture, rinse with cold water, and wipe. Remove cover, loosen mixture around edge with a knife, and invert on chilled serving dish. If it does not slip out easily, cover mold with cloth wrung dry from slightly warm water.

ICES

LEMON ICE

2 cups sugar	4 cups water
¾ to 1 cup lemon juice	

■ Mix ingredients stirring until sugar dissolves. Strain if desired and freeze, using an 8:1 ice and salt mixture. Twelve servings.

GRAPE ICE. Use 2 cups sugar, 2 cups water, 2 cups grape juice, ¼ cup lemon juice, and ½ cup orange juice. The orange juice may be omitted.

ORANGE ICE. Use 2 cups sugar, 3 cups water, 2 cups orange juice, and ¼ cup lemon juice. The grated rind of 2 oranges may be added.

PINEAPPLE ICE. Use 2 cups sugar, 2 cups water, 2⅓ cups crushed pineapple, and ⅓ cup lemon juice.

RHUBARB PINEAPPLE ICE

4 cups diced rhubarb	1½ tablespoons lemon juice
2 cups cold water	¾ cup pineapple juice
1 cup sugar	

■   Combine rhubarb, water, and sugar in saucepan. Simmer until rhubarb is soft. Cool. Add lemon and pineapple juices. Tint a delicate pink if desired. Freeze, using an 8:1 ice and salt mixture. Ten to 12 servings.

CIDER ICE

¾ cup sugar	¼ cup lemon juice
1 cup water	2 cups sweet cider
1 cup orange juice, strained	

■   Mix ingredients, stirring until sugar dissolves. Freeze, using an 8:1 ice and salt mixture. Ten servings.

CRANBERRY ICE

4 cups cranberries	¼ cup lemon juice
4 cups water	2 teaspoons grated orange
2 cups sugar	rind

■   Cook cranberries with ½ of the water until soft. Rub through a sieve. Add sugar, remaining water, lemon juice, and orange rind. Cool. Freeze, using an 8:1 ice and salt mixture. Ten to 12 servings.

SHERBETS

Use any recipe for an ice, making the mix slightly sweeter and stronger in flavor. When mixture is partially frozen, add 2 stiffly beaten egg whites to amount suggested in ice recipes, then complete freezing. A finer texture is obtained if ¼ cup of the sugar is added gradually while the egg whites are beaten. Substitute 1 tablespoon gelatin for the 2 egg whites if preferred. Soften gelatin in ¼ cup cold water, disperse over hot water, and add to mixture before freezing. Mixture to which gelatin is added should be at room temperature.

Milk and Cream Sherbets

Substitute milk, cream, or ½ of the milk and ½ of the cream for the water in any recipe for ice. Less fruit juice may be preferred. Egg whites or gelatin may be omitted. Orange, grape, and lemon juices are good in milk or cream sherbets.

ORANGE CREAM SHERBET

1½ cups sugar
¼ cup lemon juice
1¾ cups orange juice

1 cup milk
1 cup thin cream
1 egg white, beaten stiff

■ Dissolve 1⅓ cups sugar in fruit juice. Add to milk and cream gradually. Partially freeze. Beat egg whites until they begin to hold soft peaks. Beat in remaining sugar gradually. Add egg whites, and complete freezing. Ten servings.

TROPICAL SHERBET

2 cups milk
¾ cup sugar
2 eggs
1 cup apricot pulp
1½ cups mashed banana

½ teaspoon almond extract
1 teaspoon lemon juice
Grated rind of ½ orange
1 egg white, stiffly beaten

■ Make a soft custard of milk, sugar, and eggs. Add apricot pulp, mashed banana, almond extract, lemon juice, and orange rind. Freeze until mushy. Add stiffly beaten egg white and continue freezing until stiff. Eight servings.

MINTED PINEAPPLE SHERBET

1⅓ cups milk
1⅓ cups crushed pineapple
1 cup sugar
5⅓ tablespoons light corn
  syrup

1⅓ cups thin cream
Peppermint flavoring
Green food coloring

■ Mix ingredients. Add few drops of peppermint flavoring carefully and taste to obtain desired flavor. Tint a *delicate green* with food coloring. Avoid excess color. Freeze. Eight servings.

BUTTERMILK SHERBET

2 cups buttermilk
⅔ cup sugar
1 cup crushed pineapple

1 teaspoon vanilla
1 egg white

■ Mix buttermilk, all but 2 tablespoons of sugar, pineapple, and vanilla. Partially freeze using an 8:1 ice and salt mixture. Beat egg white stiff, adding the remaining 2 tablespoons sugar. Add to the partially frozen mixture and complete freezing. Eight servings.

ICE CREAMS

PHILADELPHIA OR PLAIN ICE CREAM

4 cups thin cream
¾ cup sugar

1¼ teaspoons vanilla
1 pinch salt

■   Mix ingredients, stirring to dissolve sugar. Freeze, using an 8:1 ice and salt mixture. Ten servings.

COFFEE ICE CREAM. Dissolve 1 to 1½ tablespoons instant coffee in 2 tablespoons hot water, and add to cream. Complete as for Philadelphia Ice Cream.

CRUMB ICE CREAM. Add 1 cup cooky or graham cracker crumbs to Philadelphia Ice Cream.

GRAPENUT ICE CREAM. Soak ¾ to 1 cup grapenuts in cream 15 minutes before mixing Philadelphia Ice Cream.

NUT ICE CREAM. Before freezing add 1 cup finely chopped nuts to Philadelphia Ice Cream.

PEANUT BRITTLE ICE CREAM. Substitute ½ pound crushed peanut brittle for sugar in Philadelphia Ice Cream.

PEPPERMINT STICK ICE CREAM. Substitute ½ pound crushed peppermint stick candy for sugar and vanilla in Philadelphia Ice Cream. A little pink coloring may be added if desired.

STRAWBERRY ICE CREAM

1 cup sugar
1 to 2 cups strawberries, crushed

2 cups thin cream or
1 cup thin cream and
1 cup milk

■   Add sugar to berries, let stand 15 to 20 minutes. If sweetened, frozen berries are used, sugar should be decreased. Add cream, and freeze as for Philadelphia Ice Cream (p. 168). Ten servings.

APRICOT ICE CREAM. Substitute apricot pulp for strawberries in Strawberry Ice Cream. Sweeten as desired.

BANANA ICE CREAM. Substitute 1 cup banana pulp for strawberries in Strawberry Ice Cream. Decrease sugar to ⅔ cup, and add 1 tablespoon lemon juice.

CHOCOLATE ICE CREAM

1 square unsweetened chocolate, melted
⅔ cup sugar
⅓ cup boiling water

1 pinch salt
2 cups thin cream
⅔ teaspoon vanilla

■   Cook chocolate, sugar, water, and salt until smooth and glossy. Add cream and vanilla. Freeze as for Philadelphia Ice Cream (p. 168). Six servings.

AMERICAN ICE CREAM (CUSTARD FOUNDATION)

1 egg or 2 egg yolks, slightly   1 cup milk, scalded
   beaten   2 cups thin cream
½ cup sugar   1½ teaspoons vanilla
1 pinch salt

■ Make a Foundation Custard (p. 154). Cook as for Soft Custard (p. 154). Cool. Add cream and vanilla. Freeze, using an 8:1 ice and salt mixture. Eight servings.

CARAMEL CUSTARD ICE CREAM

2 eggs or 4 egg yolks,   ½ cup sugar, caramelized
   slightly beaten   (p. 103)
½ cup sugar   2 cups thin cream
1 pinch salt   1 tablespoon vanilla
2 cups milk, scalded

■ Make Foundation Custard (p. 154). Cook as for Soft Custard (p. 154). Add caramel, and cool. Add cream and flavoring. Freeze, using an 8:1 ice and salt mixture. Twelve servings.

FRENCH ICE CREAM

Make as for American Ice Cream (p. 169), increasing egg yolks to 4 and using all cream. Eight servings.

Mixtures Frozen in the Mechanical Refrigerator

Satisfactory frozen desserts may be made by freezing rapidly a suitable mixture in the trays of a mechanical refrigerator. The mixture is necessarily one that encloses a large amount of air in such a way that it is distributed evenly in very small bubbles. These bubbles separate the ice crystals and prevent a coarse, crystalline texture. Ingredients such as gelatin, marshmallows, eggs, or flour, act somewhat in the same way but are less effective. Mixtures that are not too sweet freeze more rapidly than very sweet ones.

Parfaits, mousses, and frozen puddings can all be frozen successfully by mechanical refrigeration. Place mixtures in freezing trays and allow to stand in freezing unit for the required time with occasional stirring instead of packing in ice and salt as suggested in recipes.

Special recipes for ices, sherbets, and ice creams have been developed for use in mechanical refrigerator.

VANILLA ICE CREAM (MECHANICAL REFRIGERATOR)

⅔ cup sweetened condensed
   milk
⅔ cup water

1½ teaspoons vanilla
1 cup heavy cream,
   whipped

■ Combine milk and water. Add vanilla. Fold in whipped cream. Pour into refrigerator tray. Stir occasionally from sides and bottom of tray. Allow 2 to 4 hours for freezing. Eight servings.

CHOCOLATE ICE CREAM. Prepare Vanilla Ice Cream, add 1 to 1½ squares of unsweetened, melted chocolate to condensed milk.

FRUIT ICE CREAM. Prepare Vanilla Ice Cream. Omit vanilla, and add 1 cup crushed fruit sweetened to taste.

LEMON ANGEL CREAM

½ cup sugar
2 eggs, well beaten
1 cup milk
1 cup thin cream
⅔ cup light corn syrup

⅓ cup lemon juice
1 rind of lemon, grated
2 teaspoons gelatin,
   softened in
2 tablespoons cold water

■ Beat sugar gradually into eggs. Add milk, cream, syrup, lemon juice, and rind. Blend. Mix in softened gelatin that has been dispersed over hot water. Pour into tray. Allow 3 to 5 hours to freeze, stirring occasionally from sides and bottom. Eight servings.

BRAZIL MOCHA ICE CREAM

1½ cups milk
2 teaspoons instant coffee
1 cup sugar
2 egg yolks, beaten
¼ teaspoon salt

1½ cups heavy cream,
   whipped
1 cup Brazil nuts,
   chopped

■ Scald milk with coffee in double boiler. Caramelize ½ of the sugar to light brown syrup stage (p. 103). Stir in remaining sugar. Be sure it is dissolved. Add to heated milk, then combine with egg yolks and salt. Cook as for Soft Custard (p. 154). Cool. Fold in cream and nuts. Pour into tray. Freeze until firm, stirring occasionally. Ten servings.

ORANGE SHERBET

¾ cup evaporated milk,
   well-chilled
3 tablespoons lemon juice

1 cup orange juice
½ cup sugar

■ Whip chilled milk (p. 104) until very stiff. Dissolve sugar in fruit juices, and fold thoroughly into whipped milk. Turn into freezing tray. Freeze until mixture hardens on sides of tray. Remove from refrigerator. Beat.

Return to refrigerator, and continue freezing until firm. Allow 3 to 5 hours for freezing. Five servings.

ANGEL PARFAIT

1 cup sugar	2 cups heavy cream,
¾ cup water	whipped
3 egg whites, beaten stiff	1 teaspoon vanilla.

■ Boil sugar and water to soft-ball stage (p. 218). Pour slowly onto egg whites, and continue beating until room temperature. Add cream and vanilla. Pour into refrigerator tray and freeze. Ten to 12 servings.

CHOCOLATE PARFAIT. Melt 2 squares unsweetened chocolate in syrup for Angel Parfait.

STRAWBERRY PARFAIT. Add 2 cups crushed, fresh strawberries to Angel Parfait just before molding. Omit vanilla. Other fruits may be used in same way. If sweetened frozen fruits are used, sugar should be decreased.

COFFEE PARFAIT

½ cup sugar	2 egg yolks, well beaten
1 pinch salt	2 cups heavy cream,
1 cup strong coffee	whipped

■ Dissolve sugar and salt in coffee. Pour gradually over egg yolks, and cook as for Soft Custard (p. 154). Cool. Add cream, and complete as for Angel Parfait (p. 171). Eight to 10 servings.

MAPLE PARFAIT

4 eggs, slightly beaten	2 cups heavy cream,
1 cup maple syrup	whipped

■ Add syrup to eggs. Cook as for Soft Custard (p. 154). Cool. Add cream. Complete as for Angel Parfait (p. 171). Eight to 10 servings.

OTHER REFRIGERATOR DESSERTS

FROZEN LEMON PIE

2 eggs, separated	1 cup vanilla wafer or
½ cup sugar	graham cracker crumbs
½ teaspoon grated lemon rind	
½ cup lemon juice	
1 small can evaporated milk, chilled until icy cold	

■ Mix well-beaten egg yolks with ¼ cup sugar, lemon rind, and lemon juice. Stir, and cook in double boiler until thickened. Cool. Beat the egg whites until they form soft peaks. Gradually add remaining ¼ cup sugar, and beat well after each addition. Fold into cold lemon mixture. Coat bottom and sides of refrigerator tray with butter or margarine. Spread ½ of the crumbs on bottom of tray.

Whip chilled milk until stiff. Fold into lemon mixture. Pour into tray. Sprinkle top with remaining crumbs. Freeze without stirring at coldest temperature until firm. Slice diagonally across tray to form "pie" wedges. Eight servings.

CHOCOLATE ICEBOX PUDDING (CHOCOLATE ICEBOX CAKE)

2 egg yolks, beaten
½ cup sugar
½ cup milk
2 squares sweet chocolate, melted

1 cup nuts, chopped
1 teaspoon vanilla
2 egg whites, beaten stiff
6 ladyfingers or strips stale cake

■ Add egg yolks, ¼ cup sugar, and milk to chocolate, mixing as for Foundation Custard (p. 154). Cook over hot water, stirring until thick. Cool partially, and add nuts and flavoring. Beat egg whites to form soft peaks. Gradually beat in the remaining ¼ cup sugar. Fold beaten egg whites into chocolate mixture. Place a layer of ladyfingers, split in halves, into bottom of mold. Add a layer of chocolate mixture. Add the second layer of split ladyfingers and cover with remaining chocolate mixture. Cover. Let stand in refrigerator 12 hours. Unmold, and cut into slices. Serve with whipped cream or ice cream. Six to 8 servings.

ORANGE REFRIGERATOR CAKE

1 tablespoon gelatin, softened in
¼ cup orange juice
⅓ cup sugar
½ cup boiling water
¾ cup orange juice
12 large marshmallows, cut into pieces

½ cup orange sections, free from membranes, cut into thirds
1 cup heavy cream, whipped
Ladyfingers or slices of stale cake sufficient to line pan

■ Add sugar and boiling water to softened gelatin. Add ¾ cup orange juice. Cool. Combine marshmallows and oranges. When gelatin mixture begins to stiffen, beat until fluffy. Fold in marshallows, oranges, and whipped cream. Arrange ladyfingers or cake on bottom and sides of pan. Pour in filling. Top may be covered with cake or ladyfingers if desired. Chill overnight. Unmold, and garnish with whipped cream and orange slices. Eight to 10 servings.

DESSERTS WITH A BISCUIT FOUNDATION

Shortcakes

Shortcake consists of a rich, usually sweetened, biscuit mixture. Eggs may be added. It is served with sweetened fruit, either fresh or cooked.

STRAWBERRY SHORTCAKE

Use recipe for Baking Powder Biscuits (p. 50), increasing fat to 6 tablespoons and adding 1 tablespoon sugar if desired. A beaten egg may be added with the milk.

Divide dough into two equal parts. Pat, and roll out one portion to fit a pie or cake pan, making a layer ¼-inch thick. Brush top lightly with melted fat. Shape second portion of dough in same way, and place over first. Bake as for Biscuits (p. 50). When done, separate layers, put crushed and sweetened berries on one layer, and place second layer over berries. Spread top layer with fruit mixture. Serve at once, either plain or garnished with whipped cream. Other fruit may be substituted for strawberries.

Shortcake may be baked as one large cake instead of in layers. It is then made twice as thick and split in halves when used. Eight servings.

INDIVIDUAL SHORTCAKES. Make as for Strawberry Shortcake, cutting dough into individual servings.

DUTCH APPLE CAKE

Prepare shortcake and spread ½-inch thick in a shallow, oiled baking pan. Cut pared and quartered sour apples into uniform slices. Place slices, thin edges down, in parallel rows on top of mixture. Sprinkle with 2 tablespoons sugar mixed with ½ teaspoon cinnamon. Bake in a 400°F oven, 25 to 30 minutes or until apples are tender. Serve with Lemon Sauce (p. 102), plain or with whipped cream. Eight servings.

DATE ROLLS

Roll Biscuit Dough (p. 50) into oblong shape ½-inch thick, and spread with Date Paste (p. 192). Roll as for Jelly Roll (p. 187). Cut into 1-inch slices. Place rolls in oiled pan cut side down and far enough apart to allow for rising while baking. Bake approximately 20 minutes at 400°F. Serve as hot bread or as pudding with any desired sauce. Eight servings.

APPLE ROLLS. Make as for Date Rolls, substituting for date paste chopped apples mixed with sugar and cinnamon to taste. Nutmeg may be used instead of cinnamon.

BAKED FRUIT DUMPLINGS (APPLE OR PEACH)

Make Biscuit Dough (p. 50), and roll ¼-inch thick. Cut into 4-inch squares or pieces large enough to cover the fruit to be enclosed. Place prepared fruit in center of each square of dough. Add sugar as needed. Season with cinnamon, nutmeg, or lemon juice. Moisten edges of dough with cold water or milk, and bring corners together on top of fruit. Press edges together. Place in oiled pan, adding small amount of hot water, sugar, and butter or margarine. Bake at 400°F until thoroughly cooked, basting as needed. Serve with cream or a sweet sauce. Eight servings.

FRUIT COBBLERS. Use any desired fruit, fresh, canned, or frozen. If too juicy, drain off part of juice. If too bland, add a little lemon juice. Sweeten to taste. Fill shallow oiled baking dish ⅔ full of fruit and juice. Dot with bits of butter or margarine. Make Biscuit Dough (p. 50) and pat or roll ¼-inch thick to fit pan. Cut slit in center, and place over fruit mixture. Bake at 400°F, 35 to 40 minutes.

Serve warm with plain or whipped cream.

FRITTERS

Sweet fritters may be served as a dessert; vegetable fritters as a vegetable. Other fritters may be made of meat, fish, and vegetables and served as an entrée or as its accompaniment. They consist of fairly large pieces of food, dipped into a thin drop batter and cooked in deep fat; or smaller pieces of food may be stirred into batter that is then dropped by spoonfuls into hot fat.

APPLE FRITTERS

1⅓ cups flour	⅔ cup milk
½ teaspoon salt	1 egg
2 teaspoons baking powder	1 tablespoon fat, melted
1 teaspoon sugar, if desired	1 cup sliced, sour apples

■ Mix above ingredients as for Muffins (p. 48), stirring apples into batter last. Fry by spoonfuls in deep fat heated to 375°F. Serve sprinkled with powdered sugar. If desired, egg may be separated, and stiffly beaten white folded into batter just before frying. Approximately 18 fritters.

FRUIT FRITTERS. Substitute any desired fruit for apples, and make as for Apple Fritters. Pineapple, peaches, bananas, raspberries, or sections of oranges are often used.

CHEESE FRITTERS. Substitute ½ to 1 cup grated cheese for apples in Apple Fritter batter. Omit sugar.

MEAT OR FISH FRITTERS. Substitute small pieces of cooked meat or fish for cheese, and make as for Cheese Fritters.

PLAIN FRITTERS. Make Apple Fritter batter, omitting apple. Serve as suggested or with maple or other sauce.

MISCELLANEOUS DESSERTS

APPLE CRISP

½ cup butter or margarine
¾ to 1 cup brown or white
   sugar
⅛ teaspoon salt
¾ cup flour
4 cups pared and sliced apples

1 to 2 tablespoons water, if
   apples are dry
½ teaspoon cinnamon or
1 tablespoon lemon juice,
   if desired

■   Work fat, sugar, salt, and flour together until crumbly. Place apples in oiled baking dish. Add water and cinnamon or lemon juice if used. Cover with flour mixture. Bake at 350°F (moderate oven) until apples are tender, approximately 1 hour. Serve with thin cream. Four servings.

APPLE CRUNCH

4 medium apples, peeled and
   sliced thin
⅔ teaspoon cinnamon
⅔ cup flour

1 cup rolled oats
1 cup brown sugar
⅔ cup butter

■   Place sliced apples in a baking dish. Mix cinnamon with flour. Thoroughly combine flour, oats, sugar, and butter. Sprinkle this crumb-like mixture over apples and press down like a crust. Bake 35 to 40 minutes at 350°F. If apples are quite tart, sprinkle a little sugar over them before adding the topping. Six servings.

APPLE TORTE

1 egg
¾ cup sugar
½ cup flour
2 teaspoons baking powder
⅛ teaspoon salt

½ cup nuts, chopped
1 teaspoon vanilla
2 cups peeled and finely
   diced apples

■   Beat egg until light and fluffy. Gradually add sugar with continued beating. Sift dry ingredients together. Fold into egg mixture along with apples and nuts. Mix lightly but thoroughly. Pour into well oiled pan and bake at 350°F 1 hour. Six servings.

BROWN BETTY

2 cups soft bread crumbs
4 tablespoons butter or margarine
3 cups pared, sliced apples
½ cup sugar

¼ teaspoon cinnamon
½ teaspoon nutmeg, if desired
¼ cup water
1½ tablespoons lemon juice
Grated rind of 1 lemon

■   Oil baking dish. Butter crumbs (p. 60). Place ⅓ of crumbs in bottom of dish. Add half of apples, sugar, spices, water, lemon juice and rind.

Repeat. Cover top with remaining third of crumbs. Cover. Bake 30 minutes at 375°F. Remove cover, bake 30 minutes longer or until apples are tender and crumbs are brown. Serve with thin cream. Four servings.

DATE PUDDING

3 eggs, well beaten	½ teaspoon salt
1½ cups brown sugar	1½ cups dates, chopped
½ cup flour	1 cup nuts, chopped
2 teaspoons baking powder	1 teaspoon vanilla

■ Add ½ of the sugar gradually to eggs, beating well. Sift flour, baking powder, salt, and remaining sugar. Add nuts and dates. Fold into egg mixture. Add vanilla. Bake at 350°F in a shallow, oiled pan for approximately 30 minutes. Cut into squares, and serve with whipped cream. Eight to 10 servings.

DATE ROLL

1 pound graham crackers	1 pound marshmallows, cut
1 pound dates, seeded	into small pieces
1 cup nuts, chopped	¾ cup milk, approximately

■ Grind crackers and dates. Add nuts and marshmallows. Mix well, adding milk to moisten. Shape into a roll. Wrap in wax paper. Chill at least 24 hours before using. Cut into slices and serve with whipped cream. Roll will keep in cold place for some time. Approximately 20 to 22 servings.

Cakes

TRADITIONALLY cakes with shortening have been called "butter" cakes, because for many years butter was the fat most commonly used for making cakes. This class of cakes may be further divided into 2 subclasses. First is the pound cake for which the basic recipe is 1 pound each of butter, sugar, eggs, and flour, and in which no baking powder or soda is used. The cake is leavened by the expansion of moisture from the butter and eggs and the air incorporated during creaming of the butter and beating of the eggs. Second is cake that in comparison to the pound cake contains small percentages of fat and sugar, and is leavened with baking powder and/or soda and an acid. Shortened cakes may be baked as loaves, layers, sheets, or cup cakes.

Cakes without shortening, true sponge cakes, are leavened chiefly by the expansion of air incorporated in an egg foam, whereas modified sponge cakes may contain baking powder. Steam generated during baking also contributes to the leavening of true and modified sponge cakes. These cakes are baked in tube pans or as sheets or loaves.

Fine-grained sugar and high quality eggs, fat, baking powder, and cake flour are essential for good cake. Coarse-grained sugar gives a coarse texture and a hard crust. Poor quality ingredients may cause objectionable flavor, low volume in proportion to the quantity of batter, poor texture, and a tough crumb and crust. Cake flour is milled from soft wheat. The protein content is low, and the granulation fine and uniform to impart a satiny feeling. If cake flour is not available, decrease the amount of flour used approximately 2 tablespoons per cup (p. 9).

177

SHORTENED CAKES

Characteristics of a Good Cake

General Appearance. The shape is uniform with a flat or slightly round top relatively free from cracks. Color will vary according to ingredients used; however, light-colored cakes should be a uniform golden brown on top, sides, and bottom. The crust is thin and tender.

Crumb. The crumb has a medium-fine, even grain with thin cell walls, is tender, velvety, and moist but not sticky. To attain these characteristics it is necessary to have the ingredients well blended to form a structure that retains the carbon dioxide gas produced by the leavening agents. Color will vary according to the ingredients used. Aroma and flavor are pleasant.

Methods of Mixing

Conventional Method. Have ingredients at room temperature. Gradually add sugar to fat, creaming until fluffy. Add unbeaten eggs, well-beaten whole eggs, or yolks, according to the recipe. Add melted chocolate, if used. Add flavoring to milk or it may be added to the fat-sugar foam. Sift leavening agents and other dry ingredients such as cocoa or spices with flour. Add flour and liquid alternately to the fat-sugar mixture, combining with a beating motion. Cakes made with quick acting baking powder, such as tartrate, should not be beaten more than 15 seconds after the last of the flour is added. Those made with double-acting baking powder, such as SAS-phosphate, may be beaten 60 seconds. If nuts or fruits are used, they should be floured to help prevent settling to the bottom of the cake and may be added with the last of the flour. Finally fold in stiffly beaten egg whites, if used.

"One-Bowl" Method. Have ingredients at room temperature. Sift all dry ingredients into mixing bowl. Add fat and part or all of milk and flavoring. Beat vigorously with a spoon for 2 minutes (about 300 strokes), or mix with electric mixer on slow to medium speed for 2 minutes. Scrape bowl frequently. Add any remaining liquid and unbeaten whole eggs, yolks, or whites, and continue beating 2 more minutes, scraping bowl frequently. This method gives best results with formulas developed for it.

General Suggestions

Use of Electric Mixer. The electric mixer may be used for mixing cakes by either of the above methods. Generally moderate or low speed gives best results. Care is necessary to prevent over-mixing.

General Proportions. Allow ⅓ to ½ as much fat as sugar, equal amounts of sugar and liquid (including fat), ½ as much liquid or sugar as flour, and 1 to 2 teaspoons baking powder per cup of flour. Knowledge of these proportions is helpful in judging a recipe. An increase in eggs will permit an increase in sugar or fat, and vice versa.

Sour milk makes a thicker batter than sweet milk.

Fruit mixtures should be stiffer than plain ones to help prevent fruit settling to the bottom during baking.

Preparatory Steps. Measure all ingredients. Sift all dry ingredients together. Separate eggs, if desired. Bottoms of pans may be fitted with wax paper or lightly floured after oiling; sides should not be oiled. Preheat oven so that it will be at desired temperature when cake is mixed.

Filling Pans. Fill pans not more than ½ to ⅔ full; for cup cakes only ½ full. Push batter well to sides and corners of pan leaving a slight depression in the center so that cake will rise evenly. Tap pan sharply on table once or twice or cut through batter to break up large air pockets.

Baking. Cup or layer cakes of average size should bake at 350° to 375°F for 20 to 30 minutes, and loaf cakes of average size should bake at 350°F for 40 to 45 minutes. If oven temperature is too low, the cake may be coarse or overlight and crumbly; if too high, cake may be compact or crack on top.

Optimum results usually are obtained when cakes are baked alone. Place pan as near center of oven as possible to insure even baking. After cake begins to rise do not move it until it is fully risen and the structure slightly set, then, if necessary, the oven door may be opened and closed carefully without causing the cake to fall.

Test for Doneness. When a cake is done, it springs back quickly when pressed lightly with finger, or it begins to pull away slightly from the sides of the pan. A clean toothpick inserted into the center of the cake comes out clean when the cake is done.

Care after Baking. Let stand 5 minutes after removing from oven. Loosen edges with spatula, and invert cake on wire rack to cool. If there is any tendency for the cake to stick, turn pan on its sides successively and allow it to stand in each position long enough for cake to loosen itself by its own weight.

POUND CAKE

1 pound butter (2 cups)	10 eggs, separated
1 pound sifted cake flour (4 cups)	1 pound sugar (2 cups)
	1 teaspoon vanilla

■ Cream butter, work in flour until mixture is mealy. Beat egg yolks, sugar, and vanilla until thick and fluffy. Add gradually to butter and flour, beat thoroughly. Fold in stiffly beaten egg whites, and beat vigorously 5 minutes. Bake in 2 loaf pans lined with wax paper at 325°F for 1¼ hours. Makes 2 loaves (8- x 4-inches).

PLAIN CAKE

1 cup sugar
½ cup fat
2 eggs
1 teaspoon vanilla

1 teaspoon salt
3 teaspoons baking powder
2 cups sifted cake flour
¾ cup milk

■ Use Conventional Method of mixing (p. 178). Bake at 365°F. Two round 8-inch layers or 12 to 16 cup cakes.

CHOCOLATE CAKE. Add 1 to 2 squares melted unsweetened chocolate to Plain Cake. Decrease flour by 1 tablespoon or increase liquid 2 tablespoons, as chocolate thickens mixture.

FRUIT CAKE. Add ½ cup raisins or currants to Plain Cake. Sliced citron, dates, or other fruits may be used.

MARBLE CAKE. Add ½ to 1 square melted unsweetened chocolate to ½ of the recipe for Plain Cake. Add milk to thin as needed. Put mixtures into pan alternately to give marbled effect.

NUT CAKE. Add ½ cup chopped nuts to Plain Cake.

SPICE CAKE. Add ½ teaspoon cinnamon and ¼ teaspoon each of cloves and nutmeg to Plain Cake.

TEA CAKE. Make as for Plain Cake. Put into shallow, oiled pan, making layer of batter about 1-inch thick. Top with thin layer of melted butter, and sprinkle with sugar and cinnamon to taste while cake is warm.

"ONE-BOWL" CAKE

2¼ cups flour
3 teaspoons baking powder
1½ cups sugar
1 teaspoon salt

½ cup fat
1 cup milk
1 teaspoon vanilla
2 eggs, unbeaten

■ Have ingredients at room temperature. Mix according to "One-Bowl" Method (p. 178). Bake at 365°F. Two round, 9-inch layers.

BURNT-SUGAR CAKE. Add 3 tablespoons Caramel Syrup (p. 103) to milk in recipe for "One-Bowl" Cake.

CHOCOLATE CAKE. Add 6 tablespoons cocoa to dry ingredients, and increase milk to 1¼ cups in recipe for "One-Bowl" Cake.

SPICE CAKE. Add 1 teaspoon cinnamon and ⅓ teaspoon each of cloves and nutmeg to recipe for "One-Bowl" Cake.

LAZY DAISY CAKE. Make a topping of ½ cup brown sugar, ¼ cup butter, ¼ cup milk, and 1 cup coconut. Mix, and spread on hot baked cake, return to hot oven or broiler until coconut browns.

WHITE CAKE

1 cup sugar
½ cup fat
4 egg whites
½ teaspoon almond, lemon,
    orange, or vanilla extract

¼ teaspoon salt
2 teaspoons baking powder
2 cups cake flour
⅔ cup milk

■   Use Conventional Method of mixing (p. 178). Bake at 365°F. Two round 8-inch layers or 12 to 16 cup cakes.

GOLD CAKE

1 cup sugar
½ cup fat
8 egg yolks
⅔ cup strained orange juice
1½ teaspoons grated orange
    rind

1 teaspoon lemon extract
2¼ teaspoons baking powder
1 teaspoon salt
2 cups cake flour

■   Use Conventional Method of mixing (p. 178). Bake at 365°F. Two round 8-inch layers.

CHOCOLATE SPICE CAKE

2 cups sugar
½ cup fat
4 egg yolks
2 squares unsweetened choco-
    late, melted
1 teaspoon vanilla

4 egg whites
¼ teaspoon salt
3 teaspoons baking powder
½ teaspoon cinnamon
2⅓ cups cake flour

■   Use Conventional Method of mixing (p. 178). Beat 1 cup of sugar with the egg whites. (Two cups of sugar is too much to cream with ½ cup fat.) Bake at 350°F. Three round, 8-inch layers.

BOSTON FUDGE CAKE

2 cups brown sugar
½ cup fat
3 eggs
2 squares unsweetened choco-
    late, melted
½ teaspoon vanilla

2¼ cups cake flour
½ teaspoon soda
1½ teaspoons baking powder
¼ teaspoon salt
1 cup sour milk

■   Use Conventional Method of mixing (p. 178). Fat, sugar, and eggs may be creamed together. Bake at 350°F. Three round, 8-inch layers.

ITALIAN CAKE

1 cup sugar
⅓ cup fat
2 eggs
⅔ cup cold, strong coffee
¼ teaspoon salt

2 teaspoons baking powder
1¾ cups cake flour
½ cup raisins, chopped
½ cup nuts, chopped

■ Use Conventional Method of mixing (p. 178). Bake in 8 x 8 x 2-inch pan at 365°F. Cover with Mocha Frosting (p. 192).

APPLESAUCE CAKE

1 cup sugar
½ cup fat
1 egg
1¾ cups flour
1 teaspoon soda
¼ teaspoon salt
1 teaspoon cinnamon

½ teaspoon cloves
1 cup raisins, finely cut and floured
1 cup currants or nuts, finely cut and floured
1 cup thick, strained applesauce, hot

■ Have all ingredients except applesauce at room temperature. Sift dry ingredients together into mixing bowl. Add fat and ⅔ cup hot applesauce. Beat 2 minutes. Add remaining applesauce (⅓ cup) and unbeaten egg. Beat 2 minutes. Bake at 365°F. One loaf 8 x 8 x 2 inches.

WHITE FRUIT CAKE

1 cup sugar
1 cup fat
2 egg yolks, well beaten
½ cup light-colored fruit juice, such as pineapple
1 tablespoon vanilla extract
½ teaspoon almond extract
3 cups flour
2 teaspoons baking powder
1 cup fresh, grated coconut

1 cup candied citron, sliced thin
1 cup white raisins
1 cup candied pineapple, cut fine
1½ cups blanched almonds, chopped or cut into strips
1 cup candied cherries, cut fine
7 egg whites, beaten stiff

■ Use Conventional Method of mixing (p. 178), adding fruit mixture just before folding in egg whites. Bake in oiled loaf pan, lined with wax paper and oiled again, at 250°F about 2¼ hours, then increase to 300°F, 15 minutes. If preferred, the cake may be steamed for 3¼ hours instead of baked. After steaming, it should be dried for 20 minutes at 275°F (slow oven). Two loaves, 9½ x 4½ x 3 inches.

CAKES 183

DARK FRUIT CAKE

½ pound light brown sugar
1 cup fat
5 eggs
1 tablespoon molasses
¼ cup preserves
½ lemon (grated rind and
juice)
½ orange (grated rind and
juice)
2 cups flour
½ teaspoon salt
½ teaspoon soda
1 teaspoon mace
½ teaspoon nutmeg

½ teaspoon allspice
1 teaspoon cinnamon
¼ teaspoon cloves
½ pound candied cherries,
sliced
½ pound white raisins
½ pound seeded raisins,
chopped
½ pound candied pineapple,
diced
½ pound citron, diced
1 pound currants
2 cups pecans, chopped
½ cup grape juice

■ Cream fat until light, add sugar gradually while creaming. Beat well. Add eggs one at a time, beating after each addition. Add molasses and preserves, then flour, salt, soda, and spices, which have been sifted together and added to the fruit and nuts. Last, stir in the fruit juice. Let stand 24 hours to ripen before baking.

Bake in oiled loaf pan that has been lined with wax paper and oiled again. Fill pan about ¾ full. Bake in a 250°F oven until cake cracks slightly on top and breaks away from sides of pan. This will take several hours. Three loaves, 9½ x 4½ x 3 inches.

EASY FRUIT CAKE

1 cup brown sugar
½ cup fat
1 egg, unbeaten
1 cup moist mincemeat
2 cups flour
3 teaspoons baking powder

¼ teaspoon salt
¼ teaspoon cinnamon
¼ teaspoon cloves
½ cup milk
½ cup candied fruit, chopped
¼ cup nuts, chopped

■ Use Conventional Method of mixing (p. 178), adding mincemeat after egg. Fold in fruit and nuts last. Bake in oiled loaf pan that has been lined with wax paper and oiled again. Bake at 350°F for 1¾ to 2 hours. One loaf, 9½ x 4½ x 3 inches.

QUICK GINGERBREAD

1 cup boiling water
1 cup fat
1 cup molasses
1 cup sugar
3 eggs, unbeaten
3 cups flour

¾ teaspoon salt
¾ teaspoon soda
½ teaspoon baking powder
1 teaspoon ginger
½ teaspoon cinnamon

■ Pour boiling water over fat in mixing bowl. When fat is melted, add molasses, sugar, and eggs. Stir until sugar dissolves. Put remaining dry ingredients into sifter. Sift directly into mixture. Beat with rotary beater until smooth. Mixture will be quite thin. Pour into 13½ x 9 x 1¾-inch, oiled pan. Bake at 350°F, 30 to 40 minutes. Remove from pan. Cut into squares. Serve with whipped cream, Lemon Sauce (p. 102), or applesauce.

HOME CAKE MIX

BASIC MIX

9 cups cake flour
5½ cups sugar
1 teaspoon salt

¼ cup baking powder
2 cups fat that does not
    require refrigeration

■   Sift dry ingredients together 3 times. Cut in fat with pastry blender until a fine, mealy consistency is obtained. Store mix in a covered container at room temperature. Approximately 15 cups.

TYPE OF CAKE	AMOUNT OF MIX (CUPS)	AMOUNT OF MILK (CUPS)	UNBEATEN EGGS	ADDITIONS
Chocolate	3½	¾	2	2 squares unsweetened chocolate 1 teaspoon flavoring
Plain	3½	⅔	2	1 teaspoon flavoring
Spice	3½	⅔	2	1 teaspoon vanilla ½ teaspoon cinnamon ¼ teaspoon each, cloves, nutmeg, and allspice
White	3½	⅔	4 whites	1 teaspoon almond extract
Yellow	3½	⅞	4 yolks	1 teaspoon lemon extract

■   Use "One-Bowl" method of mixing (p. 178). Bake 20 to 25 minutes at 365°F. Two round, 8-inch layers.

PINEAPPLE UPSIDE-DOWN CAKE

⅔ cup brown sugar
2 tablespoons corn syrup
3 tablespoons butter
4 large slices pineapple

1½ cups cake mix
⅓ cup milk
½ teaspoon vanilla
1 egg, unbeaten

■   Melt butter, sugar, and syrup over low heat; pour into greased layer pan. Place slices of pineapple in syrup, cool. Mix batter, and pour over pineapple. Bake in one 9-inch layer pan at 350°F for 35 minutes.

SPONGE CAKES

Sponge cakes are classified as white, such as angel food, or yellow, sometimes called true sponge cake. White sponge cakes use only the whites of eggs, whereas yellow sponge cakes contain whole eggs, beaten separately. A large proportion of egg whites with a corresponding quantity of cream of tartar contribute to optimum volume, texture, tenderness, and color in angel cake. Cream of tartar stabilizes the egg foam, tenderizes the structure and whitens flour pigments. Chiffon cakes are a type of sponge cake that contain oil and baking powder.

Characteristics of a Good Cake

Good sponge cake has a thin golden-brown crust, fine texture with thin cell walls, is moist and tender, and light in weight in proportion to its size.

Mixing

White Sponge or Angel Food Cake. Sift flour and measure. Mix ⅓ of the sugar with the flour, and sift. Beat egg whites until frothy, add salt and cream of tartar, and continue beating until eggs are just stiff enough to hold their shape. Add remaining sugar to eggs, 1 tablespoon at a time, beating it in with rotary beater. Add vanilla and continue beating 2 minutes. Add flour-sugar mixture gradually, folding in lightly. Continue folding 2 minutes after last addition of the mixture.

Yellow or True Sponge Cake. Sift flour and measure. Sift sugar as needed to insure fineness. Divide sugar into 3 parts. Sift ⅓ of the sugar with flour and salt. Beat egg yolks until thick and lemon colored. Add ⅓ of the sugar, about 2 tablespoons at a time, beating thoroughly. Beat egg whites until stiff but not dry, and add ⅓ of the sugar, about 2 tablespoons at a time, beating well after each addition. To the egg white foam add flavoring such as lemon juice and grated rind, and beat. Fold in egg yolk mixture. Add flour-sugar-salt mixture gradually, folding lightly. Continue folding 2 minutes after last addition. Do not stir or beat after flour is added, or cake will be tough. Work quickly so that air will not be lost.

General Suggestions

Use of Electric Mixer. For beating eggs use high speed. For folding in flour or flour-sugar mixture, use low speed. The time required for mixing with an electric mixer is about the same as for hand mixing.

Filling Pans. Fill special unoiled pans used only for sponge cake ⅔ full. Push batter well to sides and corners of pan, leaving a slight depression in the center. Tap pan sharply on the table once or twice or cut through the batter to break up large air pockets.

Baking. An oven temperature of 375°F for 25 to 30 minutes gives a tender, moist, yellow sponge cake of good volume. For angel food, 35 to 40 minutes usually is required. A preheated oven is recommended, and overbaking is to be avoided because it toughens and dries the cake.

Tests when Done. When cake is done it pulls away slightly from the sides of pan, and springs back quickly when pressed lightly with finger.

Care after Baking. Invert on wire rack to cool. When cake is cold, remove it from pan with aid of a spatula.

Cutting. Cut with 2 forks placed back to back, working gently. If preferred, a cake cutter may be used or cake may be cut with a very sharp knife dipped in water.

TRUE SPONGE CAKE

6 egg yolks	6 egg whites
1 cup sugar	1 cup cake flour
1 tablespoon lemon juice	¼ teaspoon salt
½ rind of lemon, grated	

■ Follow method of mixing for True Sponge Cake (p. 185). Bake at 375°F, 25 to 30 minutes in an unoiled 9-inch tube pan.

SUNSHINE CAKE

5 egg yolks (⅓ to ⅜ cup)	½ teaspoon each of almond
8 egg whites (1 cup)	and lemon extract
1½ cups sugar	2 tablespoons cold water
1 cup cake flour	½ teaspoon cream of tartar
½ teaspoon vanilla	½ teaspoon salt

■ Beat egg yolks until thick. Gradually add ½ cup of sugar, and beat well after each addition. Mix water and flavoring. Alternately add flour and liquid. Add cream of tartar and salt to egg whites, and beat until stiff. Gradually add 1 cup sugar to beaten whites, and beat thoroughly. Fold egg mixture into beaten whites. Bake at 375°F in an unoiled 10-inch tube pan.

YELLOW ANGEL FOOD (EGG YOLK SPONGE CAKE)

12 egg yolks	1 teaspoon vanilla
¾ cup minus 1 tablespoon	½ teaspoon lemon extract
boiling water	1 tablespoon lemon juice
¼ teaspoon salt	1 teaspoon grated lemon
1¼ cups sifted sugar	rind
1¾ cups cake flour	
1½ teaspoons baking	
powder	

■ Mix ½ cup sugar with 1 cup flour; sift 3 times. Add water and salt to egg yolks. Beat until very light, about 5 minutes. Add ¾ cup sugar to egg mixture, 1 tablespoon at a time, beating well while adding. Add flour-sugar mixture gradually, folding in lightly. Sift baking powder with remaining ¾ cup flour. Fold into egg mixture gradually, alternating with lemon juice and lemon rind. Add vanilla and lemon extract, and continue folding 2 minutes. Bake in a 10-inch unoiled tube pan at 375°F, approximately 35 minutes.

ANGEL FOOD CAKE

1¾ cups egg whites
1 cup cake flour
1 to 1½ teaspoons vanilla
1½ cups sugar

2 teaspoons cream of
tartar
¼ teaspoon salt

■ Follow method of mixing for Angel Food Cake (p. 185). Bake at 375°F for 35 to 40 minutes in unoiled 10-inch tube pan.

CHOCOLATE ANGEL FOOD. Substitute ¼ cup cocoa for an equal amount of flour in Angel Food Cake. Sift cocoa with flour and salt.

JELLY ROLL

¾ teaspoon baking powder
¼ teaspoon salt
4 eggs
¾ cup sifted sugar

¾ cup flour
1 teaspoon vanilla
1 cup jelly

■ Place baking powder, salt, and eggs in a bowl. Place over smaller bowl of warm water. Beat with rotary beater, adding sugar gradually and continuing beating until mixture is thick and lemon colored. Remove bowl from warm water. Fold in flour and vanilla. Turn into shallow pan, 10 x 15-inches, lined with wax paper. Bake at 400°F about 13 minutes. Cut crisp edges off cake quickly. Turn from pan at once onto cloth sprinkled with powdered sugar. Remove paper quickly. Spread with jelly. Roll while warm. Wrap in cloth, and cool on rack. Fifteen servings, 1-inch thick.

CHOCOLATE ROLL. Substitute 6 tablespoons cocoa for 6 tablespoons flour in Jelly Roll. Use all-purpose flour, as cake flour makes the product too tender. Substitute any desired frosting for jelly.

CREAM ROLL. Substitute for jelly any desired frosting, cream filling, or whipped cream, plain or with added chopped candied fruit.

LEMON JELLY ROLL. Substitute 1 teaspoon lemon juice and ½ teaspoon grated rind for vanilla in Jelly Roll.

ORANGE JELLY ROLL. Substitute orange juice and rind for lemon juice and rind in Lemon Jelly Roll.

SPICED JELLY ROLL. Sift ¼ teaspoon cinnamon, 1/16 teaspoon cloves, and 1/16 teaspoon allspice with flour in Jelly Roll. Substitute 1 teaspoon orange juice and ½ teaspoon grated orange rind for vanilla.

Frostings
and Fillings

FROSTINGS or icings of various kinds are used for decorating cakes and other food. Fillings are distinguished from frostings by the fact that they are used only on the inside of cake, whereas frostings are used both between the layers and on the outside.

FROSTINGS

Frostings may be either cooked or uncooked. In any case they should be adapted to the cake or other food on which they are to be used. If the cake is rich, frosting should be less so, and vice versa. Sponge cakes and rich cakes are often served without frostings.

To Frost a Cake

Cake may be frosted warm or cold, but frosting must be thicker if applied when cake is warm. If necessary, trim cake to make it smooth and symmetrical. Remove loose crumbs. Place cake on flat, smooth surface. Have frosting sufficiently thick that when put on cake it will almost hold its shape. If too soft it will run off and tend to soak into cake. Place enough frosting on center of cake to cover top and spread it to edge with 1 stroke of spatula. A rough, glossy surface generally is preferred to a smooth one unless a design is to be applied with a pastry tube.

Small Cakes. Frost small cakes either just on top or by dipping into bowl containing frosting of sufficient depth to cover cakes. Pieces cut

189

from a large sheet of cake are more difficult to frost all over than individual ones. For general use it is better to frost only the top of such cakes and to do this while they are still in sheet form.

Layer Cake. Layers for cake should fit together evenly. Cover top of bottom layer with frosting. Allow it to set slightly, then put on next layer. Repeat, finally covering top and sides. If layers show tendency to slip, fasten together with toothpicks or skewers.

Fancy Frosted Cakes. First, cover cake smoothly with plain frosting. Let stand until firm. If an elaborate design is to be applied, trace it on frosting with skewer. Then apply decorative frosting with pastry bag and tube (p. 6). If ingredients such as nuts, small candies, or candied fruit are to be used, apply them before frosting sets.

COOKED FROSTINGS

BOILED FROSTING

1 cup sugar	A few grains salt
½ cup water	1 egg white, beaten stiff
⅟₁₆ teaspoon cream of tartar	½ teaspoon flavoring

■ Cook sugar, salt, cream of tartar, and water to thread stage (p. 218), stirring only until sugar dissolves. Use precautions given under Fondant (p. 219) to prevent large crystals. Pour in fine stream on egg white, beating constantly. Flavor. Beat until just thick enough to spread. Good boiled frosting is thick, has a glossy surface, and is creamy and fluffy.

CARAMEL OR BURNT-SUGAR FROSTING. Add 2 tablespoons Caramel Syrup (p. 103) to sugar and water in Boiled Frosting.

SEVEN-MINUTE FROSTING

2 egg whites, unbeaten	1½ teaspoons light corn
1½ cups sugar	syrup
5 tablespoons cold water	1 teaspoon vanilla

■ Put all ingredients except vanilla in top of double boiler. Mix well by beating with rotary beater. Cook 7 minutes over boiling water, beating constantly with beater. Frosting is done when it stands in peaks. Remove from heat, flavor, beat until thick enough to spread.

MARSHMALLOW FROSTING. Add 24 quartered marshmallows to Seven-Minute Frosting when it is about half cooked. Complete cooking.

CARAMEL FUDGE FROSTING

1½ cups sugar	1 tablespoon butter or
A few grains salt	margarine
½ cup milk	1 teaspoon vanilla
¼ cup Caramel Syrup (p. 103)	

■ Cook sugar, salt, milk, and syrup to soft-ball stage (p. 218). Add fat and cool. Flavor. Beat until creamy and thick enough to spread.

BROWN SUGAR FROSTING. Substitute brown sugar for white, and omit caramel in Caramel Fudge Frosting.

CHOCOLATE FUDGE FROSTING. Substitute 1 to 2 squares unsweetened chocolate for caramel in Caramel Fudge Frosting.

BAKED FROSTING (TORTE)

1 egg white, beaten stiff	¼ cup nuts, chopped
½ cup brown sugar	

■ Make a Meringue (p. 216) of egg white and sugar. Spread on top of any desired cake batter. Spice cake batter is good. Sprinkle nuts on top. Bake at 350°F until cake is done. Enough for cake 8 inches square.

BROILED FROSTING

¼ cup butter or margarine	½ cup coconut and
½ cup brown sugar	½ cup nuts, chopped
¼ cup milk	
1 cup shredded coconut	

or

■ Melt butter, and add sugar, milk, and coconut. Mix well, and spread on top of hot cake. Place in broiler until coconut browns.

REFRIGERATOR FROSTING

2 squares bitter chocolate	1 cup powdered sugar
2 tablespoons hot water	½ cup butter or margarine
2 eggs, well beaten	

■ Cut chocolate into pieces, melt in double boiler, add water, and blend. Add eggs and sugar. Remove from heat, but allow to stand over hot water, stirring constantly until thickened, about 3 minutes. Cool to lukewarm (98°F). Add fat, 2 tablespoons at a time, stirring and blending after each addition. Cover tightly, and store in refrigerator. It will keep for some time. It stiffens upon standing, therefore it should be applied to warm cake to spread easily. Two cups.

UNCOOKED FROSTINGS

POWDERED SUGAR FROSTING

3½ cups sifted powdered sugar, packed slightly	⅓ cup butter or margarine, melted
¼ cup fruit juice, cream, or milk, preferably hot	Flavoring as desired

■ Add liquid gradually to sugar, mix well, add fat. Beat until soft and creamy. Flavor. Use at once. If desired, before flavoring cook for a few minutes over hot water to remove uncooked taste.

CHOCOLATE FROSTING. Use 2 tablespoons or more of melted unsweetened chocolate and 2 tablespoons water for liquid in Powdered Sugar Frosting. Flavor with vanilla.

GOLD FROSTING. Use 2 tablespoons orange juice, 1 teaspoon lemon juice, and 1 egg yolk mixed with 1 tablespoon water for liquid in Powdered Sugar Frosting. Omit fat. Flavor with grated orange rind.

LEMON FROSTING. Use 2 tablespoons cold water and 2 tablespoons lemon juice for liquid in Powdered Sugar Frosting. Add grated rind of 1 lemon.

MOCHA FROSTING. Substitute cold, strong coffee for liquid in Powdered Sugar Frosting. Add ¼ cup cocoa to sugar. If instant coffee is used, dissolve 1 teaspoon powder in ¼ cup hot water.

ORANGE FROSTING. Make as for Powdered Sugar Frosting, using orange juice for liquid. Add grated rind of 1 orange.

ORNAMENTAL FROSTING

1 egg white, beaten stiff	Powdered sugar, sifted
1 teaspoon lemon juice	

■ Add sugar gradually to egg white, beating well. As mixture thickens, add lemon juice, a little at a time. Continue adding sugar until mixture is stiff enough to spread. This may be used in a pastry bag or cake decorator.

CREAM CHEESE FROSTING

3-ounce package cream cheese	½ teaspoon vanilla or
1 tablespoon milk	other flavoring as
2½ cups sifted powdered	desired
sugar	

■ Blend cream cheese and milk. Add sugar gradually, blending in well. Add flavoring.

CHOCOLATE CREAM CHEESE FROSTING. Use basic recipe for Cream Cheese Frosting. After sugar is blended in, add 1 square unsweetened chocolate, melted and slightly cooled. Increase vanilla to 1 teaspoon.

ORANGE CREAM CHEESE FROSTING. Use 1 tablespoon orange juice instead of milk and ½ teaspoon grated orange rind in Cream Cheese Frosting. Omit vanilla.

FILLINGS

FRUIT PASTE

1 cup dates, figs, apricots,	1 cup sugar
prunes, or raisins	3 tablespoons milk
½ cup water	A few grains salt
1 tablespoon lemon juice	

■ Cut fruit into pieces. Mix ingredients, and cook to a paste, stirring as needed.

NUT PASTE

1½ cups blanched, unroasted
   almonds, ground
¾ cup sugar
½ teaspoon salt

¼ cup water
4 drops almond extract,
   if desired

■ Combine ingredients. Cook 20 minutes over boiling water in covered double boiler. Stir while cooling. Store in refrigerator in a covered jar.

CREAM FILLING

3 tablespoons flour
¼ cup sugar
⅛ teaspoon salt
1 cup milk
1 egg, beaten or

2 egg yolks, beaten
1 teaspoon butter or
   margarine
¼ teaspoon vanilla

■ Mix flour, sugar, and salt. Add milk slowly while stirring, and cook until well thickened. Add some of the hot mixture to the beaten egg, then add egg to mixture, stirring rapidly. Add fat, and continue cooking until egg thickens, about 5 minutes longer. Remove from heat. Stir in butter and vanilla.

CHOCOLATE CREAM FILLING. Add 1 square melted unsweetened chocolate to Cream Filling.

COCONUT CREAM FILLING. Add ½ cup dry, shredded or grated, fresh coconut to Cream Filling.

Cookies
and Small Cakes

COOKIES may be classified as dropped, rolled, spread or sheet, sliced or icebox, and pressed. Drop cookies are usually of a softer consistency than the other types.

DROP COOKIES

Drop cookies are made from medium-soft dough. Drop batter from a spoon in desired size, and shape on an oiled baking sheet. Leave ½ inch or more of space between cookies as they spread when baked. Most drop cookies are baked at 350 to 375°F, but occasionally 425°F (hot oven) may be used. Bake from 5 to 30 minutes, according to kind.

COCOA DROP COOKIES

1¾ cups flour	½ cup fat, room
½ teaspoon soda	temperature
½ teaspoon salt	1 egg
½ cup cocoa	¾ cup buttermilk
1 cup sugar	1 teaspoon vanilla

■ Sift flour, soda, salt, and cocoa together several times. Gradually add sugar to fat and cream thoroughly. Add egg and mix thoroughly. Stir in buttermilk and vanilla. Gradually stir in sifted dry ingredients. Drop small teaspoonfuls on lightly oiled baking sheet. Bake at 400°F about 8 minutes or until almost no imprint remains when cooky is touched lightly with finger.

Watch carefully as these burn easily. Frost with Chocolate Powdered Sugar Frosting (p. 192). Approximately 64 cookies.

GINGER CREAMS

¼ cup fat, room temperature	½ teaspoon soda
½ cup sugar	½ teaspoon salt
1 egg	1 teaspoon ginger
½ cup light molasses	½ teaspoon nutmeg
½ cup water	½ teaspoon cloves
2 cups flour	½ teaspoon cinnamon

■ Combine fat, sugar, egg, and molasses and mix thoroughly. Stir in water. Sift remaining ingredients together and stir into mixture. Chill dough. Drop rounded teaspoonfuls about 2 inches apart on oiled baking sheet. Bake at 400°F until almost no imprint remains when cooky is touched lightly with finger, approximately 7 to 8 minutes. While slightly warm frost cookies with Powdered Sugar Frosting (p. 191). Approximately 55 cookies.

ROLLED OATS DROP COOKIES

1 cup fat, melted	½ teaspoon soda
2 eggs, beaten	2 cups sugar
⅓ cup sour milk	¼ teaspoon cinnamon
3 cups rolled oats	1 cup raisins
3 cups flour	1 cup nuts, chopped
3 teaspoons baking powder	

■ Mix as for Butter Cake (p. 178), combining rolled oats with sifted dry ingredients. Drop batter by spoonfuls onto oiled baking sheet. Bake at 350 to 375°F. Approximately 72 cookies, 2 inches in diameter.

LADYFINGERS (SPONGE CAKE MIXTURE)

⅓ cup powdered sugar	¼ teaspoon vanilla
3 egg whites, beaten stiff	⅓ cup cake flour
2 egg yolks, beaten thick	⅛ teaspoon salt

■ Add sugar gradually to egg whites, beating constantly. Fold in egg yolks and vanilla, then sifted flour and salt. Shape the fingers 4 inches x 1 inch with a teaspoon, placing on baking sheet covered with ungreased paper. A pastry tube may be used if preferred, or mixture may be put into special ladyfinger pans if available. Sprinkle tops lightly with powdered sugar.

Bake at 375°F, 12 minutes. Remove from paper while hot. Serve plain, dusted with powdered sugar, frosted, or put together in pairs with jelly or frosting. Ladyfingers are easily coated by dipping them into frosting. Approximately 30 fingers.

FRUIT DROPS

1 cup fat
2 cups brown sugar
3 eggs
½ cup warm water
3½ cups flour

1 teaspoon soda
1 teaspoon cinnamon
1 teaspoon baking powder
1 cup raisins
1 cup nuts, chopped

■ Mix as for Butter Cake (p. 178). Drop batter by spoonfuls onto oiled baking sheet. Bake at 350°F. Approximately 72 cookies, 2 inches in diameter.

DATE DROP COOKIES

2 cups flour
⅔ teaspoon soda
1⅓ cups sugar
1 teaspoon cinnamon
1 cup dates, chopped

1 cup nuts, chopped
½ cup fat
2 eggs
¼ cup thin cream

■ Sift dry ingredients together. Add chopped dates and nuts. Mix as for Butter Cake (p. 178). Drop batter by teaspoonfuls onto oiled baking sheet. Bake at 350 to 375°F. Approximately 36 cookies, 2 inches in diameter.

CHOCOLATE CHIP COOKIES

½ cup fat
½ cup granulated sugar
¼ cup brown sugar
1 egg, beaten
1 tablespoon water
½ teaspoon vanilla

1¼ cups flour
¼ teaspoon salt
½ teaspoon soda
1 6-ounce package
    chocolate bits
½ cup nuts, chopped

■ Cream fat and sugar. Add egg, water, and vanilla. Beat well. Add flour sifted with salt and soda. Stir chocolate and nuts into mixture. Drop from teaspoon, 2 inches apart, on unoiled baking sheet. Bake at 375°F, 20 minutes. Approximately 36 cookies.

CARROT COOKIES

1 cup fat, room temperature
¾ cup sugar
1 cup cooked, mashed
    carrots
1 egg, unbeaten

1 teaspoon vanilla
2 cups flour
2 teaspoons baking powder
½ teaspoon salt

■ Cream fat and sugar until fluffy. Add mashed carrots, egg, and vanilla; mix well. Sift together flour, baking powder, and salt; add to carrot mixture. Mix well. Drop batter by teaspoonfuls on an oiled baking sheet. Bake at 350°F about 20 minutes. While warm frost with Orange Frosting (p. 192). Approximately 60 cookies.

COCONUT PUFFS

1 cup sugar
1 tablespoon cornstarch
3 egg whites, beaten stiff

2 cups shredded coconut
1 teaspoon vanilla

■ Mix sugar and cornstarch. Beat gradually into egg whites. Add coconut and vanilla. Drop batter by small spoonfuls on oiled baking sheet. Bake at 300°F until delicately brown. Remove from pan while hot. Approximately 30 puffs, 1½ inches in diameter.

CHOCOLATE COCONUT MACAROONS I

2 egg whites
¼ teaspoon salt
⅛ teaspoon cream of tartar
½ cup sugar
1 teaspoon vanilla

1 6-ounce package chocolate bits, melted
1½ cups shredded coconut
¼ cup nuts, chopped

■ Beat egg white until frothy, add salt and cream of tartar, and continue beating until egg whites are just stiff enough to hold their shape or form soft peaks. Add sugar gradually, beating it in well after each addition. Add vanilla, and continue beating until mixture is stiff and shiny. Add cooled, melted chocolate, mix in carefully. Fold in coconut and nuts if used. Drop batter by teaspoonfuls on well oiled baking sheet. Bake at 325°F for 20 minutes. Approximately 25 macaroons.

CHOCOLATE COCONUT MACAROONS II

2 squares unsweetened chocolate

1⅓ cups sweetened, condensed milk
3 cups shredded coconut

■ Melt chocolate, add milk and coconut. Drop batter by teaspoonfuls on oiled baking sheet. Bake at 300 to 325°F, 20 to 30 minutes. These macaroons may seem hard at first but should become "chewy" when stored in tight container. Approximately 45 macaroons.

CORNFLAKE KISSES

2 egg whites
¾ cup sugar
2 cups cornflakes
½ teaspoon vanilla

1 cup shredded coconut
or
½ cup coconut and
½ cup nuts, chopped

■ Beat egg whites until soft peaks form. Gradually add sugar with continued beating. Fold in remaining ingredients. Drop batter by teaspoonfuls on oiled baking sheet. Bake at 300 to 325°F, 12 to 15 minutes. Approximately 30 small kisses.

ROLLED COOKIES

General Directions. Rolled cookies are made from a stiff dough. The mixture should be as soft as can be handled, as excess flour makes cookies hard and dry. It is possible to handle cookies with less flour if, after mixing, dough is chilled 15 to 60 minutes or longer before rolling. Only a small amount of dough should be rolled at one time. It should be handled as lightly as possible, working on a board floured only enough to prevent sticking. The use of a pastry cloth facilitates handling. All trimmings are combined for last rolling, as they make less desirable cookies. Bake at 425°F unless cookies contain chocolate, molasses, or considerable fruit. Bake such cookies at 375°F, as they burn easily. Allow 5 to 15 minutes for baking, according to size.

SUGAR COOKIES

½ cup fat	1 teaspoon flavoring
¾ cup sugar	1¼ cups flour
1 tablespoon milk or cream	¼ teaspoon baking powder
1 egg	¼ teaspoon salt

■   Mix as for Butter Cake (p. 178). Chill dough. Roll ⅟₁₆-inch thick. Cut into desired shapes. Place on lightly oiled baking sheet, and sprinkle with sugar. Bake at 425°F for 5 to 7 minutes. Approximately 60, 2½-inch cookies. For variety, add spices, chocolate, nuts, or raisins in quantities and combinations desired.

FILLED COOKIES. Make Sugar Cookies. Roll thin. Place ½ of the cookies on baking sheet. Put a teaspoon of filling, Fruit Paste (p. 192) or mincemeat on each. Place another cooky on top. Press edges together. Prick top with fork. Bake at 400°F. Approximately 25 cookies.

GINGERSNAPS

¾ cup molasses	4 cups flour
¼ cup hot water	1 teaspoon soda
¾ cup fat	1 teaspoon ginger
½ cup sugar	1 teaspoon salt

■   Heat molasses, add water, and pour over fat. When melted, add sifted, dry ingredients. Chill. Roll thin, cut, and bake at 375°F. Approximately 75 cookies.

ROLLED OATS COOKIES

½ cup fat
1 cup sugar
1 egg, beaten—may be
  omitted
3 tablespoons sour cream
2 cups flour
2 cups rolled oats

¾ teaspoon soda
1 cup raisins
⅓ teaspoon salt
1 teaspoon cinnamon mixed
  with
3 tablespoons sugar

■   Mix as for Butter Cake (p. 178). Roll thin. Cut into desired shapes. Sprinkle with sugar-cinnamon mixture. Bake at 375 to 400°F. Approximately 60 cookies.

SAND TARTS

2 cups cake flour
1½ teaspoons baking powder
⅛ teaspoon salt

½ cup fat
1 cup sugar
1 egg, well beaten

■   Mix as for Butter Cake (p. 178). Chill, roll ⅛-inch thick on slightly floured board. Cut into 2½-inch rounds. Brush lightly with slightly beaten egg white. Sprinkle with mixture of sugar and cinnamon (2 tablespoons sugar to ½ teaspoon cinnamon). If desired, decorate with halves of split almonds. Bake on unoiled baking sheet at 375°F about 10 minutes. Approximately 72 cookies, 2½ inches in diameter.

SHEET COOKIES

Sheet cookies are spread in shallow, oiled pans to form a sheet. They are usually baked at 300 to 350°F. Sheet cookies often cut better when warm rather than hot. If the cookies are cooled in the pan, it is advisable to loosen them while they are still warm.

BROWNIES

⅓ cup fat
2 squares unsweetened
  chocolate
2 eggs, beaten
1 cup sugar

½ teaspoon salt
½ cup flour
1 teaspoon vanilla
½ cup nuts, chopped

■   Melt fat and chocolate together over hot water. Cool. Beat eggs until light, add sugar and salt, then add chocolate mixture, and blend. Add flour, vanilla, and nuts. Mix well. Bake at 350°F in an 8 x 8 x 2-inch pan for 30 to 35 minutes. Cool and cut into squares. Approximately 16 brownies.

BUTTERSCOTCH BROWNIES

¼ cup butter or margarine
1 cup brown sugar
1 egg
¾ cup flour

1 teaspoon baking powder
½ teaspoon salt
½ teaspoon vanilla
½ cup nuts, chopped

■ Melt fat over low heat. Remove from heat and stir in brown sugar until blended. Cool. Stir in egg. Stir in flour, baking powder, and salt which have been sifted together. Add vanilla and nuts. Bake in an oiled 8 x 8-inch square pan at 350°F about 20 to 25 minutes. Cut into bars while still warm. Approximately 16 brownies.

DATE CAKES

1 cup fat
1 cup brown sugar
½ cup water
2½ cups rolled oats

2½ cups flour
½ teaspoon salt
1 teaspoon soda

■ Mix as for Butter Cake (p. 178). Divide into 2 parts. Pat half of the mixture into 11 x 16-inch pan. Spread with Date Paste (p. 192). Cover with other half of the dough patted into shape. Bake at 375°F. Cut into 4 x 1-inch strips. Approximately 50 cookies.

DATE NUT BARS

1 cup sugar
2 eggs, beaten thick
1 cup flour
¼ teaspoon salt

1 teaspoon baking powder
1 cup dates, chopped
¾ cup nuts, chopped
1 teaspoon vanilla

■ Add sugar to eggs. Fold in flour, salt, and baking powder sifted together. Add dates, nuts, and vanilla. Spread in thin sheet on oiled 9 x 15-inch pan. Bake at 300 to 325°F. Cut into bars while warm. Roll in powdered sugar if desired. Approximately 24 bars.

FRUIT BARS. Add ¼ cup each candied orange peel, cherries, and pineapple to Date Bars. These bars will keep indefinitely.

COCOA APPLESAUCE FRUIT BARS

1 cup flour
¾ cup sugar
¾ teaspoon soda
¾ teaspoon salt
2 tablespoons cocoa
¼ teaspoon each nutmeg,
    cinnamon, cloves, allspice
¼ cup fat

¾ cup unsweetened apple-
    sauce
1 egg, unbeaten
⅔ cup dates, chopped
⅓ cup raisins
⅓ cup nuts, chopped
Topping: ¼ cup nuts, chopped
1 tablespoon sugar

■ Sift dry ingredients together 3 times, and place in mixing bowl. Add fat and ½ cup applesauce, and beat 2 minutes on low speed. Scrape down sides of bowl and beater. Add remainder of applesauce and egg, continue beating 2 minutes longer. Remove bowl from mixer, and fold in dates, raisins, and nuts. Pour batter into an 8-inch square pan, sprinkle with nut-sugar topping, and bake 40 to 45 minutes at 350°F. Cut into squares when cooled. Approximately 16 bars.

ICEBOX COOKIES

Icebox cookies are made from a stiff dough. This dough may be packed firmly into molds or placed on wax paper and shaped into rolls about 1½ to 2 inches in diameter. Dough may be hard to hold together, and the paper permits it to be pressed into desired shape. The paper also prevents drying during storage. Wrap paper tightly about dough, and shape into a smooth, even roll. If preferred, aluminum foil may be used in place of wax paper. Chill. When cooky dough is to be frozen, use freezer wrapping material. Icebox cooky dough will keep a week or longer. When cookies are desired, cut into ⅛-inch slices, using a sharp knife and a sawing motion. Place slices on unoiled baking sheet. Bake at 425°F, 5 to 15 minutes, according to kind.

VANILLA ICEBOX COOKIES

½ cup fat

1 cup sugar

1 egg, well beaten

½ teaspoon vanilla

2 cups flour

1½ teaspoons baking powder

¼ teaspoon salt

½ cup nuts, chopped

■ Combine as for Butter Cake (p. 178). Divide into portions. Shape each portion, chill, and bake according to general directions for Icebox Cookies (p. 202). Approximately 80 cookies, 2⅓ inches in diameter.

BUTTERSCOTCH ICEBOX COOKIES. Use ½ brown sugar and ½ white sugar, in Vanilla Icebox Cookies.

CHOCOLATE ICEBOX COOKIES. Add 1 square melted, unsweetened chocolate to Vanilla Icebox Cookies.

COCONUT ICEBOX COOKIES. Substitute ⅔ cup shredded coconut for nuts in Vanilla Icebox Cookies.

LEMON ICEBOX COOKIES. Add 1 tablespoon lemon juice and 1 tablespoon grated lemon rind to Vanilla Icebox Cookies. Omit vanilla.

ORANGE ICEBOX COOKIES. Add 1 tablespoon grated orange rind to Vanilla Icebox Cookies. Omit vanilla.

SPICE-NUT ICEBOX COOKIES. Sift ½ teaspoon cinnamon and ¼ teaspoon nutmeg with flour mixture in Vanilla Icebox Cookies.

PRESSED COOKIES (TEA CAKES)

Pressed cookies are a popular form of tea cakes. They are made by packing a chilled, rich cooky dough, usually of shortbread type, into a cooky press. The dough is then forced through a forming plate following directions for press used. Baking sheets need not be oiled because of large amount of fat in mixture. Pressed cookies are baked at 400 to 425°F.

SPRITZ COOKIES

1 cup butter or margarine
¾ cup sugar
1 egg, unbeaten
1 teaspoon almond extract

2½ cups flour
½ teaspoon baking powder
⅛ teaspoon salt

■   Mix as for Butter Cake (p. 178). Dough should be quite stiff. Form into cookies with cooky press. Bake at 400°F, 10 to 12 minutes. Approximately 50 cookies, depending upon forming plate used.

Cookies may be decorated with colored sugar, hard candies, preserved ginger, gumdrops, nuts, or angelica.
CHOCOLATE SPRITZ. Make as for Spritz Cookies, substituting vanilla for almond extract, adding 6 tablespoons cocoa and reducing flour to 2¼ cups. Sift cocoa with flour mixture.

MOLDED COOKIES

MYSTERY COOKIES

1 cup butter or margarine
2 cups pecans, finely chopped
4 teaspoons sugar

2 cups flour
1 teaspoon vanilla

■   Cream fat, add nuts, sugar, flour, and vanilla. Roll into small balls 1-inch in diameter. Bake on oiled sheet at 350°F, 30 to 40 minutes. Roll in powdered sugar while warm. Approximately 50 cookies.

GUMDROP COOKIES

1 cup fat
1 cup brown sugar
1 cup white sugar
2 eggs
1 teaspoon vanilla
2 cups flour
1 teaspoon baking powder

½ teaspoon soda
½ teaspoon salt
2 cups rolled oats
1 cup coconut
1 cup gumdrops, cut in
   small pieces

■   Thoroughly cream fat and sugar, add eggs, and beat well. Add vanilla. Sift dry ingredients together, and add to cream mixture. Add oats, coconut, and gumdrops. Roll into small balls. Place on oiled cooky sheet. Press flat with fork. Bake at 375°F, 10 minutes. Approximately 72 cookies.

PEANUT BUTTER COOKIES

½ cup fat
½ cup granulated sugar
½ cup brown sugar
1 egg, unbeaten

½ cup peanut butter
1 teaspoon soda
1½ cups flour

■ Mix as for Butter Cake (p. 178), adding peanut butter after egg. Roll into balls not more than 1-inch in diameter. Place balls on unoiled baking sheet. Flatten with fork. Bake at 425°F, 10 to 12 minutes. Approximately 30 cookies.

MOLASSES CRINKLES

2½ cups flour
2 teaspoons soda
¼ teaspoon salt
½ teaspoon cloves
1 teaspoon cinnamon
1 teaspoon ginger

¾ cup fat, room temperature
1 cup brown sugar
1 egg
¼ cup molasses

■ Sift flour, soda, salt, cloves, cinnamon, and ginger together. Place fat, brown sugar, egg, and molasses in mixing bowl and mix until light and fluffy. Stir in sifted dry ingredients. Chill dough. Roll dough into balls ⅔ to ¾-inch in diameter. Dip tops in sugar. Place balls sugar side up, 1½ to 2 inches apart on oiled baking sheet. Bake at 375°F until set but not hard. Approximately 80 cookies.

Pastry

PASTRY, as usually defined, is a stiff dough composed of flour, salt, fat, and water and is used for pies, tarts, patty shells, and the like. In its broadest sense, pastry includes all fancy breads, cakes, and cake-like mixtures, as well as pies and tarts.

CLASSES OF PASTRY

Plain Pastry. The fat usually is cut into the flour or it may be combined with heated liquid in so-called hot-water pastry. Plain pastry is used largely for pie crusts and tarts.

Puff Pastry. For puff pastry most of the fat is worked into the dough by a process of folding and rolling. Puff pastry rises when baked, therefore it is used for top crusts of pies, for rims where extra height is desired, for tarts, patty shells, and various similar purposes.

QUALITIES OF GOOD PASTRY

Qualities of good pastry are tenderness, flakiness, and a golden-brown color. The center should be slightly less brown. Puff pastry should possess lightness as well as tenderness and flakiness. Good pastry has a rough, blistery surface rather than a smooth, firm one. It should cut easily with a fork yet not crumble when served.

Tenderness depends largely upon kind of flour and amount of fat and water used. Excess fat increases tenderness, making a crumbly pastry, and excess water gives a tough product. Too much handling or use of too much flour when rolling toughens pastry.

Flakiness is determined by kind of flour and fat, amount of water used, the size of the fat particles, and the temperature of baking. Small pieces of fat in the dough at time of rolling impart a flaky quality as the fat melts during baking. Melting provides space where steam can collect to separate pastry into layers and form flakes.

INGREDIENTS USED IN PASTRY

Fat. Almost any fat may be used. Lard, hydrogenated fats, and oils all give good results. However, different methods of manipulation may be necessary for different amounts and kinds of fat. When less than the usual proportion of fat is used, it should be well blended with the flour, or excess water will be needed to form dough.

Flour. Either all-purpose or cake flour may be used; all-purpose flour is more desirable for a flaky pastry. Cake flour gives a tender but less flaky product, which is more difficult to handle.

Water. Cold or hot water may be used for pastry. Cold water is best for pastry made using a solid fat. Hot water melts fat, and fat becomes better distributed so that crumbliness results rather than flakiness. The amount of water required varies. Less water is needed with soft fat, soft wheat flour, a warm temperature, or a mixture in which fat and flour are well blended. More water is needed when it is added slowly. There should never be more than just enough water to make ingredients stick together.

Egg Whites. Egg whites may be added with the water when mixing, using 1 egg white to 2 cups flour. This combination has been found to reduce soaking of crust in fruit and custard pies.

GENERAL SUGGESTIONS

Mixing. Sift flour and salt together. Cut fat into flour and salt mixture until particles are size of peas. Mix with a pastry blender, with a fork, or with fingers. Sprinkle just enough water over fat-flour mixture to make particles stick together, then stir lightly with a fork. Push portions that cling together to one side of bowl each time before more water is added. Mixture is sufficiently wet when particles will just cling together and form a ball when pressed lightly between palms of the hands. Such a dough is neither sticky nor crumbly. Exact quantities of water cannot be stated, as amount varies with temperature, fineness of division of ingredients, and rate at which water is added.

Preparing for Pan. Refrigerating dough for 10 minutes may facilitate rolling. Roll only enough pastry for 1 crust at a time. Allow more for the bottom crust than for the top. Sprinkle flour on board or pastry cloth. Use only enough flour to prevent sticking. Pat and roll out dough as lightly and as nearly circular as possible, making pastry about ⅛-inch thick. Do not push rolling pin off onto board, as it makes pastry of uneven thickness. When pastry is a little larger than pan, fold ½ over the other and place carefully and loosely in pan. If the pastry breaks it is better to press the broken edges together than to reroll.

Roll top crust in same way, making it smaller and cutting openings in it to allow for escape of steam. Place filling in pie, and lay top crust in position, then press edges firmly together. Knife handle may be held under pan while trimming to make pastry come as far over the edge as possible. This tends to prevent undue shrinkage.

If a single crust is to be baked before filling, it should be fitted into the pan loosely. Trim and prick with a fork to prevent loss of shape. The crust will often be more satisfactory if it is baked on the outside of pan and is pricked as suggested. Another method to insure a well-shaped crust when baked is to place a pie pan identical in size and shape on top of fitted crust. This may be removed after crust is set, to permit browning.

Baking. Pastry shells should be baked at 450°F until firm, dry, and golden brown. Two crust pies may be baked at 450°F for 10 minutes then at 375°F until done, or at a constant temperature of 400 or 425°F.

PIE CRUSTS AND PIES

PLAIN PASTRY

1½ cups flour	½ cup hydrogenated shortening
⅓ cup lard or	5 to 6 tablespoons cold water

■ Follow general directions for mixing pastry (p. 206). One 9-inch 2-crust pie.

CHEESE PASTRY. Mix ½ cup grated cheese with flour-fat mixture of Plain Pastry before water is added. Use for Apple or Pumpkin Pie.

ORANGE PASTRY. Add 2 teaspoons grated orange rind to dry ingredients for Plain Pastry. Substitute orange juice for water. Use for Cream, Banana, or Pineapple Pie.

WATER WHIP PASTRY. Substitute ⅓ cup boiling water for cold water. The minimum amount of fat is sufficient. Add to water. Beat until creamy and fluffy. Add to sifted dry ingredients, mixing lightly.

WATER PASTE PASTRY

2 cups flour	¼ cup water
1 teaspoon salt	⅔ cup fat

■ Sift flour and salt together. Remove ⅓ cup, and mix to a paste with water. Cut fat in remaining flour until particles are size of small peas. Stir flour paste into flour-fat mixture to make a dough. Form into a ball. Use as desired. One large 2-crust pie.

STIR AND ROLL PASTRY (WITH OIL)

2¼ cups flour	½ cup + 1 tablespoon oil
1 to 1½ teaspoons salt	
¼ cup + 1½ teaspoons cold milk	

■   Sift flour and salt into bowl. Pour milk and oil into a measuring cup (do not stir); add all at once to flour. Stir lightly with fork until well mixed. Form into smooth ball. Place ½ of the pastry, flattened slightly, between squares of wax paper. To prevent slipping of wax paper, place it on working surface wiped with damp cloth. With short, gentle strokes, roll to form a circle ⅛-inch thick. If bottom paper wrinkles, turn, roll on the other side. Peel off top paper. If pastry breaks, press edges together, or press piece of pastry over torn place. Lift bottom paper and pastry. Place, with paper side up, in 8- or 9-inch pie plate. Carefully peel off paper. Gently fit pastry into plate. Roll top in the same way. You may substitute 5 tablespoons plus 2 teaspoons ice water for milk. In this case, beat with oil until thickened and creamy. Add to flour all at one time then proceed as above. Makes 1 8- or 9-inch 2-crust pie, 2 8- or 9-inch pie shells, or 8 to 10 medium tart shells.

PUFF PASTRY

2 cups butter or margarine	2 teaspoons salt
4 cups flour	Ice water

■   Wash butter in cold water until pliable and waxy. Reserve 2 tablespoons. Shape remainder into a flat, circular piece. Pat between folds of clean cloth until dry. Chill. Sift salt with flour, then cut the 2 tablespoons butter into it. Add ice water to form a stiff pastry. Turn onto floured board. Knead 1 minute. Chill. Roll pastry ¼-inch thick, making as nearly square as possible. Flour outside of chilled butter, and place in center of lower ½ of the pastry. Fold upper ½ of the pastry over it. Press edges firmly together, enclosing as much air as possible. Fold 1 side of pastry over and other side under enclosed butter, making 3 layers. Chill. Pound, and roll ¼-inch thick; keep pastry square, and flour board and rolling pin as necessary. Fold from ends to center, again making 3 layers. Chill. Repeat rolling and chilling twice, turning pastry ½ the way round each time and chilling whenever fat begins to soften. After fourth rolling, fold from ends to center, then double, making 4 layers. Roll to desired thickness. Shape with floured cutter. Place on pan covered with heavy paper. Chill. Bake 475°F until delicately brown, then reduce temperature to 250°F and continue baking until golden brown and crisp.

CRUMB PASTRY

⅓ cup butter or margarine, melted
1¼ cups fine crumbs (graham crackers, vanilla, or chocolate wafers)

3 tablespoons sugar, if desired

■ Melt fat, add crumbs, and sugar, if used. Mix well. Make ⅛-inch layer of crumb mixture on bottom and sides of pie pan, pressing evenly and firmly. Chill.

FRENCH PASTRY

3 cups flour
1½ teaspoons salt
1 cup lard

1 egg
4 tablespoons water
1 teaspoon vinegar

■ Sift flour and salt. Cut in lard. Beat egg with water and vinegar. Sprinkle over dry ingredients. Mix with fork. Form into ball, flatten, and allow to stand 10 minutes before rolling out. Three 8-inch crusts.

CHEESE STRAWS

Plain pastry (1½ cups flour, p. 207)

1 cup grated cheese
Cayenne pepper

■ Roll pastry ¼ inch thick. Sprinkle with cheese and lightly with cayenne. Fold over. Roll again. Repeat 3 times. Cut into ¼ x 5-inch strips. Bake at 450°F. Approximately 50 to 60 straws.

CINNAMON STICKS

Roll Plain or Puff Pastry (pp. 207, 208) ⅛-inch thick. Spread with soft butter or margarine. Sprinkle with a 6:1 mixture of sugar and cinnamon. Cut into 1 x 4-inch sticks or other desired shapes. Bake at 450°F, 10 minutes or until brown.

APPLE PIE

4 cups sliced apples (6 to 7 medium-sized)
¾ to 1 cup sugar
2 to 4 tablespoons flour

1 teaspoon cinnamon or nutmeg
1⅓ tablespoons butter or margarine

■ Peel apples, remove cores, and slice thin. If apples are dry, sprinkle with a little water. Combine sugar, flour, and spice. Add apples, and mix. Line pie pan with Plain Pastry (p. 207), and heap with apple mixture. Dot with butter or margarine. Cover with top crust, and bake at 400°F approximately 50 to 60 minutes. One 9-inch pie.

FRESH FRUIT PIE

3 cups prepared fresh fruit
½ to 1 cup sugar, according to acidity of fruit
2 tablespoons flour or granular tapioca or

1½ tablespoons cornstarch
1⅓ tablespoons butter or margarine

■ Line pie pan with Plain Pastry (p. 207). Combine sugar and thickening agent. Add fruit, and mix. Fill pastry-lined pie pan with fruit. Dot with butter or margarine. Cover with top crust, and bake at 400°F approximately 40 to 50 minutes. One 8-inch pie.

COOKED FRUIT PIE

2 tablespoons flour or granular tapioca or
1½ tablespoons cornstarch
Sugar, as desired, depending on sweetness of fruit

¾ cup juice drained from fruit
3 cups cooked fruit, drained
1⅓ tablespoons butter or margarine

■ Line pie pan with Plain Pastry (p. 207). Combine sugar and thickening agent. Stir in juice, and cook until clear. Place fruit in pastry-lined pie pan, and pour in thickened juice. Dot with the butter or margarine. Cover with top crust. Bake at 425°F for 30 to 40 minutes. One 9-inch pie.

RHUBARB PIE

1⅓ cups sugar
4 tablespoons flour
4 cups rhubarb, cut into ½-inch pieces

1⅓ tablespoons butter or margarine

■ Combine sugar and flour, and mix with rhubarb. Line pie pan with Plain Pastry (p. 207), and fill with rhubarb. Dot with the butter or margarine. Cover with top crust, and bake at 400°F approximately 40 to 50 minutes. One teaspoon of grated orange rind may be added to rhubarb if desired. One 9-inch pie.

CRANBERRY PIE

Line pie pan with Plain Pastry (p. 207). Fill with Cranberry Sauce (p. 39). Roll pastry for upper crust. Cut into ½-inch strips, arranging them in lattice fashion across top. Bake at 425°F approximately 30 minutes. One 9-inch pie.

MINCE PIE

Line pie pan with Plain Pastry (p. 207). Fill with 3⅓ cups mincemeat. Cover with top crust. Bake at 425°F approximately 30 to 40 minutes. One 9-inch pie.

MINCEMEAT

1 pound lean beef	¼ teaspoon cloves
¼ pound suet	½ teaspoon mace
2 pounds tart apples	½ teaspoon nutmeg
1 pound currants	1 teaspoon salt
1 pound raisins	2 cups sugar
¼ pound citron	1 cup meat stock
¼ cup candied orange peel	1 cup cider or fruit juice
½ teaspoon cinnamon	

■ Cook beef, and cool it. Remove membrane from suet. Pare and core apples. Grind beef, suet, and fruit. Mix all ingredients. Cook slowly until apples are tender. Pack into sterilized jars. Seal and refrigerate. Approximately 3 quarts.

DEEP-DISH APPLE PIE

⅔ cup sugar	1 to 2 tablespoons water
1 tablespoon flour	1 tablespoon butter or margarine
2½ cups pared and sliced tart apples	

■ Combine sugar and flour. Mix with sliced apples. Arrange apples in a 12 x 7 x 2-inch baking dish, with fruit slightly heaped in center to hold top crust. Sprinkle water over fruit, and dot with butter or margarine. Lemon juice, cinnamon, or nutmeg may be added if desired. Cover with Plain Pastry (p. 207) that is cut ½-inch larger than top of dish. Press pastry to edge of baking dish. Bake at 400°F until apples are tender, approximately 35 to 45 minutes. Six servings.

DEEP-DISH BERRY PIE. Wash and pick over berries (raspberries, blackberries, blueberries). Prepare as for Deep-Dish Apple Pie. For 2½ cups fruit, use ½ cup sugar and 2 tablespoons flour.

CUSTARD PIE

Line deep pie pan with Plain Pastry (p. 207), taking care that no air is enclosed. Fill with Custard (p. 153) made by using 2 to 3 eggs to 1½ cups milk. Bake at 450°F approximately 10 minutes, until crust begins to set. Reduce temperature to 325°F, and bake approximately 30 minutes longer or until custard is firm. Filling must not be allowed to boil at any time, or pie will be watery. One 7-inch pie.

To prevent soaked crust, bake custard filling and crust separately in pans of same size with sloping sides. Use 3 eggs to 1 cup milk for filling. Cook as for Baked Custard (p. 154). Cool until pan is just warm to touch. Run spatula around edge, tilt, shake, and slide custard from pan into crust. If edge is not perfectly smooth, shredded coconut may be sprinkled around outer edge of pie. Egg white as a pastry ingredient (p. 206) has been found to reduce soaking of crust.

COCONUT CUSTARD PIE. Add 1 cup dry, shredded coconut to filling for Custard Pie.

PUMPKIN PIE

1½ cups cooked pumpkin
¾ cup sugar
½ teaspoon salt
½ teaspoon ginger
1 teaspoon cinnamon

¼ teaspoon nutmeg
¼ teaspoon cloves
3 eggs, slightly beaten
1¼ cups milk
¾ cup evaporated milk

■ Thoroughly combine pumpkin, sugar, salt, and spices. Add eggs, milk, evaporated milk; blend.

Pour into pastry-lined pie pan. Bake at 450°F for 10 minutes, then at 325°F approximately 45 minutes or until mixture does not adhere to a knife. One 9-inch pie.

SQUASH PIE. Substitute squash pulp for pumpkin.

SWEET POTATO PIE. Substitute sweet potato pulp for pumpkin.

CREAM PIE

½ cup sugar
4 tablespoons flour
½ teaspoon salt
1½ cups milk, scalded

2 egg yolks, well beaten
1 tablespoon butter or
   margarine
½ teaspoon vanilla

■ Mix dry ingredients. Add milk slowly while stirring. Cook in double boiler or over low direct heat, stirring gently, until well thickened. Pour over egg yolks, stirring rapidly. Add fat. Cook until egg yolk is thickened, about 2 minutes. Remove from heat, and flavor. Pour into baked pie shell. Cover with Meringue (p. 216). Brown at 450°F. One 7-inch pie.

CHOCOLATE CREAM PIE. Make as for Cream Pie, using 3½ tablespoons flour and adding 1 to 1½ squares unsweetened chocolate, melted.

COCONUT CREAM PIE. Make as for Cream Pie, adding 1 cup shredded coconut to cooked filling.

FRUIT CREAM PIE. Make as for Cream Pie, adding 1 cup chopped dates or 2 medium-sized bananas, sliced, to cooked filling.

BUTTERSCOTCH PIE

2 tablespoons butter or margarine
1 cup brown sugar
1 pinch salt

4 tablespoons flour
1½ cups milk
2 egg yolks, slightly beaten
½ teaspoon vanilla

■ Melt fat. Mix sugar, salt, and flour; add to melted fat. Mix well. Add milk. Cook over hot water or direct heat stirring gently, until thick and smooth. Cook 15 minutes longer. Pour a little custard over egg yolks then add the mixture to the remainder of the custard while stirring. Cook 2 minutes longer. Cool slightly. Pour into baked pie shell. Cover with Meringue (p. 216). Brown at 450°F. One 7-inch pie.

LEMON FILLING I

⅓ cup flour or
3⅓ tablespoons cornstarch
¾ cup sugar
1 pinch salt
1½ cups boiling water

2 egg yolks, slightly beaten
1 lemon rind, grated
1 tablespoon butter or margarine
4 tablespoons lemon juice

■   Mix flour, sugar, and salt, then add hot water gradually while stirring. Cook over boiling water or direct heat until thickened, stirring as needed to prevent lumping. Cook 5 minutes longer, then pour slowly over egg yolks. Add fat, lemon juice, and rind and cook until egg yolk is thickened. If a double boiler is used allow longer time for cooking. Cover with Meringue (p. 216). Brown at 450°F. One 7-inch pie.

LEMON FILLING II

¼ cup lemon juice
1 lemon rind, grated
⅛ teaspoon salt
1 cup sugar
4 egg yolks, beaten thick
    and lemon colored

2 tablespoons butter or
    margarine
4 egg whites, beaten stiff

■   Add lemon juice, rind, salt, and ½ of sugar to egg yolks. Cook in double boiler, stirring until thickened. Add butter. Cool. Beat remaining sugar gradually into egg whites. Fold ½ of this meringue into yolk mixture. Pour into baked shell. Cover top with remaining meringue. Brown at 450°F. If desired, all the meringue may be folded into yolk mixture. It is then baked as above until puffed and brown. One 7-inch pie.

LEMON CHIFFON

4 egg yolks, beaten
1 cup sugar
½ cup lemon juice
⅛ teaspoon salt
1 tablespoon gelatin, softened in

1 cup cold water
½ lemon rind, grated
4 egg whites
1 cup heavy cream, whipped,
    if desired

■   Cook egg yolks, ½ cup sugar, lemon juice, and salt in double boiler. Stir while cooking until thick and creamy. Remove from heat, add gelatin, and lemon rind. Cool. Beat remaining ½ cup sugar gradually into egg whites until stiff. Fold into gelatin mixture when it begins to thicken. Pour into baked Pastry or Crumb Shell (p. 209). Chill 2 to 3 hours. Cover with whipped cream. One 9-inch pie.

BANBURY TARTS

Plain Pastry (1½ cups flour, p. 207)
1 cup raisins, chopped
1 cup sugar
3 tablespoons cracker crumbs
1 tablespoon butter or margarine, melted

1 egg, slightly beaten
3 tablespoons lemon juice
1 lemon rind, grated
⅛ teaspoon salt

■ Roll pastry ⅛-inch thick. Cut into 3-inch squares. Mix remaining ingredients in order listed. Put 2 teaspoons mixture on each pastry square. Wet edges with cold water. Fold over to form triangle. Press edges together with a fork. Prick top several times. Bake at 425°F. Eight to 10 tarts.

Meringues

MERINGUES are stabilized egg white foams and are classified according to texture as soft or hard. Soft meringues are used as topping on cream pies, tarts, or puddings. For variation, they may be folded into pie fillings or puddings. Hard meringues serve as the base for a filling such as fruit or ice cream.

The ingredients used in both types of meringues are egg whites, salt, sugar, cream of tartar, and flavoring. Hard meringues contain more sugar than soft meringues. Meringues should be beaten at high speed throughout the preparation of the foam. Sugar and cream of tartar increase the stability of egg white foams and increase the beating time. The amount of sugar used per egg white varies from 2 to 3 tablespoons depending on the type of meringue desired. Two tablespoons of sugar gives the most stable meringue with the least amount of leakage. Two and one-half tablespoons produces a meringue of good appearance and excellent cutting quality. Three tablespoons of sugar per egg white results in increased tenderness and leakage. Soft meringues are better if the egg whites are beaten until they hold a soft peak before the addition of sugar than if not beaten at all or beaten to the stiff but not dry stage.

Soft meringues spread on warm fillings rather than cold result in less leakage and slippage of the meringue on the filling. Soft meringues may be baked over a wide range of temperatures (325 to 425°F) if the baking time is varied. A higher internal temperature in the meringue and less leakage is obtained with the lower than with the higher oven temperatures. Meringues baked at higher oven temperatures are less sticky and more tender than those baked at lower oven temperatures. Soft meringues to be used as garnishes for puddings may be floated on water for baking. A baking temperature of 250°F or lower is used for hard meringues.

SOFT MERINGUES

2 egg whites
⅛ teaspoon salt
⅛ teaspoon cream of tartar

4 to 6 tablespoons sugar
¼ teaspoon vanilla

■   Beat egg whites with salt and cream of tartar. After the foam forms soft peaks add sugar gradually. Continue beating until stiff but not dry. Flavor. Spread on food and bake at 325°F for 16 to 18 minutes or at 425°F for 6 to 7 minutes or until delicately brown. Sufficient for 1 9-inch pie.

HARD MERINGUES

4 egg whites (½ cup)
¼ teaspoon salt
¼ teaspoon cream of tartar
1 cup sugar

½ teaspoon vanilla
1 cup nuts, chopped, if
   desired

■   Beat egg whites with salt. Add cream of tartar when the egg whites are frothy. After the foam forms soft peaks, add sugar gradually. Continue beating until stiff. Flavor. Cover baking sheet with brown paper or dust oiled baking sheet with cornstarch. Mark into circles or shapes. Kisses are usually 2-inches or less in diameter; meringues are often twice this size. Drop meringue mixture into desired spaces on baking sheet. Shape meringues into flat circles with a spoon or pastry bag and tube. Bake 1 hour at 250°F. Remove from paper or pan while hot to avoid breaking. Meringues may be stored in refrigerator 24 hours for ease in cutting and eating. Approximately 16 meringues.

ANGEL PIE. Prepare as for Hard Meringues. Bake as a pie shell. Cool, and fill with Bavarian Cream (p. 162), Gelatin Whip (p. 160), or Gelatin Sponge (p. 162) of any flavor. If whipped cream is not used in filling, pie may be frosted with it.

DATE KISSES. Prepare as for Hard Meringues, fold in 1 cup finely chopped dates. Shape into small mounds with a teaspoon. Bake.

NUT KISSES. Prepare as for Hard Meringues, fold in 1½ cups finely chopped nuts or crushed nut brittle. Shape into small mounds with a teaspoon. Bake.

Candy and Nuts

CANDY

Candies are classified as crystalline and noncrystalline. Crystalline candies, such as fudge, fondant, and panocha, contain small sugar crystals that should be imperceptible to the tongue. Noncrystalline candies, such as butterscotch and caramels, should be free from crystals and may be "chewy" in texture.

General Suggestions for Candy Making

Utensils. Pans chosen for candy making should be large enough to allow space for "boiling up." A pan made of heavy gauge metal is desirable.

Wooden spoons are preferable for stirring candy, as they do not scratch the pan and do not get hot when stirring. A marble slab provides a large, smooth surface, which is advantageous for working candy; but a baking sheet, large platter, or other smooth surface may be substituted. A thermometer is desirable to use in making candy.

Ingredients. Cane and beet sugar are equally good. When brown sugar is used, a light brown is preferable, as the flavor is more delicate. For the same reason, light-colored molasses is desirable. The flavor of butter is pleasing in candies. When oiling pans, use butter or margarine.

Substitutions for certain ingredients may be made as indicated in the table on p. 219.

217

Tests for Stages of Sugar Cookery

Tests for stages of sugar cookery are made with a thermometer or by dropping a small portion of syrup into cold water. Each stage corresponds to a temperature range as indicated by a thermometer. Temperatures, however, vary with altitude and with ingredients used, therefore temperature ranges should be determined for each recipe in a given locality. Temperatures should be decreased 1°F for each increase of 500 feet in elevation. On humid or rainy days cook to a temperature approximately 2°F higher than usual. Temperatures listed in the accompanying table are correct at sea level for a mixture of sugar and water but are still subject to variations if other ingredients are used.

TEST	DESCRIPTION OF TEST	TEMPERATURE OF SYRUP AT SEA LEVEL (INDICATING CONCENTRATION DESIRED) °F
Thread	Mixture spins 2-inch thread when dropped from fork or spoon	230 to 234
Soft ball	Mixture forms soft ball when dropped into cold water but loses shape when removed from water	234 to 240
Firm ball	Mixture forms firm ball in cold water and holds shape when removed from water	244 to 248
Hard ball	Mixture forms hard ball in cold water	250 to 266
Soft crack	Mixture will separate into threads when it strikes cold water and will crack or break when crushed with fingers	270 to 290
Hard crack	Mixture is very brittle when dropped into cold water and will not stick to teeth	300 to 310
Caramel	Mixture passes hard-crack stage and begins to brown	320 to 348

CRYSTALLINE CANDIES

Fine crystals are desired in crystalline candy. Crystalline candies should not be stirred after the sugar is dissolved. Sugar crystals that form on the sides of the pan can be removed with a clean, wet cloth or by tightly covering the pan for a few minutes to allow steam to dissolve the crystals. The presence of a single crystal in the syrup after boiling may start a chain of crystals.

When the candy syrup has been cooked to the desired concentration, it is poured from the pan without scraping and is cooled without stirring. Scraping or stirring tends to start crystallization. The extent to which syrup is allowed to cool is the principal factor that determines the number and size of crystals that form at one time. If syrup is beaten while hot, relatively few crystals form at one time and they increase in size; therefore the candy is coarse and grainy in texture. If syrup is allowed to cool until lukewarm (104°F) before it is beaten, many tiny crystals form at one time and the candy is smooth and creamy. Beating is continued until crystallization is complete, in order to prevent clumping of small crystals, which also produces a grainy candy.

The presence of other substances in sugar syrup helps to produce a creamy candy by interfering with the tendency of small crystals to group together to form aggregates. There are two methods of introducing these interfering agents. One method is to add an acid ingredient such as cream of tartar, vinegar, or lemon juice. When acid and sugar syrup are cooked, a small portion of the sugar (sucrose) is converted to a mixture of fructose and glucose called invert sugar. Fructose also absorbs moisture from air and tends to prevent drying during storage of candy. The second method is to add small amounts of butter, cream, corn syrup, chocolate, or egg white directly to the sugar syrup. Cream of tartar or egg white make the fondant whiter than other interfering agents. In the accompanying table proportions of these ingredients are suggested for one cup of sugar.

Approximate Equivalents to Prevent Crystallization in Candy Making

INGREDIENTS	AMOUNT
Cream of tartar	$\frac{1}{16}$ teaspoon
Vinegar	$\frac{1}{2}$ teaspoon
Lemon juice	$\frac{1}{2}$ teaspoon
Corn syrup	1 tablespoon
Glucose	1 tablespoon

FONDANT

1 cup sugar
$\frac{1}{2}$ cup water

$\frac{1}{16}$ teaspoon cream of tartar
or
1 tablespoon corn syrup

■ Mix ingredients, stir, and heat to boiling point. Cook, without stirring, to soft-ball stage (234 to 240°F). Wash crystals from sides of pan as they form, or cover pan a few minutes while cooking to dissolve them. Pour mixture onto a platter rinsed with cold water. Cool to 104°F. Work back and forth until mixture is white and creamy. Then knead until smooth.

Place in an airtight container and allow to ripen at least 24 hours before using. Fondant may be kept a long time if tightly covered. If it dries, a damp cloth may be placed over it. If ⅛ teaspoon of glycerine is added to other ingredients when fondant begins to boil, a creamier product results, which is suitable for centers of bonbons. It must be worked up at once, however, as it softens upon standing and therefore is difficult to handle. If fondant should "sugar," add water and cook again. Seven-eighths cup.

BROWN SUGAR FONDANT. Make as for Fondant, substituting brown sugar for ½ of the white sugar.

CHOCOLATE FONDANT. Add 1 to 2 squares melted unsweetened chocolate to 1 cup finished fondant. Knead until well mixed.

COFFEE FONDANT. Make as for Fondant substituting strong, clear coffee for water.

EASY FONDANT. Make as for Fondant, cooling and working in pan in which it is cooked. Spread 1 egg white, beaten stiff, over cooled fondant before working.

MAPLE FONDANT. Make as for Fondant, adding ⅓ cup maple syrup and decreasing water to ⅓ cup.

CARAMEL FONDANT. Make as for Maple Fondant, substituting Caramel Syrup (p. 103) for maple syrup.

OPERA OR CREAM FONDANT. Make as for Fondant, substituting heavy cream for water.

UNCOOKED FONDANT

1 egg white, unbeaten	2½ cups powdered sugar,
½ tablespoon cold water	more or less accord-
¾ teaspoon flavoring	ing to size of egg

■ Put egg white, water, and flavoring into bowl. Beat well with rotary beater. Add sugar gradually until stiff enough to knead. Use at once. Seven-eighths to 1 cup.

BUTTER CREAMS

3½ cups powdered sugar	4 tablespoons fruit juice
¼ cup butter or margarine	1 teaspoon vanilla,
1 pinch salt	if desired
3 tablespoons boiling water	
or	

■ Make mound of sugar on board or marble slab. Put remaining ingredients in center of mound, adding liquid as needed. Knead until smooth. Mixture should not stick to fingers when kneaded. Shape as desired. One and ¾ cups.

CHOCOLATE FUDGE

1 cup sugar
½ cup milk or
⅜ cup evaporated milk and
　¼ cup water
1 tablespoon corn syrup
A few grains salt

½ to 1 square unsweet-
　ened chocolate
1 tablespoon butter or
　margarine
½ teaspoon vanilla

■ Mix sugar, milk, corn syrup, salt, and chocolate. Stir frequently until sugar dissolves and chocolate melts. Cook to soft-ball stage (234 to 240°F). Add butter. Remove from heat. Cool. Add vanilla. Beat until it is creamy and has lost its gloss, then pour quickly into oiled pans, making a ¾- to 1-inch layer. Cut into 1-inch squares when nearly cold. It may be kneaded and molded if preferred. Ten to 12 1-inch squares.

CARAMEL FUDGE

1 cup sugar
⅓ cup milk

2 tablespoons butter or
　margarine
A few grains salt

■ Caramelize ⅓ of the sugar (p. 103). Add 2 tablespoons hot water to form syrup. Add remaining sugar and milk. Finish as for Chocolate Fudge. Eight to 10 1-inch squares.

PANOCHA

1 cup brown sugar
⅓ cup milk or thin cream
½ teaspoon vanilla
1 tablespoon butter or
　margarine

¼ to ⅓ cup nuts,
　chopped

■ Boil sugar and milk, stirring as needed to prevent curdling and scorching. Cook to soft-ball stage (234 to 240°F). Remove from heat. Add butter, cool, then flavor. Beat until creamy. Add nuts. Pour quickly into oiled pan. Ten to 12 1-inch squares.

ALOHA PANOCHA

½ cup brown sugar
½ cup crushed pineapple,
　drained
½ cup nuts, coarsely chopped

1 cup sugar
1 tablespoon butter or
　margarine
½ teaspoon vanilla

■ Cook sugar and pineapple to soft-ball stage (236°F). Remove from heat. Add butter. Beat until thick and creamy. Add nuts and vanilla. Pour into a loaf pan lined with wax paper. Cool. Slice when ready to serve. If preferred, pour it into a shallow, oiled pan and cut into squares. One loaf.

CARAMEL NUT LOAF

2 cups white corn syrup
6 cups sugar
3 cups evaporated milk,
   undiluted

3 cups mixed nuts,
   coarsely chopped
1 teaspoon vanilla

■ Mix syrup, sugar, and milk. Bring to a boil over low heat. Increase heat, and cook to firm-ball stage (244°F). Cool (104°F), add nuts and vanilla. Beat until stiff enough to knead. Form into 2 rolls.

DATE LOAF

2½ cups sugar
1 cup milk

½ pound seeded dates
¾ cup nuts, chopped

■ Cook sugar, milk, and dates to soft-ball stage (234 to 240°F). Stir as needed to prevent burning. Remove from heat. Cool to 104°F. Beat until it begins to harden. Add nuts, and turn onto a damp cloth. Shape into a roll 2-inches in diameter. Let stand until firm. Cut into slices as needed. This candy will keep some time if tightly covered. Approximately 25 to 30 slices.

DIVINITY

3 cups sugar
¾ cup light corn syrup
¾ cup water
3 egg whites, beaten
   stiff

1 cup nuts
1 teaspoon vanilla

■ Cook sugar, syrup, and water to hard-ball stage (250 to 266°F). Pour slowly, with constant beating, over egg whites, continue beating until candy begins to hold its shape. Add nuts and vanilla. Pour into oiled pans. Cut into squares when cold. Candy may be shaped into a loaf or formed into irregular pieces by dropping it from tip of spoon onto wax paper. Approximately 50 pieces.

NONCRYSTALLINE CANDIES

Formation of crystals is avoided in noncrystalline candies by use of fairly large quantities of such substances as corn syrup, acids, or fat.

PLAIN CARAMELS

1 cup sugar
1 cup white corn syrup
1 cup thin cream or
   evaporated milk

¼ cup butter or margarine
½ teaspoon vanilla

■ Mix ingredients. Cook to firm-ball stage (244 to 248°F). Stir occasionally at beginning of cooking and constantly toward end of process.

Flavor. Turn into oiled pan. Cool. Cut into ¾-inch squares. Remove from pan. This is a soft, rich, chewy caramel. Approximately 30 pieces.

COCONUT CARAMELS. Add 1 cup dry, shredded coconut to mixture for Plain Caramels just before pouring into pan. Coconut may be toasted if desired.

FRUIT CARAMELS. Add 1 cup coarsely chopped dried fruit, such as dates or raisins, to mixture for Plain Caramels just before pouring into pan.

NUT CARAMELS. Add 1 cup chopped nuts to mixture for Plain Caramels just before pouring into pan.

CHOCOLATE CARAMELS

1 cup brown sugar	¼ cup corn syrup
1½ squares unsweetened chocolate	⅓ cup butter or margarine
¼ cup milk or cream	½ teaspoon vanilla

■ Mix ingredients except butter and vanilla. Bring slowly to boiling point. Cook to soft-crack stage (270 to 290°F), adding butter toward last of cooking. Stir as needed to prevent scorching. Remove from heat, add vanilla, and pour into oiled pan. Cut into ¾-inch squares. When mixture is cool, remove from pan. Wrap in wax paper. If desired, ⅓ cup coarsely chopped nuts may be added before pouring into pan. Approximately 20 to 24 pieces.

BUTTERSCOTCH

2 cups brown or white sugar	⅓ cup butter or margarine
1 cup corn syrup	¼ teaspoon salt
1 cup water	¼ teaspoon vanilla

■ Cook sugar, syrup, and water to firm-ball stage (244 to 248°F). Stir as needed to prevent scorching. Add butter and salt. Continue cooking to hard-ball stage (250 to 266°F). Add vanilla. Pour into oiled pan, making a ¼-inch layer. Cool. Cut into squares. Approximately 60 pieces.

MOLASSES TAFFY

3 cups sugar	½ cup butter or margarine
1 cup molasses	¼ teaspoon soda
1 cup hot water	½ teaspoon vanilla
1 tablespoon vinegar	
½ teaspoon cream of tartar	

■ Heat sugar, molasses, water, and vinegar. When mixture boils, add cream of tartar. When candy is nearly done, add butter and soda. If chewing taffy is desired, cook to soft-crack stage (270 to 290°F). Cook hard taffy to hard-crack stage (300 to 310°F). Pour into oiled plates. When it is cold enough to handle, flavor and pull. When taffy is light colored and porous, stretch it into a rope. Cut off piece about 1 inch long with scissors, turn rope half over, and cut another piece. Continue turning after each cutting. Place on oiled plate to cool. If taffy is to be kept for a time, wrap each piece in wax paper. Place in tight container. Approximately 125 pieces.

WHITE TAFFY

2 cups sugar	1 tablespoon vinegar
1¾ cups white corn syrup	1 teaspoon vanilla

■   Cook sugar, syrup, and vinegar to hard-crack stage (300°F). Stir only until sugar dissolves. Finish as for Molasses Taffy (p. 223). Approximately 75 pieces.

AFTER DINNER MINTS

2 cups sugar	2 tablespoons vinegar
¾ cup water	5 to 10 drops oil of
4 tablespoons butter or	peppermint (strength
margarine	varies)

■   Mix sugar, water, butter, and vinegar together. Stir until sugar dissolves. Boil rapidly, keeping sides of kettle free from crystals. Cook without stirring to hard-ball stage (261°F). Pour into oiled platter. When it is cool enough to handle, add peppermint, color as desired, and pull. When candy is stiff, stretch it on the table into a rope, and cut it into 1-inch lengths. Wrap in wax paper. Place in tight container to cream. Approximately 125 pieces.

PEANUT BRITTLE

1 cup sugar	1 teaspoon butter or
½ cup corn syrup	margarine
½ cup water	½ teaspoon vanilla
1 cup raw peanuts	1 teaspoon soda
(Spanish preferable)	

■   Cook sugar, syrup, and water to soft-ball stage (234 to 240°F). Add unblanched peanuts. Continue cooking until syrup is light brown and meets hard-crack test (300 to 310°F). Remove from heat. Add vanilla and soda. Mix ingredients well. Pour onto oiled baking sheet, spreading thin as possible. When mixture is nearly cool, wet hands in cold water, and turn candy over, stretching to desired thinness. Cut into squares or break into pieces. Approximately 48 pieces.

LOLLYPOPS

2 cups sugar	Flavoring
⅔ cup white corn syrup	Coloring
1 cup hot water	

■   Cook sugar, syrup, and water to extreme hard-crack stage (310°F). Stir only until sugar is dissolved. Remove any crystals that form on sides of pan. Cook slowly toward end of process in order that syrup may not scorch. Remove from heat, add coloring and flavoring, stirring only enough to mix.

Drop mixture from tip of a tablespoon onto a smooth, oiled surface, taking care to make drops round. Press a toothpick or skewer into edge of each before it hardens. Any decorations are pressed on at same time. Candies should be loosened from slab before they are quite cold to prevent cracking.

Candied cherries, shredded, blanched almonds, and any small, fancy candies are suitable for decoration. Approximately 30 lollypops, 2 inches in diameter.

ENGLISH TOFFEE

1½ cups blanched almonds   ¼ teaspoon salt
¾ cup butter or margarine   5 tablespoons water
1 cup sugar   Milk chocolate, melted

■ Brown almonds lightly in oven. Put ½ through food chopper. Split remainder into halves. Melt butter. Add sugar, salt, and water. Stir until sugar dissolves. Cook to hard-crack stage (300°F). Stir constantly. Add split almonds. Pour into oiled pan 8 x 8-inches. Spread chocolate over top, sprinkle generously with ground nuts. Cool. Turn toffee upside down on wax paper. Spread this side with chocolate, and sprinkle with nuts. When it is cold, break into pieces. One sheet, 8 x 8-inches.

MARSHMALLOWS

2 cups sugar   2 tablespoons gelatin,
½ cup hot water   soaked in
A few grains salt   ¾ cup cold water
                              1 teaspoon vanilla

■ Cook sugar, salt, and hot water to soft-ball stage (234 to 240°F). Add soaked gelatin. Pour into large bowl. Beat until mixture holds its shape, adding vanilla toward last. Coloring may be added, if desired. Pour into pans dusted with powdered sugar. When marshmallows are set, remove from pans. Cut them into squares and roll them in powdered sugar or in grated coconut or finely chopped nuts. They may be dipped in chocolate if desired. Approximately 36 marshmallows.

MISCELLANEOUS CANDIES

APRICOT ROLL

3 cups sugar   apricots, drained, cut
1 cup milk   into pieces
1 cup soaked dried

■ Cook sugar and milk to firm-ball stage (246 to 250°F). Add apricots. Continue cooking until firm-ball stage is reached again. Cool. Beat until thick. Shape into a roll. Slice when ready to serve. One roll, 16 inches long, 2 inches in diameter.

BRAZIL NUT RICE CANDY

¾ cup corn syrup
½ teaspoon salt
1¼ cups sugar
2 tablespoons butter or
   margarine

2 tablespoons vinegar
4 cups puffed rice
¾ cup Brazil nuts,
   coarsely chopped
½ teaspoon vanilla

■ Boil syrup, salt, and sugar to firm-ball stage (248°F). Add fat and vinegar. Blend well. Remove from heat, add puffed rice, nuts, and vanilla. Pour into oiled pan 8 inches square. When mixture is nearly cold, cut it into squares or sticks. Sixteen servings.

CANDIED ORANGE PEEL

1½ cups sugar
¾ cup water

Peel from 4 medium-sized
   oranges

■ Remove peel in quarters. Cover with cold water. Bring slowly to boiling point. Boil until tender. Drain. Cut into narrow strips with scissors. Make syrup of sugar and water. Water in which peel has been cooked may be used in syrup, if stronger flavor is desired. Add orange strips. Cook until syrup is nearly absorbed. Lift out, drain, and roll each piece in granulated sugar. Grapefruit or lemon peel may be prepared in same way. Three and ½ cups.

PARISIAN SWEETS

1 pound figs
1 pound dates

1¼ cups nuts, chopped
Powdered sugar

■ Grind figs, dates, and nuts several times. Knead on board dusted with powdered sugar. Roll ⅛ inch thick, and cut into fancy shapes; or pat into pan, and cut into 1-inch squares when nearly cold. Roll in sugar if desired. Approximately 25 pieces.

POPCORN BALLS

1 cup sugar
1 cup brown sugar
½ cup white corn syrup
½ cup water
2 tablespoons butter or
   margarine

½ teaspoon salt
½ teaspoon vanilla, if
   desired
Popcorn as required,
   about 3 quarts

■ Cook sugar, syrup, and water to soft-crack stage (270 to 290°F). Watch carefully, and stir occasionally toward last of cooking to prevent burning. Add butter and flavoring. Stir only enough to mix. Pour slowly over popcorn, which has been sprinkled with salt. Mix well, then form into

balls with hands, pressing as little as possible. Puffed rice may be substituted for popcorn. Approximately 10 balls, 3-inches in diameter.

TURKISH PASTE

2 cups sugar	Grated rind and juice of
½ cup hot water	1 lemon
2 tablespoons gelatin, soaked	Grated rind and juice of
in	1 orange
½ cup cold water	Coloring

■   Heat sugar and hot water to boiling point. Add soaked gelatin. Boil
slowly 20 minutes. Remove from heat. Add fruit juices, grated rind, and
coloring. Strain into pan rinsed with cold water, making layer ½- to 1-inch
thick. When mixture is firm, turn onto a board, cut into squares, and roll
in powdered sugar. If desired, ½ cup chopped nuts may be added. Approximately 33 pieces.

NUTS

BLANCHED ALMONDS

Cover shelled almonds with boiling water. Let stand until skins will
slip. Drain, put in cold water, and rub off skins. Dry between towels.

Allow almonds to stand in cold water overnight. The skins will then
pop off and thus eliminate the boiling water procedure. To sliver blanched
almonds, do so while they are moist and warm.

SALTED ALMONDS

Place blanched almonds, a few at a time, in a small mesh frying basket;
fry (360 to 370°F) to a delicate brown, avoid overbrowning. Drain.
Sprinkle with salt. Nuts also may be browned in a small amount of fat in
oven (300°F) or on surface units. Occasional stirring is necessary. (Other
nuts may be salted in the same way.)

ROASTED NUTS

Spread nutmeats in a shallow pan in a thin layer. Heat at 250°F,
stirring occasionally until nuts are light brown in color.

SPICED NUTS

1 cup sugar	½ teaspoon nutmeg
1 teaspoon cinnamon	1 teaspoon ginger
1 cup nut halves	1 unbeaten egg white
¼ teaspoon cloves	1 tablespoon cold water

■   Combine sugar, cinnamon, cloves, nutmeg, and ginger. Add water to
egg white and mix nuts with egg white. Coat with sugar mixture. Spread
in thin layer on baking sheet. Bake at 300°F, 30 to 35 minutes.

Preservation of Foods

SPOILAGE of foods is caused by enzymatic action and/or microbial growth. Enzymes occur in all fresh fruits, vegetables, and meats. Enzymatic action is necessary for the ripening of fruit and the maturation of vegetables, but can be a cause of spoilage if permitted to continue indefinitely. Therefore, enzymatic action must be controlled. The application of heat is one way to control it.

Microbial spoilage is due to the growth of yeast, mold, or bacteria. Yeasts and molds most frequently cause the spoilage of acid foods, such as fruits; whereas, bacterial growth usually is the cause of spoilage of vegetables and meat. Microorganisms may occur in the vegetative or growing state, or in the spore or resting state. Vegetative microbial cells are readily destroyed in a reasonable length of time by boiling temperatures. Freezing inhibits and may destroy cells. Spores are more difficult to destroy and may be a problem in food preservation.

Since enzymes are abundant in foods, and microorganisms occur in air, in water, in soil, and on food, preservation depends upon controlling enzymatic action and destroying or retarding growth of microorganisms. It is usually accepted that all methods of food preservation will destroy or control the growth of spoilage microorganisms but none improves the food product. Therefore, food should be preserved as soon after harvesting as possible. Canning, drying, and freezing are common methods of preserving foods.

CANNING

Canning may be defined as the preservation of food in jars or cans by applying heat and forming a hermetic seal. For successful canning of foods, enzyme action must be stopped or controlled and microorganisms must be destroyed or their growth prevented. The spoilage of canned fruits and acid vegetables (pickles) is usually caused by yeasts and molds which can grow in the acid environment. If these foods are thoroughly processed and properly sealed in sterilized containers, they usually keep as both yeasts and molds are killed easily by pasteurization and boiling temperatures. Bacteria thrive on low or non-acid foods, such as peas, corn, beans, and meats. Bacterial spores are more difficult to destroy than yeast and mold spores. Therefore, for processing low-acid or non-acid foods it is necessary to use temperatures above that of boiling water. To obtain such temperatures, a pressure cooker is used.

Processing consists of heating food for a given time in a can or jar to prevent spoilage, and is done in a water bath or pressure canner depending on the type of food. Pasteurization is used for fruit juices and similar products because boiling temperatures affect their flavor. The food is placed in containers, heated, and held at a specific temperature for a specific length of time sufficient to destroy pathogenic microorganisms and to arrest fermentation. The time and temperature varies with the food and pack.

TYPES OF CANNERS

The heat processing of foods in cans or jars requires a container or canner that holds the filled jars or cans with sufficient water to cover them, or that holds steam under pressure. The water bath can be used safely for acid foods with a pH 4.5 or lower such as fruits, acid vegetables (pickles), and tomatoes. The steam canner or pressure cooker is used for less acid foods with a pH of 4.5 or above, such as vegetables and meats. To insure the safety of the product, the low-acid or non-acid foods cannot be processed in a reasonable time in boiling water. The high temperature of the pressure canner permits processing food in jars or cans in a reasonable length of time and insures the safety of the food. The safety of the food refers to the destruction of *Clostridium botulinum* bacterial spores. This bacterium is an anaerobe, which if not destroyed, produces a very poisonous toxin. Therefore, all home processed non-acid food should be boiled for 10 minutes before tasting to destroy any toxin that may be present.

Water-Bath Canner. The water bath is the simpler and cheaper of the 2 types of canners. It has 3 essential parts: container or kettle, rack, and tight cover. The kettle should be deep enough to permit 1 to 2 inches of water over the top of jars or tins for brisk boiling.

Pressure Canner. The pressure canner is usually of heavier gauge metal than the water bath. The principal parts of the pressure canner are the container, rack, lid, gasket, and gauge. The lid and gasket are so designed that steam cannot escape. Accurate gauges are necessary to measure the pressure of the steam within the container. Steam at a given pressure is related directly to a particular temperature. The gauge may read as pressure only or as both pressure and temperature. Gauges should be checked regularly. Weighted ones need only be checked to determine if they are thoroughly clean. Dial gauges can be tested for accuracy by a Home Economics Agent, dealer, or manufacturer. If the gauge is not off more than 4 pounds, it may be used by allowing for the inaccuracy in the reading. A new gauge should be purchased if it is off 5 pounds or more. Directions for processing are usually for 10 pounds pressure or 240°F. For each 2000 feet above sea level 1 pound pressure is added to obtain the desired temperature.

Pressure Saucepan. Pressure saucepans are being recommended for the heat processing of canned food. The saucepans heat and cool rapidly; therefore processing time varies from those recommended for pressure canners. The directions given by the manufacturer of the saucepan should be followed.

CONTAINERS FOR FOOD

Glass Jars and How To Use Them

Jars are used more extensively in some areas of the country than others for heat processing of foods. It is preferable that jars be colorless, wide mouthed, and free of chips and cracks. Jar lids with sealing compound and screwbands often are used to insure a hermetic seal. Other types of lids are sometimes used but commonly are not available through retail markets. Instructions supplied by the manufacturer for using jar lids of a given type should be followed.

Jars should be cleaned thoroughly by washing with hot water and a soap or detergent, then rinsing with boiling water. The temperature of the jars should be near that of the food to be placed in them.

Filling Jars. Jars may be filled with food using a jar filler, being careful not to pack too tightly. Heat penetrates slowly to the center of a tight pack. Head space is left at the top of jar for the food and liquid or juice to expand. Canning tables as found in government bulletins, indicate whether or not liquid is to be added as well as the head space needed for each food. Glass jars may be fitted with different types of lids that are adjusted in various ways. The manufacturer's directions should be followed for each type.

Sealing Jars. When using the flat metal lid with sealing compound, the lid is dipped into boiling water, and placed on the mouth of jar with sealing compound next to the glass. The metal band is screwed on firmly and the food processed for a given time at the recommended temperature. When taken from the canner the seal must not be tightened further or it may be broken. Twenty-four hours after processing the metal band may be removed. If band sticks it can be covered with a hot damp cloth for 1 to 2 minutes to loosen, being careful not to break the seal.

Handling Jars. Glass jars are handled with tongs when placing in or removing from a canner. The tongs are used to grasp the shoulder of the jar to prevent interference with the seal.

Cooling Jars. Jars are cooled in an upright position on a rack and out of drafts. However, it is necessary to permit air to circulate around the jars. Covering the jars with a towel increases cooling time.

Tin Cans and How to Use Them

Tin cans, either plain tin or enamel-lined, may be used in canning. Tin cans are desirable for canning large quantities of food. They do not break, do not lose liquid, are economical of space, generally require less processing time than glass jars, and may be cooled quickly. Plain tin cans may be used for most fruits, vegetables, and meats. Enamel-lined cans are used for foods that react with tin to darken food or corrode the can. A deep gold enamel lining with a bright finish known as R enamel is used to keep red color from fading, as in beets or red berries, and such food as pumpkin or squash, from corroding the can. Enamel of a dull, light gold, known as C enamel is used to prevent corn, lima beans, and some other foods from discoloring. Avoid use of C enamel with acid or fatty foods, as they cause enamel to peel. All cans should be free of dents, rust or scratches.

Filling Cans. Cans should be filled without packing. Head space should be provided according to size of jar or can and food being packed. Most of the air should be removed (exhausted) from can before sealing.

Sealing Cans. All cans should be sealed immediately after exhausting while cans are hot to insure a vacuum seal. Tin cans require an instrument for sealing. Before starting to can the sealer should be in good working condition. Test the sealer for proper adjustment, by placing a little water in a can, sealing it, then submerging the can in hot water for a few minutes. If air bubbles rise from around the lid of the can, the seal is not tight and the sealer needs further adjusting according to manufacturer's directions. After sealing, follow directions for processing the specific food.

Cooling Cans. Cans are lifted from the canner and placed in cold, clean water to cool quickly. Cans should be removed from cold water while still warm to air dry, then staggered to allow air to circulate.

Approximate Yield of Home-Canned Products From Raw Fruit and Vegetables *

PRODUCT	POUNDS OF FRESH PRODUCT NEEDED TO CAN 1 QUART	QUARTS OF CANNED FOOD TO 1 BUSHEL OR CRATE	APPROXIMATE WEIGHT OR MEASURE
Apples	2½ to 3	16 to 25	1 bu (48 lbs)
Berries, except strawberries	1½ to 3	12 to 18	24 qt crate
Cherries (canned unpitted)	2 to 2½	22 to 32	1 bu (56 lbs)
			1 lug (22 lbs)
Peaches	2 to 3	16 to 24	1 bu (48 lbs)
			1 lug (20 lbs)
Pears	2 to 3	17 to 25	1 bu (50 lbs)
Plums	1½ to 2½	22 to 36	1 bu (56 lbs)
			1 lug (24 lbs)
Tomatoes	2½ to 3½	14 to 22	1 bu (53 lbs)
			1 lug (32 lbs)
Asparagus	2½ to 4½	9 to 16	1 bu (40 lbs)
Beans, lima in pods	3 to 5	6 to 10	1 bu (32 lbs)
Beans, snap	1½ to 2½	12 to 22	1 bu(30 lbs)
Beets, without tops	2 to 3½	14 to 24	1 bu (52 lbs)
Carrots, without tops	2 to 3	17 to 20	1 bu (50 lbs)
Corn, sweet, in husks (canned whole-kernel style)	3 to 6	6 to 10	1 bu (35 lbs)
Okra	1½	16 to 18	1 bu (26 lbs)
Peas, green, in pods	3 to 6	5 to 10	1 bu (30 lbs)
Pumpkin or winter squash	1½ to 3	15	50 lbs
Spinach and other greens	2 to 6	3 to 8	1 bu (18 lbs)
Squash, summer	2 to 4	16 to 20	1 bu (40 lbs)
Sweet potatoes	2 to 3	16 to 22	1 bu (50 lbs)

* From "Home-Canning of Fruits and Vegetables," United States Department of Agriculture, Home and Garden Bulletin 8.

GENERAL PROCEDURE

Preparing the Foods

Fruits, Tomatoes, and Pickled Vegetables. Select and prepare containers as indicated under "Containers for Food" (p. 231). Choose fresh, sound, firm, ripe products. Work with only enough food for 1 canner load at a time. Before peeling and cutting, thoroughly wash the food through several changes of water by dipping and lifting the product rather than pouring water off the food. Be careful not to bruise fruits. Sort according to size.

Sugar or sugar syrup often is added to fruits when canning to help them maintain their shape, color, and flavor. If the fruit is juicy and packed hot, ½ cup sugar per quart of raw prepared fruit may be added before cooking. Sugar syrup is made by boiling together, for 5 minutes, sugar and water or juice extracted from the fruit. Proportions for 3 types of syrup commonly used are:

Syrups for Fruits *

TYPE OF SYRUP	SUGAR (CUPS)	WATER OR JUICE (CUPS)	YIELD OF SYRUP (CUPS)
Thin	2	4	5
Medium	3	4	5½
Heavy	4¾	4	6½

* From "Home Canning of Fruits and Vegetables," United States Department of Agriculture, Home and Garden Bulletin No. 8.

Vegetables. Select and prepare containers as indicated under "Containers for Food" (p. 231). Choose young, tender vegetables.

Process as soon after harvest as possible because vegetables mature rapidly. Work with only enough food for 1 canner load at a time. Wash thoroughly by dipping and lifting vegetables in and out of water instead of pouring off liquid. Use particular care with vegetables from the ground, as soil may carry bacteria that are hard to destroy. Prepare as for cooking: peel, pod, tip, etc. Work quickly. Add 1 teaspoon salt per quart.

Meat. Select and prepare containers as indicated under "Containers for Food" (p. 231). Select fresh, clean, wholesome meat: beef, veal, lamb, pork, or poultry. Variety meats such as heart and tongue also can be canned. After slaughter, meat should be chilled immediately at 40°F or below until canning time but not longer than a few days.

Frozen meat may also be canned. Cut fresh or saw frozen meat into 1- to 2-inch cubes or can-length strips. Cut the strips with the grain of the meat. Clean meat with damp cloth. Trim fat and cut meat from bone. Add ½ teaspoon salt per pint jar or No. 2 plain tin can.

Packing the Containers

Raw-pack. Raw-pack consists of placing uncooked prepared food into jars and adding hot water, juice, or syrup to fill the container. Minimum head space is allowed as necessary, before placing the lid on the container. If tin cans are used, raw meat or other raw food is placed in the tins. The filled, open cans are placed in a kettle with a rack and a tight fitting cover. Water is added to 2-inches below the can tops. The water and food are heated to attain 170°F in the center of the canned food.

Hot-pack. Hot-pack is recommended for practically all foods. This method reduces air in jars to a minimum and shortens time required to reach desired processing temperature. A short precooking period precedes placing the hot food into a container. The food is heated in steam or in boiling water to shrink and wilt it. The preheated food is then packed boiling hot into jars, adding precooking liquid, boiling water, or syrup to cover. Head space is left, as indicated by recipe for specific vegetable.

Processing the Food

Specific directions for a particular food may be found in the United States Department of Agriculture Home and Garden Bulletins that may be obtained from the Government Printing Office, Washington, D.C., or your Home Economics Agent. Always follow the most recent edition.

Water Bath. After packing, place the containers of food in the canner so that water can circulate around them. Count the time of processing from the time the water reaches a rapid boil. Keep the water boiling briskly throughout the processing period. A definite length of time is recommended for processing each food. When that processing time is completed, remove the jars from the water bath with a pair of tongs. Cool the jars on a bread board, rack, or folded cloth away from drafts.

Pressure Canners. The manufacturer's directions for the canner should be followed for processing. A few pointers on the use of any steam-pressure canner:

Use 2 to 3 inches of water in the canner so that it will not boil dry during processing.

Place containers in canner so that containers do not touch.

Fasten lid securely.

Let steam escape from open petcock or weighted gauge opening for at least 10 minutes; then close the petcock or put weighted gauge in place.

When the recommended pressure is reached, adjust heat to keep pressure constant.

Begin to count processing time when the recommended pressure is reached.

When processing time is completed, slide canner from heat.

Cool undisturbed at room temperature until gauge registers zero. After 1 or 2 minutes slowly open petcock or remove the weighted gauge.

Remove lid by tilting far side up to keep any steam away from operator.

Remove jars with tongs, being careful to grasp jars by shoulders and not by lids.

Cool jars out of draft and uncovered.

Care of Food after Canning

Examine the cooled containers for leaks the day after canning. It is essential to use food at once if container leaks. Label each container, giving contents, date, and lot number if more than 1 batch was processed that day.

Store in a cool, dark, dry, clean place. Any bacteria that survived processing are more likely to grow and cause food to spoil or to lose quality, if stored in a warm rather than a cool place. Light may fade the color of food in glass jars and cause the loss of vitamins. Dampness may corrode tin cans and metal lids. Freezing does not spoil canned food for use, but it may cause a jar to crack or break a seal so that spoilage microorganisms can invade the container.

Before opening any glass jar or tin can for use, inspect it carefully. There should be no leaks. A glass jar with bulging lid or with gas bubbles may mean that the food has spoiled. A tin can with either end bulging should be suspected. Spurting liquid, when the container is opened, and "off" odor or color, or mold are danger signals. If spoilage is suspected save the container of spoiled food and its contents for investigation by health authorities.

It is possible for foods to contain the toxin that causes botulism without showing any visible signs of spoilage. As a safeguard, boil all home canned low-acid foods for 10 minutes before tasting or serving. This boiling will destroy both the growing microorganisms and the very poisonous botulism toxin. If the food is not turned over to the health authorities, destroy spoiled foods by burning or heating them with lye and then burying both container and food so that it will not be eaten by human beings or animals.

FREEZING

Freezing is a means of preserving food through the application and maintenance of extreme cold or below "freezing" temperatures. It is effective because most of the water of the food tissue is changed from the liquid to the solid state. This change in the physical state of the water retards enzymatic action and stops microbial growth, the causes of food spoilage; thus preserving the food. However, upon defrosting the spoilage agents can be reactivated. Therefore, defrosted frozen food should be used and not stored or refrozen.

The original quality of fresh food is best retained if the food is frozen within 24 hours. The lower the freezing temperature the more quickly the food will be frozen. Further, the frozen food should be stored at 0°F or lower with minimum fluctuation. Long storage should be avoided.

Generally, foods are prepared for freezing much as they would be prepared for serving. The food is placed in moisture-proof packaging material. Depending on the food, as much air as possible is excluded from the package. The package is sealed and the food is frozen. Detailed directions for freezing specific foods should be followed. Check with your Home Economics Agent for the most recent state or federal bulletins available.

Selecting the Food. Select only foods of high quality for freezing. The quality of food does not improve with freezing. Fruits and vegetables should be of optimum maturity. Not all varieties freeze equally well. Consult the

Home Economics Agent or write the state experiment station for recommended varieties to freeze. Choose eggs that are clean, sound, and Grade A quality for freezing.

Selecting Container. Desirable containers are moisture-proof, are free of odor and flavor, do not break readily, pack into freezer to give maximum use of space, and are easily filled and emptied. Containers may be of polyethylene, pliofilm, plastic, glass, aluminum foil or any one of many specially prepared papers.

Preparing the Food. Fruits and vegetables should be frozen soon after harvesting. They should be carefully and thoroughly cleaned and made ready for cooking or serving. Those of large size may be sliced. Vegetables should be scalded before freezing to help retard enzymatic action. Scalding periods vary. Heating in boiling water should be sufficiently long to cause some inhibition of enzymes, but not so long that there is an excessive destruction or extraction of water soluble nutrients. The amount of vegetable scalded at one time should be small enough that there is not an excessive drop in the temperature of the water when vegetables are added. Immediately after scalding, vegetables should be plunged into cold running water for the same length of time as they were scalded; so that there is not an excessive extraction of water soluble nutrients.

Quality beef and lamb may be hung in a cooler for 10 to 14 days to ripen before freezing. Beef, pork, and lamb should be cut into pieces of suitable size for cooking. Many cuts may be boned to conserve freezer space. Poultry should be thoroughly chilled immediately after killing and dressing. Birds should never be cut up until chilled. Broilers should be chilled 6 to 8 hours, and roasters and turkeys 12 to 18 hours. Fish are best frozen as soon as possible after they are caught.

Whole eggs may be frozen by breaking the eggs into a container and beating. However, it is recommended that 1 teaspoon of salt or 1 tablespoon sugar or corn syrup be added for 1 cup of whole eggs. If the eggs are separated, the whites need no special treatment. It is necessary to add 1 teaspoon of salt or 2 tablespoons sugar or corn syrup to 1 cup of egg yolks.

Packaging the Food. Following scalding, vegetables are packed dry. Fruits may be packed dry, in sugar or in syrup. If packed dry, a common proportion is 1 pound sugar to 3 pounds fruit, although 1 to 2 may be used. Fruit and sugar should stand 1 to 2 hours after mixing or long enough for part of the sugar to dissolve and syrup to penetrate fruit before freezing. Fruits that discolor readily, such as peaches, should be packed in syrup. Concentration of syrup varies from 2 cups sugar to 1 quart water for a 30% syrup to 3¾ cups sugar to 1 quart water for a 50% syrup. When syrup is used, fruit is placed in container, syrup is poured over it, and the whole is allowed to stand in a cold place long enough for the syrup to penetrate the fruit before freezing. An antioxidant such as ascorbic acid may be added to the syrup to retard darkening.

Meats, including fish and poultry, should be packaged to exclude as much air as possible and to prevent drying of the food. Usually meat is tightly wrapped in moisture-proof paper. However, when aluminum foil is used the foil should be molded to the shape of the cut of meat rather than pulling it tightly around the piece of meat.

Eggs should be packaged in containers of such a size that the entire contents will be used at one time and immediately after defrosting. Head space must be left, especially in a rigid container, for expansion during freezing.

All wraps and containers should have a tight closure or seal. If liquids are packaged in a rigid container allowance must be made for head space as specified by the manufacturer. The containers or wraps should be labeled specifying contents and date.

Freezing and Storing. All foods should be frozen immediately after preparation. If any delay is necessary, the prepared packages should be stored in a cold place. If food is frozen in a home freezer, only a limited quantity of unfrozen food should be put in the freezer at one time, and space should be allowed between packages for circulation of air. For storage, the packages should be packed as tightly as possible. A storage temperature of 0°F or lower is desirable and should be maintained. Storage time depends on the particular type of food.

DRYING

Drying is another method of preserving perishable foods. No other method of preservation develops the distinct flavor of the home-dried product. An oven that can be maintained at a temperature of 150°F for a period of 3 to 6 hours may serve as an adequate source of heat to dry either fruits or vegetables. The prepared products should be spread out in a single layer on a rack so that there can be maximum circulation of air and quick drying can occur. Apples, peaches, and pears need a special anti-browning treatment prior to drying; such as treating with sodium sulfite. Fruits become tough and leathery when dried sufficiently, whereas vegetables become brittle. After drying the products must be cooled and stored in an airtight container.

PRESERVING WITH ADDITIVES

Jellies, Jams, Preserves, Conserves, Fruit Butters, Marmalades

Sugar contributes to the preservation of jelly, jam, preserves, conserves, fruit butter, and marmalade. So much sugar is added to these products that the ordinary spoilage organisms, yeast and bacteria, cannot grow. Mold can grow on their surfaces if the sugar concentration is 65% or greater. Differences among the products depend upon kind of fruit used, way in which it is prepared, proportion of ingredients, and method of cookery.

Jelly is made by combining certain fruit juices with sugar in correct proportions under proper conditions. A good jelly is clear, tender, and translucent. It holds its shape when unmolded or cut, yet is so delicate it quivers. Jam is a "spread" made from small fruits, usually berries, which have been crushed and cooked to a pulp with a large amount of sugar. Preserves are whole fruits or large pieces of fruit in a thick, slightly jellied syrup. Marmalade consists of thin slices or small pieces of fruit, usually citrus fruit, in a clear jelly or jelly-like syrup. Conserves are similar to marmalade but often are made from a mixture of fruits with addition of chopped nuts and raisins. Fruit butter consists of fruit pulp cooked in a comparatively small amount of sugar until it is thick and butter-like.

The correct proportions of 4 essential ingredients are needed for a jellied fruit product: fruit, pectin, acid, and sugar. The fruit used gives the characteristic flavor as well as furnishing at least part of the necessary pectin and acid for the jellied product.

Pectin is a carbohydrate possessing jellying properties, when combined in the right proportions with acid and sugar. Pectin does not occur in all fruits. It frequently is not found in juices of raw fruits, yet it appears in abundance in these same juices when extracted by cooking. Fruit should therefore be thoroughly cooked to insure a good extraction, but if over-cooked, pectin is weakened. Pectin is much more abundant in underripe than in ripe fruits, therefore underripe fruits are preferable for jelly making. Pectin generally is believed to occur in 3 forms. The parent substance, protopectin or pectose, is associated with the hardness of green fruits; pectin is formed from protopectin by ripening or boiling; and pectic acid is formed from pectin in overripe fruit.

If either pectin or acid is lacking or is insufficient in amount, it should be added. Commercial pectins are available at the market so that the home-maker may test the fruit juice for pectin content and add more if needed. Fruits rich in both pectin and acid are crab apples, sour apples, cranberries, currants, Concord grapes, gooseberries, loganberries, blackberries, oranges (including skin), and sour plums. Fruits rich in pectin but low in acid are quinces, sweet apples, and sweet guavas. Fruits rich in acid but low in pectin are strawberries, cherries, rhubarb, pineapple, raspberries, apricots, and sour peaches. Fruits low in both acid and pectin are peaches, overripe fruits, and elderberries.

Tests may be used by the homemaker to determine whether or not there is sufficient pectin in the juice to make a jellied product. Such tests include the jelmeter and Epsom salts. For the jelmeter test, a device known as a jelmeter measures the viscosity of the fruit juice. The juice is permitted to flow through the jelmeter for 1 minute and the reading obtained indicates amount of sugar needed per cup of juice when making a jelly. Juices that are high in pectin are viscous and will flow slowly through the jelmeter. Those juices will require more sugar for jelly than those that flow through rapidly. For the Epsom salts test, make an Epsom salts solution by adding 1 teaspoon sugar and ½ tablespoon Epsom salts to 1 tablespoon fruit juice. Stir until salts dissolve. Let stand 20 minutes. A heavy precipitate indicates abundant pectin. Little or no precipitate indicates pectin should be added.

The acid content of fruit varies with the fruit used. More acid is found in the underripe than in fully ripe fruits. When fruits are low in acid, lemon juice or citric acid is sometimes added to the fruit juice to supply the needed acid. However, if commercial fruit pectin is used, it contains some acid. There is no scientific test for acidity that is practical for home use. Acidity usually is judged by taste. If juice tastes as sour as a tart apple it contains enough acid. If not, add acid in some form, preferably a fruit acid. If the fruit is known to be deficient in acid, 3 tablespoons of lemon juice may be added to each pound of fruit before cooking.

Sugar serves as the preservative, aids in gel formation, contributes to the flavor of the product, and has a firming effect on the fruit in preserves. Either cane or beet sugar may be used.

Directions for making jelly, jam, preserves, and other jellied fruit products are presented in detail in the United States Department of Agriculture, Home and Garden Bulletin 56, which can be obtained from the Government Printing Office, Washington, D.C., or your Home Economics Agent.

PICKLES

Pickles are preserved by means of salt and acid. The acid may be the result of fermentation or it may be added. Pickles are classified according to flavor. The fermented or brined pickle may have a pleasant tart and tangy flavor, the quick-process or fresh-pack pickles a tart and pungent flavor, fruit pickles a spicy, sweet-sour flavor, and fruit and vegetable relishes a hot and spicy flavor. Apples, cherries, crab apples, fresh figs, grapes, peaches, pears, and watermelon rind are suitable for pickling. Crisp vegetables such as cucumbers, green tomatoes, onions, cabbage, cauliflower, and beets most often are used. Several of them may be combined for mixed pickles.

Good quality ingredients must be used and proper procedures followed to obtain satisfactory products. For best flavor fresh spices should be used because spices lose their pungent flavor rapidly during hot and humid weather. Too much salt toughens and shrivels pickles or may retard fermentation unduly in fermented pickles. Use pure granular salt if available. Materials added to salt may darken pickles. Too strong vinegar may bleach or shrivel pickles. A high-grade cider or white distilled vinegar of 4 to 6 per cent acidity (40 to 60 grain) is desirable for a well-flavored pickle. Do not dilute the vinegar unless so specified in the recipe. Instead, sugar may be added to make a less sour pickle. Use enameled, stainless steel, glass, or other utensil not attacked by the acid of vinegar, and wood, enamel or stainless steel spoons. Store pickles in sterilized glass jars and seal them; or place them in tightly covered crocks. Storing in sterilized glass jars is preferable.

Recommended procedures for successful pickling may be found in "Making Pickles and Relishes at Home," United States Department of Agriculture, Home and Garden Bulletin 92.

Causes of Defects in Pickles

Softening usually results from microbial action. It may be caused by too dilute a brine, by exposure of pickles above brine, by scum throughout the brine during fermentation, insufficient heat treatment, lack of airtight seal, moldly garlic, or spices.

Shriveling is caused by use of too strong a solution of salt, sugar, or vinegar, especially at the beginning of the pickling process. It is more likely to occur in sweet pickles.

Hollow pickles may be due to poor development of the cucumbers, allowing too much time between gathering and brining, too rapid fermentation, or too strong or too weak a brine during fermentation.

Scum consists of wild yeasts, bacteria, and molds, and should be removed. It will attack the food beneath it and weaken the acidity of the brine, thus causing spoilage.

Temperature is an important factor in fermentation. A temperature of 86°F is favorable for lactic acid fermentation. Higher temperatures result in poor flavor and spoilage, and lower ones retard fermentation.

Index

243